KYLE SPENCER

SHE'S GONE COUNTRY

Kyle Spencer lives in New York City with her very Northern fiancé. She is still an avid fan of country music and returns to North Carolina regularly.

SHE'S GONE
COUNTRY

DISPATCHES FROM A LOST SOUL

IN THE HEART OF DIXIE

BASED ON A TRUE STORY

KYLE SPENCER

VINTAGE DEPARTURES
Vintage Books
A Division of Random House, Inc.
New York

A VINTAGE DEPARTURES ORIGINAL, MAY 2002

Copyright © 2002 by Kyle Spencer

All rights reserved under International and Pan-American Copyright
Conventions. Published in the United States by Vintage Books, a division
of Random House, Inc., New York, and simultaneously in Canada by
Random House of Canada Limited, Toronto.

See pages 289–90 for permissions.

Vintage is a registered trademark and Vintage Departures and colophon are
trademarks of Random House, Inc.

Library of Congress Cataloging-in-Publication Data
Spencer, Kyle.
She's gone country : dispatches from a lost soul in the heart of Dixie /
Kyle Spencer.
p.   cm.
"A Vintage original"—T.p. verso.
ISBN 0-375-70904-5 (trade pbk.)
1. Spencer, Kyle.   2. Journalists—United States—Biography.
3. Raleigh (N.C.)—Social life and customs.   I. Title.
PN4874.S594 A3 2002
070'.92—dc21
[B]
2001045507

Vintage ISBN: 0-375-70904-5

Book design by Debbie Glasserman

www.vintagebooks.com

Printed in the United States of America
10   9   8   7   6   5   4   3   2   1

for

Mark
Lisa
A.C. Sheffield

and for Seth

DISCLAIMER

I ain't got a witness and I can't prove it
But that's my story and I'm sticken' to it.

COLLIN RAYE

Not everything in this book is true. I changed some things. And I made some stuff up.

I also altered identifying characteristics of certain people—and in some cases took several real people I knew and created one exaggerated person.

She's gone country, look at them boots,
She's gone country, back to her roots,
She's gone country, a new kind of suit,
She's gone country, here she comes.

ALAN JACKSON

My Dysfunctional Family Tree

The Connecticut Socialite

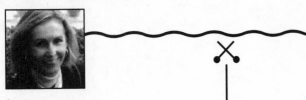

MY MOTHER EDIE
Makes a mean martini. Wonders: "What kind of people summer in South Hampton?"

The Nice, Normal, All-American

The Cape Cod Recluse

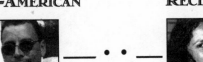

MY BROTHER-IN-LAW MICHAEL
A.k.a. The Family Outsider.

MY SISTER ELIZABETH
Spent $10,000 last summer to fence in her yard.

The Pampered Pet

JETT
Gets Christmas presents.

THE REBEL WASP

THE SOHO DRAMA QUEEN

MY FATHER GEORGE
Abandoned tennis and sailing in 1973. Can still be spotted in khakis.

MY STEPMOTHER SHELBY
Has connections to the finest gourmet grocery stores in the city. Buys illegally imported cheese.

THE GHETTO DWELLER

THE EXPOSER

THE CONSERVATIVE

MY BROTHER GEORGE
Swears his Brooklyn neighborhood is going to be the next SoHo.

ME
I confess writing books about my family is cheaper than therapy.

MY HALF-BROTHER PHILLIP
Diehard Howard Stern fan, even after Howard's divorce.

KEY:

 = SHAKILY MARRIED

 = SHAKILY MARRIED, THEN DIVORCED

•• = HAPPILY MARRIED
(at least, that's what they say)

I guess I should explain something up front. I'm a Lois. Picture Superman's sidekick without a romantic hero to save her from self-destruction.

Loises are manlier than magazine girls, who wear stilettos to work, rowdier than Wall Street writer girls, who wear suits. We do beepers and boots. These low-key getups work well for us on our newspaper jobs in the Wisconsins and Texases where we're sent, young and driven, to flex our writerly muscles and dig up dirt where no one thought there was any.

Being a Lois is more of a philosophy, really, than a job. Loises always choose "never done that before" over "the sure thing"—because they know that's how they'll get ahead. New experiences, after all, are currency in Newspaperland. They boost your résumé and your reputation. (They also sink your social life.) That's how we end up in small-town Southern bars on Saturday nights, with hard-to-explain crushes on buff men with badges and gun-toting members of the NRA.

It's a tough life. And, quite frankly, it's a little unfair. The thing is, the boys with the Woodward-and-Bernstein complexes get to drag their arty girlfriends to the hinterlands with them. The Suzies and the Annies of this world knit scarves and write poetry, while the boys investigate.

But Loises are not so privileged. They have trouble convincing the men they love to jump in their suitcases—especially when the bags are headed for the hills of Tennessee, or the barren plains of South Dakota. And anyway, we don't go for men who knit sweaters. So, we ride solo, titillated by our macho careers, deeply depressed by our inability to sustain something very obscure that we hear about on trips home: a relationship. The only thing that makes it all worthwhile is a good scoop. That's when the Lois feels so utterly like a stud she doesn't need to be sleeping with one.

SHE'S GONE
COUNTRY

1

Who doesn't know what I'm talking about
Who's never left home, who's never struck out
To find a dream and a life of their own
A place in the clouds, a foundation of stone?

DIXIE CHICKS

I'll have you know that I don't usually drink in semiprofessional situations. But seeing as this pig pickin' is being held in my honor, and a handsome man in a seersucker suit is eyeing me intently as he pours me a tasty mint julep from an icy pitcher, I've decided to leave my newspaper ethics at home.

I notice how pleasing his muscles look in his suit. And I'm sure he notices how stunning I look in my buttercup brown cowboy boots and my powder pink hat—the size of a Frisbee—which hangs over my head in a slightly funky, slightly elegant way.

I'm feeling rather relaxed as I gaze up from my cushioned lawn chair at this giant Italianate mansion in front of me.

Green sheets of Japanese kudzu are dripping down the walls by the columned front steps, and two hundred purple rhododendrons line the brick walkway.

I'm nibbling delicately on a heaping plate of food: crackling, crisp pieces of pig, baked beans dripping with molasses, and pieces of fried okra that are soft in the middle and crunchy on the outside.

Meanwhile, all around me on the lawn, violas and snapdragons reach up out of the earth, and the fragrance of the hickory wood coals from the pig pit mixes with the minty smell of late afternoon. The scents wrap around me like a summer shawl, and a few feet away from me my new editor is telling everyone I'm the most exciting thing that has arrived in North Carolina since General Sherman.

Fortunately, I've been too busy to pay attention to this cornucopia of compliments—which I find rather embarrassing, considering that I'm really quite new at this. For a while, I was playing putt-putt with Michael Jordan—on the tarmac by the garage. He flew in last night to welcome me to his hometown state. Then I was chatting with the North Carolina Young Heifer Star of the Year. A few minutes ago, she ceremoniously threw off her jean jacket and tossed it my way—in case I got chilly. I blew her a few kisses and agreed to add the jacket—which happens to have a wonderful sequence of rhinestone inlay—to my collection of preferred outerwear.

I'm delighted to be here, but I must confess I have a bit of a hangover. The truth is, I haven't stopped partying since I crossed the state line. First, there was a cocktail party with Jesse and Dot Helms—who have put aside their general ire at the North to welcome me. Then last night, the raucous race car wanna-be Buckshot Jones dropped by my hotel room for a nightcap. We had a few whiskeys, then slid into his $200,000 Dodge and whizzed over to a racetrack in Durham to do some laps. My limbs would be aching a lot less if we hadn't stopped at the Have a Nice Day Café to gulp down these fruity alcoholic beverages from plastic cups in the shape of the state of North Carolina. I guess my insistence that Buckshot teach me the shag may also have something to do with it. At one point, I seem to remember I was air-bound on the dance floor.

Anyhow, I think Buckshot has a thing for me. But I told him that he didn't have a chance, seeing as I just moved to North Carolina and wanted to launch any new romantic liaisons slowly. He said he understood and gave me his red Winston Cup baseball cap as a welcoming gift—even though I refused to let him slip his hand down my blouse on the ride home.

Anyway, this is all to explain why I'm resting on this lawn chair rather than getting down with the bluegrass band by the pool.

Oh, look. There's Tammy Faye. You know—the former wife of that mischievous Charlotte preacher Jim Bakker. Tammy's famed for her mascara-drenched eyelashes—but that's old news. It's a little-known secret that Tammy has a fabulous shoe collection. The woman makes Imelda Marcos's shoe closet look like a used clothing store.

Since my arrival, Tammy and I have talked several times on the phone—and once in person. I chose to make contact with her as a means of gathering information about the state before I came on as a metro reporter at the Raleigh daily, where I am scheduled to start working in a few days. She's a great listener. And in addition to giving me historical background on North Carolina, she's been grilling me about my foibled upbringing in lower Manhattan. She loves the stuff.

"Not everyone grew up with a backyard and a car," I yell across the lawn, repeating a comment I made to her a few days before at the Hayes Barton Grill, where we were downing Bloody Marys. It made her cackle so hard she nearly fell off her chair.

She bumbles over and wraps her arms—lined with bangle bracelets—around me.

"Tammy, don't get me wrong, I'm not trying to elicit sympathy," I mumble, my head buried in her chest. "But I wouldn't mind some understanding—now that I've moved ten hours from home. And I have no family to speak of within six states."

"Darlin'," Tammy coos, "in that fabulous getup you've got on, you couldn't elicit sympathy if you wanted to."

We both chuckle and the mayor, a Bobby Brady look-alike sporting a patterned sweater with several yellow geese on it, overhears this. He pats me gently on the back and says: "We're going to take care of you, don't worry."

I smile at the mayor. And now that I have his ear, I decide to fill it with info about what attracted me to the South.

"Mayor," I begin, recalling the speech I wrote a few weeks before to use on occasions like this. "I've never interviewed a sheriff, kissed a man in a Stetson, or owned a pair of hiking boots, let alone worn a dress that wasn't black." I take a sip of my julep and bolt out of my lawn chair. Then I make a broad stroke in the air with one of my manicured hands and prepare for the grand finale of my speech. "But here I am ready to explore. Some people go to Europe to find adventure, take safaris in Africa or visit ashrams in India. For me, adventure has always meant the sticks."

Cheers erupt, even though I think a few people were slightly offended by the reference to "the sticks." And I realize that the entire picnic has been listening to my conversation. Several well-wishers rush to embrace me. I feel a wave of calm sweep over me as James Taylor grabs my hand and begins to whisper the lyrics to his hit "Carolina in My Mind" into my left ear. He and I slip into the Italianate mansion—together—to have a little private chat. And before you know it, we're kissing up a Carolina storm while Buckshot is outside tapping against the drawing room windowpane. "What the hell are you . . ."

"Are you doing?" my best friend Mark hollered as he banged his fist against the bathroom door. I stuck my tongue out and stared at myself in the mirror, did a clean-teeth, smudge check, and jammed my lipstick back into my pocket. I wasn't wearing a straw hat or a pair of cowboy boots. I had on my black leather pants, my Doc Martens, and the suede coat I bought in Spain with the fuzzy collar. I was in New York City, in the women's bathroom at Odeon, my foot on the garbage can, applying lipstick and talking to myself.

Mark had chosen the venue for my two-person farewell party. I guess he figured they didn't have brasseries—or anything else a girl from New York would want—in North Carolina. It was a ploy. And, frankly, it wasn't working.

"The whole idea of moving to North Carolina is making you sick to your stomach, isn't it?" Mark inquired, when I flung open the door and exited the bathroom. "Moving so far away from New York City—any city, I mean."

Mark—who was still living on the Manhattan block where he had learned to ride a two-wheeler—was having trouble coming to terms with my plan to take a reporting job in Raleigh. He had taken to pronouncing Raleigh as if he were saying "war-torn Bosnia." That's when he wasn't referring to it as "down there."

"You know you don't have to go down there?" he said. "You can always stay in one of my parents' apartments and freelance. In case you're worried about that."

"Worried? What are you talking about?" We were back at our table. I took a sip of my now warm beer. "When was the last time you had the opportunity to stick your tongue down James Taylor's throat?"

"What?"

I raised a brow. "Just forget it."

Mark and I have been best friends since we were fourteen. And he purports to know me well: the overdeveloped fantasy life, the way I tend to optimistically assume every man I meet is going to marry me, the way I embellish events for the sake of the story. These are the parts of my personality he finds most entertaining. He laughed for weeks in high school when I told him Darryl Strawberry was going to take me to the prom. I didn't think it was very funny, particularly since I ended up going with a kid from my AP history class who had failed gym—twice.

When Mark and I first met, I was not the semiadjusted person I am today. I wore black lipstick and yelled a lot. I don't remember why. But Mark says I was enormously angry with my parents. As for Mark, he was not the model of stability, either. He wore the same Hanes T-shirt every day and nibbled on little balled-up pieces of loose-leaf paper. *Anxious* is the word I would use to describe his general teenage mood. We've matured a lot since then. Now, when I get upset I try to "center myself" and "find my breath." When he gets worked up, I tell him: "You're not your thoughts. Let it go." Or sometimes I just tell him: "Don't worry. Girls think you're hot." He loves that last part. As for making me feel better, Mark says if I'm thirty-eight and still unwed, he'll marry me. Mark is my insurance policy. And I'm his.

Mark put his beer down and suddenly got somber. "Kyle, I think this North Carolina stuff is a pretense."

I furrowed my brow. "For what?"

"Maturing. I think you're trying to move on with your life, figure out what you want."

"So, what if I am?"

Mark threw his hands up in the air. "Then I have to do it too, numbnuts. Or else you're going to leave me behind. And the only woman in my life will be my sister. And she doesn't even know when my birthday is."

I looked at him intently. Jane Goodall, ready for another journey to Tanzania. "Mark, you've got to set me free! I'm a journalist! I'm supposed to be exploring foreign lands. That's my job."

Mark was silent for a second. He took a sip of his drink—then launched into a rendition of the Simple Minds tune from the movie *The Breakfast Club:* "Don't you forget about me."

> *Walk my way*
> *Don't walk on by*
> *Rain keeps falling,*
> *Rain keeps falling down, down, down, down,*
> *Don't you forget about me.*

After three minutes of hellish singing, I jumped up. "Listen, I gotta go finish packing. I'll call you when I get there."

I grabbed my things, gulped down my drink, and flew out of there—leaving Mark gawking at some woman at the table next to us. I wasn't too worried about my best friend. He just had a little trouble with good-byes. But he'd figure things out on his own. I knew that. As for me, I was feeling so brave. So together. So girl-on-the-move. . . . But frankly, I was also feeling scared. What I hadn't told Mark—or anyone else, for that matter—but I can tell you, is this: Moving to North Carolina wasn't just an adventure, it was also an escape.

————

If you feel like you entered this story through the back door, don't worry. You have. Let me fill you in. My name is Kyle Spencer. I'm twenty-seven, and *dysfunctional* would be a kind way to describe my family. I was raised in a loft in lower Manhattan by my father, a frustrated investment banker who worshiped Pablo Picasso, and my stepmother, Shelby, an underground theater actress whose stage name was Stardust.

In my world, *avant-garde* was a household word. Andy Warhol was a hero. And putting anything with artificial ingredients in your mouth was a sin. My childhood was populated by artists, drag queens, and intellectuals threatening to move to Cuba.

"That's it," my parents' philosopher-plumber friend Kevin would shout every time another Republican was elected to office, slapping his half-finished manuscript against our dining room table and waving his fork in the air. "I'm getting out of here!" As a recovering bank robber who had spent ten years behind bars, Kevin was lucky to be going anywhere. But since his troubled youth, he had matured. In prison, he started a world-renowned theater group that later became the focus of a feature-length film.

All I wanted was to be surrounded by manicured lawns, tree houses, and normal adult role models—like doctors, teachers, and policemen. I was not so lucky. Our neighbors were temperamental artists, people who "experimented with mediums," and musicians who gave us contact highs when their pot smoke drifted down the air shaft and slipped into my parents' bedroom on Saturday nights, while we watched *The Love Boat*. Our dinner guests were people like Sur Rodney Sur, the artist who showed his works in his bathroom and wore a telephone cord around his neck as a piece of mobile art.

While this eccentricity might have appealed to other young people, it did nothing but disappoint me. Perhaps I would have felt differently about the nonconformity my parents found so appealing if it hadn't been coupled with a marriage that entailed a great deal of high-energy hysteria. There were few things my parents found more satisfying than a good knock-down-drag-out fight. You know. Beams out the window. Milk cartons across the room. Police bumbling into our house to talk about why plates were crashing against walls.

While other people celebrated birthdays and graduations, we hosted annual Divorce Week. The time once a year when my father, bleary-eyed and bloated, would announce from his spot on the guest bedroom bed that he couldn't hold on any longer to the abysmal relationship he had with "the histrionic shrew he had married." Or my stepmother would drag us to a friend's house, and announce along the way that she had made a terrible mistake marrying my father, a "passive-aggressive misogynist."

I tell you all this because I maintain a great deal of ire against the people I hold responsible for my miserable upbringing, ire which perhaps I should have unloaded by now. But I haven't. And this story is partially about that.

Here's a family *Who's Who* (a.k.a. "My Sob Chart"), in case you need help sorting out the kooks in my life.

1. Meet my father, George, a handsome WASP from Rochester, who left my mother and our Upper East Side apartment when I was three to join my stepmother—a bohemian from the West Village—because it was 1973 and he needed to be "free."

2. Say hello to my mother, a pretty WASP from Connecticut who fell apart when my father unexpectedly left. To cope, she joined the Upper East Side cocktail circuit, and almost forgot she had three kids. Having garnered a strong and unfounded sense of entitlement at an early age, I considered the level of attention I was receiving unacceptable. And at my father's prodding I left my mother's house at age eight and moved downtown.

3. In walks my stepmother, Shelby, a tall, loquacious left-winger, famed for her killer red lipstick, fake eyelashes, and six-inch heels. Shelby saved my neglected young soul by showering me with attention, French films, and chocolate-covered raisins. Among other things, she taught me to read, signed me up for my first writing class, and introduced me to "well-made" children's clothing—which was all she said a stepdaughter of hers should be wearing.

4. Welcome my half brother, Phillip, born when I was nine

and rumored to have been a last-ditch effort to save my father and Shelby's failing relationship. Throughout his childhood, he paid back the favor by maintaining a level of low-grade anger toward everyone in the family and assumed the role of "problem child"—even though his IQ is probably double all of ours combined. He has since taken a great interest in the American military and harbors political beliefs that are perilously close to those held by members of the Christian Coalition.

5. Also in the picture is my older brother, George, who shares my father's name. He is six years my senior, and my mother's only son. George stayed with my mother when I went to live with my father, visiting my father only on weekends. Today, he is an artist who paints bloody-faced boxers and moonlights as a real estate mogul who buys dilapidated buildings in Brooklyn ghettos and fixes them up.

6. On the sidelines is my older sister, Elizabeth, seven years my senior. She escaped us all by practically moving in with her best friend, Gretchen, when my father first left—and never really returning.

A note: My mother doesn't figure in this story. When I told her I was writing an "exaggerated memoir," she begged to be left out. "Listen, Kyle, I know I was not the best mother to you when you were young. But it was the seventies. All the professionals were telling us how resilient you kids were. If I'm in that book, I know you're going to make me a whore or something."

Nor does Elizabeth. She works at a preppy catalog company and lives on Cape Cod with her husband and dog. She's so normal that basically she skews the whole story. So, I let her off the hook, too.

———

A day after my talk with Mark, I sped into downtown Raleigh, almost out of gas, and parked my car in front of a large, picturesque town square. Curious but tired, I peered sheepishly out of my window. Above the square—and a little to the left—was the Raleigh skyline. Nothing towering or monumental, just a few gleaming office complexes and a cylinder-shaped Holiday Inn reaching toward the heavens. Lining the square were sidewalks—clean, wide, and roomy. And in the distance I spotted a snake-shaped railroad track that looped around the city. Raleigh would never be a beautiful city. But it had a slow, meandering pace that appealed to me.

I cracked open my window. The scent of lemons and lavender filtered through the afternoon air. It was so much fresher and cleaner than New York City air. I breathed a sigh of relief and pulled out a cigarette. Here, I thought, unbuckling my seat belt and throwing my safety club in the backseat, you could actually stroll down the sidewalk without bumping into one of those frenzied New York pedestrians ready and willing to ram her purse into your groin. I was looking forward to leaving behind those superdriven New Yorkers—so beautiful and so brilliant and so brutally ambitious they'd sacrifice their firstborn (and your life) for a walk-on in an afternoon soap opera. Not to mention the last container of milk at the grocery store.

With these thoughts floating through my head, I crushed my cigarette out and drove to the nearest gas station. Then I tanked up and headed out of town. I passed a Hardee's and an IHOP, and then a row of large, cube-shaped suburban homes showcasing faux Greek columns and Federalist porches. Eventually, I fell onto a rural road with long stretches of tobacco fields and potato patches that seemed to go on forever. I pictured myself, straw in mouth—frolicking through the pastures, making cheese or maybe milking cows, finding solace and serenity. I would be cool, collected. I would adopt a happy, slow-paced life in which I would read self-help books and do things like think about my inner self and achieve a permanent state of well-being.

Back in the city, I spotted the block-letter sign for my hotel. I pulled out my duffel bag and clicked back to reality. The hotel lobby had tangerine carpeting and a nightly happy hour and dance party in the bar, which was named Bowties. I resisted the urge to partake in the Bowtie happy hour and headed to my room. I inserted my card into the door slot and pulled open the curtains.

Here before me was the city where I would be living for the next two and a half years. The Raleigh Plastic Surgery Center and a Christian chain bookstore were staring up at me. I switched the lights off and noticed a twinkling from the Denny's below.

I centered my gaze on the glow from downstairs and thought of the chaos back in New York, the tension between Shelby and my father, the silent anger that oozed through our house, the way Phillip was growing tattoos on his arm and had just announced he wanted to spend the summer at a military camp in Texas.

It was during a family dinner—minus Phillip—a few weeks before in a crimson-walled Indian restaurant in the East Village that I realized how utterly unbearable the heaviness had become. We'd walked there together—the three of us. Me in the middle, because Shelby and my father could no longer bear to stand next to each other. My head snapped back and forth during the entire walk, and my mind juggled two separate thoughts and ideas as I tried to carry on two conversations at once while staving off whiplash. The two warring factions weren't just refusing to talk, they were refusing to acknowledge each other's existence.

Back in Raleigh, my hotel room felt peaceful and calm. Free

of worry and stress. Safe. It buzzed with the hum of the air conditioner and the tap-tap sound of water in the bathroom sink.

"I'm home," I said to the highway that stretched before me. Then I slipped under the crisp hotel sheets of my king-size bed and fell into a restful sleep.

———

I didn't just wake up one morning, point to a map, and announce I needed to seek solace in Raleigh, North Carolina. But the fact that I would seek solace somewhere far away, where I could work long hours, pour all my energies into writing and reporting, dissect other people's lives—not my own— was nothing new. It was my pattern. Newspaper work was an all-consuming, almost addicting way for me to keep my mind off my family and to keep me growing intellectually. And during my twenties, I embraced that life wholeheartedly. I lived for dead bodies, car chases, elections, and anything controversial or flashy.

For the first part of my journalism career, I freelanced in Prague. I ate cheese patties and potato chips for a whole year while I watched Communism die. I shipped articles back to the States in hopes of accumulating enough of a clip file to get a job at a top paper. Things weren't so rosy on the home front, but I ignored those problems. I was having an exhilarating, once-in-a-lifetime experience. And that was all that mattered. My work in Europe landed me a two-year internship at *The Philadelphia Inquirer*, where I wrote about school board squabbles and traffic woes. Philadelphia wasn't exactly glam central—but I was working with some of the best editors in the country, and for a cub reporter it doesn't get much better than that.

When my two years were through, I had hoped to stay on in Philadelphia, but "the best editors in the country" were kind enough to help me realize that I needed to aspire higher, elsewhere. Gentle, like boyfriends right before they dump you.

"You have so much raw talent, so much potential, so much energy. . . . We're not hiring you."

That honest appraisal sent me on yet another job hunt. I interviewed with a Wall Street wire service that wooed me with a job covering the commodities market from a room they referred to as the dungeon. I then sent my résumé to several Manhattan magazine editors who encouraged me to come and join their staffs of "girls" who write "creative copy" about Russian bikini waxers and Brazilian boob jobs. I sent one résumé to Newark and another to Bergen County—not the most thrilling areas in the world, but both house well-respected feeder papers—that's what they call papers that train young reporters.

Mark was gung ho about these jobs. So was everyone else I knew. The general feeling was that I was ready to settle down, stop running around. But the idea of finishing off my twenties on or near the urban island where I had spent most of my life just didn't sound that titillating to me. After all, I already knew how to finagle my way into a New York City nightclub, what to wear to an East Village art gallery opening, and where to buy the best Italian bread at three in the morning. By twenty-seven, I'd already dated a French photographer, a fashion designer, and a kid who augmented his allowance by providing hallucinogens to my high school class. As far as I was concerned, life in the big city was boring and passé. It was also riddled with bad memories. Sometimes, it seemed like every street corner had borne witness to moments when I—as a child—had felt sad, anxious, and worried. With one divorce under my belt and another one closing in on me, I myself had—in New York City—witnessed enough tension between lovers to last me a lifetime. I wanted to experience something new. And I guess there was a strong part of me that felt I needed to get as far away, physically and culturally, from New York City as I could get.

A call from Kip Kane, an editor at a newspaper that had just won a prize for a series on pig manure scandals in the Tar Heel State, gave me my chance. "Have you ever been to a pig pickin'?" Kip asked me gruffly. I took the job.

———

I lasted three nights above Bowties, then decided it was time to find a real home. After a quick search, I settled on a knobby-hilled neighborhood a few minutes from downtown built in the 1910s on a former tobacco plantation. Boylan Heights was shaded with dogwoods and dotted with restored bungalows and a few Victorian mansions that overlooked the city skyline. But, most important, it housed dozens of the one Southern amenity that I longed for: a porch. On every street there were wraparound porches, side porches, two-story porches, and upstairs porches. I saw myself on one of these porches slapping hamburgers on and off a barbecue grill, meeting and greeting men, knitting, drawing, crocheting, and doing lots of other things that I didn't know how to do, but that a few months in Raleigh would surely teach me.

After a few circles around the 'hood, I found a For Rent sign in front of a rust-red bungalow with a creaky screen door and a gravel driveway. If Raleigh had a poster home, this was it. Peeling paint, wrought-iron fence, a little pale-blue shed in the back.

I called the number. And before I knew it, I was standing on the bungalow porch—face-to-face with my new landlords: Beau and Suzie Burns.

"Welcome," Beau said, offering me a beefy handshake.

"Hello!" boomed Suzie, waving her clipboard in the air and flashing me a smile. She had clear braces on her teeth and a strawberry-blond bob.

Beau and Suzie paraded me through the house like two game

show hosts. I gawked at the recently redone hardwood floors, the fireplace, the swishing ceiling fans, complimenting them on their work. I tapped seductively on the air-conditioning unit while Suzie flung open the washer and dryer lids. Finally, Beau tugged slowly at two sliding doors, revealing a tiny closet. Then, apologetically and tentatively, they told me the price: $540 a month.

"It's a lot," Suzie noted.

"But we think it's worth it," Beau piped in.

"I mean, we did the work ourselves," Suzie added.

I was silent. Then I coughed. "What do you mean?" I shouted, banging on Suzie's clipboard. "Five forty? That's less than the cost of a New York City parking spot."

They both smiled.

"The only thing I should mention is that the kitchen is in the bedroom," Beau warned as he and Suzie led me toward the back of the house.

"But a lot of people like that," Suzie chimed in. "You know, especially people who like to eat late at night. If you get hungry the fridge will only be a few steps away."

For a split second, I was a little worried. But as we headed into the bedroom, I realized that Beau had been overly cautious. The fridge was really about ten feet away, which to my New York real estate eye was a different part of the house. A lot of my friends don't even have kitchens, I thought to myself. Some wash their dishes in the bathtub. This is good, you won't shock your system with a whole separate kitchen.

"I'll take it," I said, digging into my bag for my checkbook.

I filled in a check, ripped it off, and handed it to a smiling Beau.

"Thanky," he said, as he and Suzie jumped into their Suburban and sped off.

I stood on the porch of my new house, admiring its laid-back feel. The whole thing felt totally luxurious. I had my own bedroom and a landlord who knew my name. And I had just learned my first local expression.

"Thanky," I whispered into the afternoon air.

I spent the next few afternoons unpacking the boxes that had arrived from New York. I hung my Dog Faced Herman poster above my bed, put my coffee grinder in the kitchen. I placed my banana yellow couch circa 1960s into the living room and positioned my ceramic ashtray from Spain on the coffee table I had found at a postfuneral sale in Philadelphia. I drove to Kmart and bought lawn chairs and tiki torches for my first party, a paper towel holder for the kitchen, and a tablecloth for when I made intimate dinners for my friends and dates. On my last night of unpacking, I crawled into bed in my new house. I was happy.

I fell asleep to the liquid chirping of a mockingbird outside my bedroom window.

About an hour later, I woke up.

"Lights out," a voice crackled into my ear.

"They're out," I mumbled, pulling my pillow over my head.

"Shut-in starts in three minutes," the voice bellowed.

Shut-in? Oh God, did I shut the door? I threw off my pillow and leapt out of bed. I am, by the way, a confirmed checker.

"Shut-in till six A.M." the voice continued.

I was getting worried.

I opened my back door. A strobe light swept over my fence. It caught me in the eye and blinded me for a moment. The voice I was hearing was coming from a loudspeaker. Curious, I pulled on my sneakers and ambled down my back steps in my cotton nightgown. I lifted myself up onto the fence, pushing aside some bushes. In the distance, I noticed a watchtower and a razor-wire fence.

My backyard fronted the North Carolina state prison.

———————

I woke up three times that night: once to wonder what the prison escape rate was in North Carolina. Another time, to contemplate the chances an escapee would hide in my basement. Finally, to take a Tylenol P.M. for my pounding headache.

I was furious at Beau and Suzie—but mostly at myself for being so naïve. Certainly I was wary of New York landlords, who seemed to delight in lying to you, kicking you out, keeping your security deposit forever. But that was easy. They were mean. Beau and Suzie had duped me by being nice.

———————

The next morning I woke up, groggy and a little out of sorts, but ready to give Raleigh another go. I had to start working in two days, and I figured before I did that I might as well spend some time driving around and figuring out where the main roads were. Certainly my house situation was a disappointment—but if I could just learn to enjoy the pace, the warm weather, and my new neighbors, I would be fine. I could already feel myself adjusting. In a few short months I'd be totally in time with the rhythm of the place. I just needed to stop imagining men in orange jumpsuits hanging their heads over my fence during their gym breaks to chat with me while I gardened.

To empty this thought from my brain, I turned on the radio and began singing. Feeling relaxed, I sped up, switched lanes, then switched again. Then, realizing I was on the wrong road, I made a U-turn and kept going. When I looked into my driver's side mirror, I noticed a police car, siren blaring, behind me. With the radio on I hadn't heard the noise.

A buff North Carolina state trooper in a crisp uniform, a crew cut, and a pair of menacing plastic glasses approached me. I smiled gently and cranked down the window.

"Ma'am, do you know what you are doing?"

"Driving?" I offered, sure that this was just a routine stop.

The officer pulled out his leather ticket book and a pen, and slapped it against my car.

"Don't worry, old car," I said, making a little joke to lighten things up.

"Now, don't get sassy with me, young lady. You're doing eighty in a forty-five zone. That's no small matter. I hope you have a license."

I pulled out my wallet and handed it over. He grabbed the plastic-coated card and sauntered back to his cruiser.

This was no mere donut-downing officer. This was a man on a mission. I flipped the radio on and off. To soothe my rattled nerves, I began to think about all the things I needed to do: call Mark, send out résumés, get a lock for my door. I pulled out a cigarette, lit it, and took a few fast drags. Finally, the trooper stepped out of his car and walked slowly my way.

"Officer," I began. "I am so sorry. I know I did a bad thing. But . . ." I chuckled a little and took another drag of my cigarette. "But I am having a really crazy day. I've been racing around, trying to get all this shit done." I was feeling alive and animated and hoping the New York attitude I'd been so happy to escape was working for me now. "See, I just moved here. And then—well, you know . . . moving is expensive. So I certainly can't afford a ticket. And anyway, I really didn't expect you to stop me. I'm used to NYC, where you've got to rob someone at gunpoint to get a cop to pay the slightest amount of attention to you. I know things are different here. But just cut me this one break, please. . . . I've got so much stuff to do today. And . . ."

The officer glared at me, obviously unimpressed with my booked schedule.

"Ma'am," he interrupted, handing me back my license.

"You've got only one thing you need to do now that you're here with us." He paused for a second. "You have got to calm yourself down."

I looked down and realized that my car radio and my blinkers were still on. Ashes from the cigarette in my hand were dripping on my skirt. And I was talking very loud and very fast.

The officer handed me my ticket, then eyed me sympathetically. "Or hell, you're gonna give yourself a heart attack."

I eyed the officer's crisp blue suit and silver name tag. Behind him on the hill above the highway, brightly colored vehicles lined the parking lot of the area's newest car dealership. There were lanes and lanes of roads in front of us, and large neon green signs in the distance indicating nearby towns and cities, each one more foreign to me than the next.

My ticket cost $250. I tossed it on the seat next to me and mashed out my cigarette.

"Thanky, Officer!" I mumbled as I cranked up my window and sped off. Once on the road, I couldn't help wondering why I had had to go five hundred miles from New York to escape my family. What was so wrong with New Jersey?

I've got friends in low places.

GARTH BROOKS

Hector clicked his chains good-naturedly against the partition that separated the sheriff's lobby from the Wake County Jail and flashed me a gap-toothed grin. "Do I look like a killa?"

I eyed Hector closely. His hands were all scratched up. His eyes were beady and bloodshot. He was sporting paper slippers, prison chains, and an electric orange jumpsuit. I decided not to answer the question.

"The police, they say you strangled those girls." Saliva was clogging my throat. "With your hands. . . . They say you did it with your bare hands."

"I didn't do no murders. . . . They liars."

"So, what are you going to do about this?"

Hector glared at me through the glass—wild-eyed and bubbly. I was wearing baggy pants and an oversize T-shirt. No makeup. I was hoping to appear nonthreatening, even a little repulsive, to a serial killer. (It was a fashion balance I had never experimented with before.)

"I'm going to do you," he whispered.

"Actually I don't think that's a good idea," I said, jolting out of the jail, my heart pounding against the strap of my reporter bag.

———

It was my third week in Raleigh, and I was spending it with a man the police referred to as the Human Carver. I hadn't exactly chosen a date with a homicidal maniac. But I had agreed to go on it for the reason most young reporters agree to do the things they do: I had been suckered into it.

A few days earlier my editor, Kip, had shuffled up to my corner desk in his usual uniform: high-tops, khakis, and a coffee-stained oxford, and tossed a ten-page arrest warrant on my lap. "First big cop assignment," he had grumbled, in a lame effort to excite me.

The highlighted words on the warrant read: ruthless killer, psychopath, highly dangerous. I cringed.

Kip found a spot on my forehead and avoided my pleading eyes. "Kyle, you're the only one we feel can really do this Saturday evening interview," he lied.

I was still new enough at the paper to be sensitive to flattery and eager to please, but I was not delusional. In national newspaper speak, Kip had just said: "No one else wants to go near the guy, and you're the lowest one on the office hierarchy."

I smiled dryly. "When does my insurance kick in?"

Kip dug his hands in his pockets and jangled his coffee quarters.

"You'll be fine," he muttered. "The guy's behind bars." Then he shuffled off, his high-tops making brush marks on the glossy linoleum floor.

Needless to say, my glamorous new job as cub reporter was turning out to be a lot less glamorous than I had thought. My desk consisted of a dusty piece of metal cluttered with ripped phone books and half-empty bottles of Pepto-Bismol. My assignment: general news on weekdays, cops on weekends. My days off: Monday and Tuesday. Essentially, I was charged with doing all the stories no one wanted to do, on all the days no one wanted to work.

Still, it didn't seem that horrific until I saw the office props I would be dragging with me everywhere: beeper, cell phone, and police scanner. I had more tools than a TV repairman.

"You'll get used to the noise," Kip had told me apologetically. "You only have to keep the scanner on five days a week."

————

When I got back to the office after declining Hector's generous invitation, I was pleasantly surprised to discover that Kip was off for the weekend. I figured with him gone I wouldn't have to stress about my empty notepad. I'd do an eight-inch brief. The story would be buried. And I could pour my energy into an article with more potential.

Kip's opinion of me was key. He was why I had come to Raleigh. The paper had a good reputation around the country. But Kip had cult status. His specialty was hiring inexperienced reporters and churning out journalistic prodigies with immeasurable loyalty to him. When I'd come for my interview, several reporters had told me: "Make Kip happy, and you'll go to whatever paper you want next."

Impressing Kip was a challenge, and Loises like challenges.

But so far, I hadn't had a chance to produce anything that was capable of impressing anyone. The most intriguing thing I'd done was grill the victim of a chitlin' and beefstick holdup in a small town forty minutes outside of Raleigh for a 3B story. The owner—worried about how a news story on the holdup would affect business at his country store—had completely clammed up.

"How could you have forgotten? It was only a few hours ago," I inquired.

The man smiled at me dumbly. "Gosh, it feels like it was weeks ago. Really, I've already told you more than I know."

GUY WON'T TALK went the less than scintillating headline in our paper.

In Raleigh they have a name for such responses: the limp gambit. It is a football term; it means pretending to be wounded to get the opponent off guard, then going for the touchdown.

A few days later a long, flattering feature about how courageous the store owner had been during the holdup was printed in the local daily.

MAN TELLS ALL read the subhead.

Anyway, considering that I was having yet another "bad copy day," it was good to know the object of my professional wooing was not around to witness it. But alas, my relief was short-lived. As I approached my desk, a high-pitched cackle floated heavily through the otherwise sleepy newsroom. I was doomed. The office cackler was a leggy Mexican named Maria—known for her snakeskin stilettos, skintight blouses, and impressive collection of journalism awards. She was the paper's investigative reporting editor, and she happened to sit on the other side of my cracked partition. Her presence in the office on a Saturday indicated she was on weekend duty, replacing Kip.

My dreams of a go-easy day were gashed. Maria wasn't just a looker. She was a ball-buster, too. Since I'd arrived she'd sent a reporter on a canoeing expedition down the Neuse River and ordered him to swim around with a glass jar to collect chemical pollution samples. She had ordered another reporter—an avid animal lover—into a coastal town where turtles were being brutalized. And at one of the 10:30 meetings, where editors went to critique the morning paper, Maria hit like a stealth bomber. "Whoever edited today's front-page feature must have been on drugs," she exclaimed. "Is this English?"

Maria slammed down the phone. "Fuck me. Fuck me to tears."

She saw me and flashed a superior grin. It went from my toes to the tip of my head, as if to say: Nice shoes, nice skirt. I do have a better ass than you, though.

"How did it go?" she asked.

I noticed Sunday's budget—a list and description of the stories slotted for the next day's paper—on her desk. "Page One," it read. "WHO IS THE HUMAN CARVER? Spencer does in-depth interview with serial killer, talks with him at length about what possessed him to kill, whether he has any regrets, and how he plans to defend himself in court. She writes a long, intimate profile."

Suddenly, the cafeteria's watery coffee machine, three stories down, was beckoning me like a supercharged magnet.

"Well, he wouldn't talk," I said.

Maria picked up a Number 2 pencil from her copy-strewn desk and pointed the lead tip at my forehead. "Did you ask him why? Did you ask him if he was sorry? Did he tell you about his family? Any tattoos? . . . I mean, didn't you try to butter him up a little?"

I imagined Maria in leather stilettos, buttering up the Human Carver. *You really have a knack for fine razor cuts. I mean, slitting skin without making a big mess has got to take a lot of practice. Which you clearly have had, Mr. Carver.*

"I tried, really."

Maria was looking eager to inflict torture. And I was starting to look like her next victim. She sniveled. "I'm holding the story. You need to get out there. Go to the men's shelter tonight and look for the guy's friends. Do you think you can handle it?"

I assumed she didn't want an honest answer. I grabbed Hector's arrest warrant from my desk and hobbled toward the elevator.

The arrest warrant showed Hector to be a ruthless killer with a weakness for street women and mind-numbing acts of misogyny. Officials alleged he had chosen each of his victims carefully and then meticulously tortured them. He scarred them with deep razor cuts that crisscrossed their bodies like lines on a road map. He raped them. Then he strangled them to death, leaving their necks with red-patterned hand marks—not unlike the finger painting children do in kindergarten. On a few of the occasions, the police had found a slab of masking tape on the victim's dead lips.

Murder was not the only thing Hector was meticulous about. A search warrant, attached to the back of the arrest warrant, suggested that the guy was also a neat freak. Inside a plastic grocery bag at the shelter where he lived, officials found combs, toothbrushes, tissue packs, cotton balls, and a bottle of hand lotion.

When I finished flipping through the tissue-thin document, I headed for the Raleigh homeless shelter, vowing never to date a man who carries toiletries around with him in a plastic bag.

The men's shelter was housed in an old warehouse building on the edge of a wide, underutilized road that led to a pet food factory and an X-rated video store. The shelter had pigeon gray cement floors and off-white walls. It was a high-ceilinged desert of army cots, bulging garbage bags, and men with watery eyes and skullish grins. I flashed my laminated press pass and forged briskly past a sign that read: PLEASE LEAVE ALL DANGEROUS WEAPONS AT THE FRONT DESK.

I was trying to be inconspicuous. One hundred rheumy eyes stared at me.

Spontaneous interviews are tricky. You have to be in the mood to badger strangers. I wasn't. I pulled my sweater tightly around me and found myself face-to-face with a guy whose natty head was buried inside a 1997 copy of *House & Garden*. I leaned against the metal table where he and several other men were gathered and pulled out my pad.

"Excuse me, sir. Did you know Hector?"

The man plopped his magazine down and began twisting the tips of his pencil-thin mustache—as if each twist was jogging his weakening memory. "You mean the guy who's in the slammer?"

I nodded a yes and sucked in the shelter's musty air.

Mustache Man glared at the cement ceiling in what I assumed was a gesture of his disgust. I braced myself for the worst. Lost fingers, missing toes, horrific anecdotes about how Hector practiced his razor cuts on his buddies while they slept in their stiff cots.

Mustache Man flashed me a grin. "Nicest guy in the world."

Surprised, I rested my elbows on the table and leaned toward him. The scent of stale bourbon flew up into my nostrils. "Really?"

"Generous too. Passed you a Washington when you needed one."

A kid in a skullcap and purple plastic jogging pants, who had been listening to our conversation, sauntered up to the table. "Hector was always givin' me free shit. He used to flip burgers at Wendy's down on Capital. He'd bring me those big-ass Wendy hamburgers. You know, those square mommas. Man, it's too bad he ain't 'round no more."

The kid's raspy voice was echoing through the shelter. And his comments, coupled with my presence, were attracting listeners. Before I knew it several men were huddled around the table voicing their opinions.

"He was the funniest motherfucker, wasn't he?" I heard someone bellow.

"I never met a fellow who showered so much in my life."

"Shit he was a good cardplayer."

"And popular with the ladies."

I looked at my new friends in disbelief. Either Human Carver was a regular Horatio Alger, or I was up against the best PR team in the state of North Carolina. Either way I was screwed. I hadn't garnered one single quote that shed light on the charges lodged against Hector. I slumped down on the bench next to Mustache Man and took a deep breath.

"He's in jail for murder and rape, you know?" I coaxed, hoping to jog someone's memory. "Surely, there were signs."

"Nope."

"I neva woulda thought he'd dun that shit."

I was losing my patience now. "Come on. The guy's a maniac."

Mustache Man was unfazed by my outburst. He eyed me suspiciously. "Listen, lady, we don't want no trouble. No one here needs to be in the paper."

"Can I use that as a quote?" I asked feebly.

"Nope," he blurted out. "That was off the record."

I stood upright again, crossed my arms against my chest—hoping to appear powerful and menacing. "Listen, you." I pointed at the kid in the skullcap. "Just give me your name and I'll use one of those nice quotes about how Hector brought you burgers all the time."

Mustache Man tugged a comb out of his pants pocket and began sliding it through his hair. "He ain't stupid. None of us need the police coming down here, poking around, gettin' into our business."

I saw Kip shoving a ticket in my hand and throwing me on an afternoon 747, bound for New York. He would pronounce me unsuited for newspaper work and wave good-bye from the glass airport wall.

"I can't use your remarks without names," I pleaded, sitting down in one of the empty chairs at the table and burying my hands in my face. "I need to be able to I.D. you guys. It's newspaper policy." When I looked up, Mustache Man and his followers were gone.

I remembered one of the pamphlets I'd read during orientation about not using quotes or background information from sources who refuse to reveal their identities. "In this profession, credibility is key," it began.

I was starting to sense my own credibility slipping away. I was not looking forward to telling Kip or Maria about this. I tossed my pad of unusable quotes in the trash and scampered out of the shelter, slamming the steel doors behind me.

The next day I strolled into the newsroom—fantasizing that members of the newspaper staff had come down with a horrible case of amnesia, brought on by the cafeteria's hugely popular oatmeal raisin cookies. The entire third floor, it would turn out, had forgotten about the Human Carver.

Real life was not so rosy.

"Can't wait to see your profile," the executive editor said, patting me encouragingly on the back as I skulked past his office.

"Looks promising," one of the managing editors said, giving me big thumbs-up as he brushed past my desk on his way to lunch.

"Glad someone is finally getting those folks at the shelter to open up to us," a veteran reporter said on his way to his afternoon coffee break.

Petrified, I went home early and called Mark.

———

My best friend was now interning for the most feared director in America, pretending to be a movie mogul—even though he spent his days and nights with a beeper glued to his underwear in case the guy needed a fax sent at midnight, or some microwave popcorn at three in the morning.

As for me, I was still playing CNN foreign correspondent on a special detour from my reporting duties in Bosnia. We share a zest for grandiosity, Mark and I.

"Say what you will, buddy, but I am really feeling intellectually challenged. I'm having a lot of contact with members of the dispersed populations. People with a lot of poverty and substance abuse issues. It's the underbelly. And wow is it powerful."

Mark laughed. "Did you spend another night in a homeless shelter? . . . I thought after all those nights in that Philly shelter, they'd at least promote you to a soup kitchen or something."

Mark is usually generous enough to pretend to believe my lies. This time, he was not in a generous mood.

"Don't underestimate the dilemmas that face this forgotten population," I offered defensively.

"Did I ever tell you, your voice squeaks when you're bullshitting me?" he asked.

"No, you didn't," I squeaked.

"So when are you coming home? I want you to meet Chantal."

Chantal was Mark's newest love interest: thirty-six, retired banker, Harvard B.A., fluent in Russian, competent in Korean.

He had met her at a dinner party with his parents, where she was quick to point out that she abhors foul language. I pictured Mark, naked, prancing around Louis XIV furniture in a Park Avenue apartment, yelling "phooey" and "fudge."

Whatever. I was not letting his brush with a sexy, genius, Ivy League bazillionaire make my life, which now included stints at the Raleigh homeless shelter, seem shabby or trivial in comparison. "She sounds underexposed," I said dismissively.

He graciously ignored me.

I could hear Mark's director hollering—something about lukewarm coffee.

"I think you have coffee—I mean *movies*—to make," I retorted before hanging up.

————

When I got back to work, I had two e-mails from Kip.

"How's it coming?" asked the first.

Translation: You better produce that serial killer story soon.

The second e-mail read like this: "We'll budget it for Monday."

My computer said the second one had arrived at four-thirty. That was right after the afternoon budget meeting. Otherwise known as the "fudge it" meeting. Kip had clearly been throttled into coming up with copy from his reporters. He'd sacrificed me.

When I'd finished reading my e-mails, he charged over. "Do you have enough info on the guy?"

Kip was an editorial mumbler. The thing was, when you got him interested in a story, he could muse with you about it for hours. But if you didn't, you could spend days two desks away from him without so much as exchanging a few words. In any event, a conversation initiated by him, about the whereabouts of a long overdue story, was the equivalent of a screaming drag-out fight with any other editor.

I smiled faintly.

Kip took that to mean yes.

"Good. I got a call today about Hector. He had a girlfriend at the women's shelter. Why don't you go see if you can find her. You can write the piece tomorrow."

I nodded obediently.

No matter how much pressure you are under, one thing you should never do as a reporter is pretend you have a great story you don't have.

I patted Kip on the shoulder and smiled. "This is going to be good."

———

The doors at the Raleigh women's shelter were bolted. A young girl in a green parka and a knit cap banged on the door. "Sheryl, let us in. I need to watch my shows."

I scanned the faces, dour and owlish, and imagined which one had routinely made love to the Human Carver. At six sharp, Sheryl clicked open the doors. We piled in. Some headed for beds in the back. A few grabbed for toiletry buckets and strolled toward the showers, plastic caps already on their heads. The woman in the green parka switched on the TV.

I sat down by Sheryl's desk, intent on making my inquiry discreetly. "I'm with the paper," I said, scratching the desk's plywood paneling. "I'm looking for the girlfriend of the . . . hmm . . . the guy who whacked all those homeless women."

Sheryl furrowed her brow. "A real sadness," she said.

"Oh, yeah," I said, feeling about as sensitive as Jesse Helms on the topic of welfare reform. "It must be very scary for people here."

"Kelly's over there," Sheryl said, turning her eyes sideways, toward a natty couch in the corner.

Kelly was a fat, snaggle-toothed woman in a heather gray jogging suit. She was stuffing a hamburger into her face and stammering into the shelter's portable phone. I had expected her to be, well, more appealing. I don't know why. But I guess after I'd seen how popular Hector had been among the men at the shelter, I figured he'd be dating a real babe.

"Hi!" I said, a third-grader, new at school. "My name is Kyle. I'm a reporter."

Kelly nodded, as if she only half-heard me, and sank down low on the couch.

I joined her, my throat tightening, as the unappetizing aroma of processed-cheese and french-fries invaded my lungs. This was the woman my story was hinging on, my last-ditch effort. And I was already worried.

"Who were you talking to?" I asked, my voice crackling with nerves.

"Boyfriend."

"You mean the guy . . . the killer?"

Kelly nodded glumly.

I pictured Kip circling my desk with a deadly stapler in his hand. *Get this interview*, he ordered. Then he mumbled something about my imminent death.

I sat up. "Maybe we should call him again," I suggested.

"No," Kelly barked. "He said he wasn't talking to no fuckin' newspaper reporter."

"Okay, okay . . . that's fine too," I said, letting my pen drop to the floor.

I slithered back down on the couch next to Kelly; I was exhausted. I scanned the shelter living room and let my eyes wander back to the bedroom. Suddenly, a picture of razor-toting Hector and big-bosomed Kelly getting it on in the other room flashed through my head. The vision repulsed me. Beady-eyed Hector. Kelly's rolls of fat. Then it scared me. I jumped up. "Kelly," I blurted out. "Aren't you freaked out? The guy could have killed you."

Kelly crumpled up her hamburger wrapper in a little ball

and stuck it in her pocket. "Of course I'm freaked out," she said, glaring at me as if I was a total moron. "I just didn't know he hated women."

"Some things are dangerously universal," I quipped.

Kelly let out a sad laugh. "They don' tell you that when they trying to git sum."

"Nope," I said, laughing a little too. "Those bastards never do."

Kelly handed me a Merit Light. We settled in, two sad sacks on a Saturday night, our fags glowing in the dark like little car lights.

Time is a source opener. People get warmed up by the silence. Then, sometimes, they talk. I waited.

Kelly peeled off her sneakers and a pair of crusty tennis socks and scanned her living room.

I waited some more. Finally, I was the one who broke the silence.

"He sweet-talk you?" I stomped my cigarette out.

Kelly nodded. "Yeah. I mean, girl, he was the shit." She paused for a second, then took a drag off her cigarette. "You never done gotten some man all wrong?"

"Oh, I have. You know, it's my specialty. Last guy I dated—a photographer. All sweet. Then one day he puts a pillow over my head, says: 'I could kill you like this.' Then he goes: 'I was just joking.'"

Kelly looked at me like suddenly I was unpalatable to her. "Girl, you're lucky to be alive. He sounds like a crazy ass." She squeezed her cigarette between her pinkie and her forefinger and took another drag. "Hector, he waz nice—at first. Brought me food. On Valentine's Day, he brung me a teddy bear with twenty-dollar G's in its paws. Nah, he don' look like a killa—he musta had sum bad-ass split personality. 'Cause, girl, you know what? I waz in luv with him." Kelly smudged her cigarette out on the floor with her fingers and breathed, deeply, like her lungs were sinking.

I touched her shoulder lightly, where her jogging suit puckered up from the hood strings. I was at a loss for words.

"I'm sorry," I finally whispered.

"Sorry?" Kelly said. "I'm the one he spared. I feel sorry for those girls. They died."

I cringed.

Kelly peered down at her watch. "I've got to go to bed," she said, matter-of-factly. "They kick us out at five. And I gotta get crackin' on my new job."

I followed her through a narrow corridor, into the back of the women's shelter. She found a plastic pillow on the floor and settled on a children's bed by the wall.

I stood beneath the faux wood-paneled doorway, plucked my map book out of my shoulder bag, and scanned it for directions home.

Kelly leaned a scaly elbow on her pillow and lifted her head up from the wood bed. "Hey, reporter girl," she called to me. "Are you okay?"

She was still wearing her sneakers.

"Yeah, why?"

"Well, you look kinda lost."

A fluorescent overhead light shone down on the shelter bedroom, illuminating Kelly's face and the bodies of a dozen lanky women. Their teeth were the color of brown sugar. Their arms and legs were poking out of ratty nightgowns. Everything they owned was crumpled inside used suitcases and plastic bags by their beds.

"No, I'm fine," I said, shoving my now-crumpled map back into my bag. "Just new in town."

"Oh, I hate that," Kelly said, dropping her head back on her plastic pillow. "Always have trouble getting acclimated."

I scrambled to my car, noticing that the stars were sparkling against slivers of parking lot gravel. As I careened out of the lot, my wheels crunching against the driveway stones, I couldn't help noting that the moon was a large and airy ball of blue.

Like a piece of dust on a four-lane road,
Honey, I was blown away.

PAM TILLIS

The serial killer story got buried. It fell from 1A to 1B, eventually to the back of the metro section, bumped by an article on a level-one hurricane that never landed.

"Don't take it personally," the lead copy editor told me. "People really care about that weather stuff."

Copy editors are charged with making late-night decisions about where stories ought to be placed. Then, the next afternoon, they are charged with lying to crushed reporters about why they made the decisions that they did. About as truthful as they will ever get is to talk in terms of "strong." As in: "The weather story was stronger." Or: "We just thought your story wasn't quite strong enough."

If you haven't guessed, *not* and *strong* are two words you don't want uttered together anywhere near your pod. Unfortunately, they were together a lot that day, with my name attached.

Maria took an unusually kind approach. Instead of needling me about my poor reporting skills, she pretended I no longer worked at the paper.

Kip was his usual two-sentence guide. "Could have been worse," he said, hovering over my desk. "Now, how 'bout doing a feature?"

Editors steer you toward features for one of two reasons: They think you have a special knack for writing—or they consider you a total flake.

I followed him to the copy machine. "I'm sorry, Kip," I said, leaning against the newsroom bulletin board covered with forms for national journalism conferences. "The story just wasn't happening. I really didn't expect to be filibustered by every homeless person I encountered."

Kip was fiddling with the plastic buttons on the machine. "Some stories are harder to crack than others," he said, avoiding my gaze.

Kip was a master at tough love. He was not one to soothe your reporter soul when you screwed up. I realized this as I scanned his humorless face, looking for a hint of sympathy or collegial understanding. My eyes fell on the thin, silver cross dangling from his neck. It was the first time I'd seen it. Suddenly, I remembered that the week before Kip had mentioned something about going to confession with his kids at their Catholic elementary school. He himself had been educated by a band of Jesuits at a college in Massachusetts.

I had found my saving grace. Kip believed in salvation.

I patted him lightly on his shoulder. "Can I repent?"

Kip cracked a small smile. "Write something I can put on the front page, please."

I chose the Deep River Clay Pigeon Sporting Center in Sanford for the feature that would resurrect me. A story about New York's native bird crashing and dying seemed kind of poetic.

I was on the knobby course before sunup, stomping around in my Doc Martens looking for some action. Before I'd even finished my coffee, a golf cart whizzed by, almost running me over. I realized I was going to need a set of wheels. When the next cart zipped by me, I jumped in front of it and waved my hands in the air. A hunter in leather lace-ups, tight Wranglers, and carrying a big gun stopped the cart. I wanted an in—someone who would let me shadow him and give me the insider scoop.

"Reporter!" I said, flashing my notepad.

"Dexter," he shouted back, removing his beer cooler from the passenger seat. I jumped in. I'd found my man.

Clay shooting is not exactly a fringe sport. In fact, three million Americans—that's one out of every eighty-seven people in this country—participate in the activity. I found all this out while thumbing through a clay pigeon shooting magazine. Fascinated by this tidbit, I had added the magazine to my pile of Dixie research material along with *Southern Living* magazine and a series of Civil War, race car, and doll collectors' fanzines.

To write a decent feature, your subject must include four things: good photos, good quotes, a fair number of obsessed people, and an eccentric spokesperson. Here's why clay shooting passed my test.

1. Clay shooters wear weird stuff: orange plastic glasses, cactus-colored caps with brass buckles on the back, fluorescent shoulder bags with water bottle holders attached.

2. Shooters are full of adages, witticisms, and long-held truisms that make for good quotes. "Shoot, shoot, shoot. And don't stop shooting, till you're done," was a quote I'd read in my clay pigeon shooting magazine.

3. There are a substantial number of people who aren't just into shooting but have slipped unwittingly into the obsessed category. During my research I found dozens of special clay pigeon chat rooms on the web where serious shooters were swapping stories about the best Gore-Tex jackets to wear, and how shooters with bad shooting hands can deal with their carpal tunnel surgery. On one site shooters were exchanging firing techniques that had names like the shallow saucer approach or the deep dive shoot, and on another, they were brainstorming about how to tame unruly, bad-boy shooters who curse during competitions.

4. Finally, the sport has a zany spokesperson: My favorite clay pigeon shooting reporter is a progressive athlete who has long advocated a more holistic approach to the sport. In one of his monthly columns, he went so far as to suggest that his fellow shooters take advantage of massage therapy, psychoanalysis, stream-of-consciousness writing exercises, and ultrasound.

"I know these ideas sound 'squishy,' " he mused. "But heck, they keep you loose and flexible. And they may help you save a target. One target at the right time is worth a lot."

––––––––––

"Boom!" Dexter bellowed, squinting his eyes as he shot the first flying pigeon. It soared out of a clay pigeon trap, fast like a tennis ball from a practice machine. "Boom! See, cowgirl, it's kind of like, you know, boom, boom, boom. Point. Shoot. Bang. Ouch. Hee-haw!"

The quote was perfect for my story. Even more perfect when I noticed Dexter's bulging biceps. I wanted to slip my hands around them and squeeze. How long had it been since I'd seen a man, really seen one? I flipped open my notepad and scribbled some words: "Pigeons—Fragile! Dexter—Available?"

At the next station, Dexter hopped out of the cart and handed me the long-barrel shotgun. "I'll make sure you don't shoot yourself."

I fired nervously in the air, missing the clay bird completely and hitting the trunk of a nearby oak tree.

Dexter made a sound like a buzzer at the state fair. "Pay attention, cowgirl. This is no time for woolgathering." Then he pressed his fingers gently around my waist.

Dexter smelled of sweat, or cow manure, or something really masculine like lawn fertilizer. He was the kind of guy who probably read *Playboy* on the john and patted women on the ass. He would protect you in a hurricane or on a cold winter night.

I didn't need to ask to know that Dexter came from somewhere rustic: a cabin in the Carolina mountains or a farm in the Piedmont region. Or maybe a forest in Virginia. I could almost see him now—gnawing on a slice of meat from a turkey he had shot himself, or clutching an ax as he chopped wood for his campfire. He didn't worry about environmental issues or political reform. Dexter worried about outsmarting Mother Nature. To me, he was a modern-day Thoreau, and I was grateful I had met him.

Dexter grabbed the gun, and we jumped into the cart. We whizzed to the next station. When he stopped, he turned to me slowly to make sure I was paying close attention. He picked up the gun and waited. When the pigeon flew out, he pulled the trigger, and the clay bird exploded.

I looked at the fallen pigeon shards and thought, for a second, about my story, a unique look at the ramifications of the shooting life. It would be intellectual and well-written, introspective and thought-provoking. I would wow Kip with it. He'd want to promote me right away.

Then I saw Dexter's ass. He was brushing shards of clay pigeon off his back pockets. I pictured that ass naked. I was a goner.

————

I've always liked the idea of slipping into a foreign world, like adjusting the lens on your camera so something far away is suddenly up close. It makes the universe seem smaller. It also creates the illusion of options. As a fourth-grader I sometimes imagined myself changing lives with the gifted Gabbie Hershman, waltzing around her spacious Park Avenue apartment, wearing one of her ironed turtlenecks and her matching hair clips made of painted ribbon. I imagined myself doing homework assignments that would get triple stars glued onto them and owning all of her sticker books.

When I was in high school, trading places did not lose its appeal. While my father and Shelby duked it out in SoHo, I'd hang out in Washington Heights, sipping espresso and watching Spanish soap operas with my Dominican boyfriend's mother. She would slap slabs of pork in a frying pan with chopped onions and peppers. Black beans would stew in a pot on the stove. "*Mi amor,*" she would say. "How was school?" I pretended to be the daughter of this serene Dominican soul.

Then, when I became a reporter, I got permission to do the camera lens trick on a regular basis. You can get face time with Michael Jordan, envisioning that you are part of the posse that plays miniature golf with him at three in the morning. You can spend hours with a construction union president, touring work sites and pretending you are a girl builder with muscles in your fingers. You can peek inside people's fridges, the backs of restaurant kitchens, the factories where things are made. As long as you are just reporting—and you keep your clothes on— it's acceptable to really, really want that contact. I don't want to sound like a perv, but for me that second part has always been a bit of a challenge.

At the next station Dexter grabbed me by the shoulder and pulled me toward him so my back was propped up against his chest. He wrapped his arms around my front—his biceps pushing against my breasts. "Don't worry, little lady. I'm one jump ahead of you." He took the shotgun, gently placed my fingers on the trigger, and squeezed his hands tightly around mine.

"Ready?" Dexter whispered into my ear.

"Sure am," I shouted back.

We watched the pigeon shoot out of a brick cage. As it flew through the air, Dexter pressed my trigger finger and then jumped back a bit. I went with him. A bolt of electricity ran through my body.

"Oh Jesus!" he yelped.

"Oh God!" I screamed.

The pigeon flew up and then down and then crashed to the ground.

"We're out there!"

"We're alive!"

"Yee-haw!"

Dexter gave me a little pat on the butt with his shotgun.

I gave him a little friendly pat on the behind in return. "We're under the sky," I said. "Just breathing the air."

And just as I was about to tackle this cowboy and cover him with kisses, I recalled the first words of advice my editor in Philadelphia had given me: "Remember, you're not in this to make friends!"

I removed my hand from Dexter's behind and pulled out my pad. I was perilously close to committing a professional faux pas. I saw Kip standing over my desk, woefully disappointed at my lack of self-control. Then I recalled a chat I had once had with Jane, a more experienced female reporter, on the topic of risky situations.

"Let's face it, finding yourself naked with a source in work boots is an occupational hazard," she had said, having fallen several times herself. "Who wouldn't want to do one of those guys? I mean, look at our options: a broad-shouldered fireman who lifts flaming SUVs for a living or your potbellied office mate. The most exercise he's gotten all week is turning on his Power Book. One's buff and bronzed by the sun and can't wait to show you the goods. The other's got chalk-colored linguine legs and he wants to impress you with his intellectual prowess. No contest."

———

I looked down at my watch; it was already noon. I banished unruly thoughts from my mind and tugged the cap off my pen.

"So, why do you like shooting, Dexter?" I asked, leaning a boot against his golf cart.

Dexter brushed a hand through his hair and looked up at the sky. "The fun of it."

"Mmmmm . . . ," I said, smiling encouragingly.

Dexter coughed, then continued. "I think clay shooting is gaining in popularity because of its inherent down-home nature." He squinted his eyes a bit. "There's something simple—almost primitive—about it. You know, it harkens back to a time when a man wasn't judged on boardroom deals or Internet inventions—but on the power of his pistol and the precision of his aim."

I was impressed—and pleased. "Can you just repeat that last bit," I said, pulling out my pad. This was quote material.

Dexter repeated his sentence, and I jotted it in my pad. Then we sat down together on the edge of the cart. He put his gun on the ground and pulled a can of beer from his cooler. He handed it to me. I smiled. He touched my lips with icy fingers, rested a thick leg against mine. He snapped his beer open. "Thirsty?" he asked. Just a word, concise like his body.

"Yeah," I said smiling.

Cowboys and Indians. Boys and Girls. Pigeons and Guns. I thought about my friends in New York. Bland suits and ties, sipping martinis in posh bars after work. I imagined the lame parties, pretentious get-togethers, brushing shoulders with wimpy Woody Allen types and urban intellectuals unable to communicate with nature.

I took a sip of beer. Dexter nudged me with a hard shoulder. Beer spittle dribbled down my chin. Dexter wiped it off.

"You're dribbling," he said.

"You're dribbable," I replied.

Dexter dove off the cart, a cowboy leaping from his horse. "You've shot me in the heart, cowgirl."

My own heart skipped a beat. Then I fell too—sucking in the sun as I landed on the ground. The grassy slope of the shooting range rose above me. The trees jutted out of the sky. The soft dirt seeped into my back, and the clouds hugged my chest. Bones and muscles, sun and steam. I was not a reporter. Not someone worried about redeeming herself in her editor's eyes. I was Dexter's cowgirl.

I made a bad miscalculation.

RASCAL FLATTS

I drove home, adrenaline zipping through my body like splashy waves on a water slide. I passed the OfficeMax, the Wendy's, the Beautiful Church of Heavenly Saviors. Their windows glowed like amusement park lights as the day's delicious moments looped across my windshield.

A good story high lasts an hour—two if the topic is sex or the body count is in the double digits. If you've just fallen for your source, you can add on another sixty minutes.

By the time I'd stopped off at work and driven home, I was coming down. I fixed a screwdriver, smoked a cigarette, and listened as my prison neighbors got called to dinner. In other words, I faced another night alone. And that was when I began to wonder what exactly I had just done.

Sex with strangers is like Chinese for dinner. It's satisfying for the first two hours—three go by and you start to feel empty inside. Don't get me wrong, I'm not opposed to sexual dalliances. In fact, I'm all for them—in theory. In practice, however, I have come to understand that they make *me* feel like shit. In my early twenties, I used to rage against this man-woman inequality in relation to postsex sentiment. I slept with whomever I could beckon my way and then pretended the shitty feeling wasn't there. The problem is I was assuming that men were right all along, that it was normal and well-adjusted not to feel any emotional connection the morning after romping around naked with another human being. But by twenty-five, I had begun to think that the men weren't right. And that this morning-after sexual inequality existed. It was not that men didn't feel anything emotional after sex. It was just that they were better at keeping what they felt hidden from themselves. Unfortunately for me, the result of my increased self-awareness was not that I avoided sex with strangers. It was that I felt like shit the day after *and* I felt really guilty, and pissed too that I wasn't doing what my stepmother Shelby referred to as "taking care of myself."

With these unpleasant thoughts rumbling through my head, I decided to hit the tub. This was where I was spending most of my nights those first six months—doing just about everything but eating. So, familiar with the bathing routine, I knew exactly how many minutes it took for the hot water to turn cold. Lying there, it occurred to me that I may have flubbed the possibility of seeing Dexter again—and that was a bummer.

By the time I climbed out, my skin was the texture of dried apricots. I checked to see if the phone had rung while I was submerged underwater shampooing. Phoning was my other favored Raleigh sport. And even though I still got the jitters when I hadn't wrapped my fingers around a cord in a few hours and AT&T had already sent me a preferred customer gold card, I was pretty sure I wasn't using it as a crutch.

"Listen, Dad," I said into the receiver, drying myself with a towel. "I know we chatted this morning. But what do you think about artificial insemination? I was just wondering about it— thought I'd get some feedback."

My father, who considered North Carolina about as primitive as a tribal village in Africa, sounded noticeably concerned. "Are you okay?"

"No," I replied.

I hung up and dialed my brother, George, who had just bought an old warehouse building in Brooklyn and was fixing it up. "The next SoHo," he confided in me. "Give me five years. This place is going to be big."

"So, George," I said. "How is the Sheetrocking coming?"

My brother was installing a toilet and was talking to me on the speakerphone. It soon became clear that he was also reading a plumbing manual and arguing with his girlfriend about where to put the porcelain bowl.

"You seem busy," I said.

He agreed, and hung up.

My half brother, Phillip, whom I bothered at military school, was characteristically blunt. "Don't you have anything to do, you loser?"

"No," I replied. "I don't. Now entertain me, you little shit. Tell me what you ate for breakfast this morning."

"Listen, some of us have lives."

"Phillip, I'm bored," I whined. "Talk to me, please!"

"The Knicks, they're choking again in the play-offs."

My younger brother had been talking like an ironworker

from Queens since he was seven. Growing up in SoHo with two angry nonconformist parents can do that to you.

"Phil!"

"What? You wanted to talk. We're talking."

"Phil. I hate baseball."

"I was talking about basketball."

Phil was fiddling with his remote, flipping channels. I could tell I was about to lose him.

"If you hang up on me, Phil, I'm going to kill you. Phil? Phil?"

I pulled on some clothes and lay in my bed, hoping that Mark—who had just moved to Los Angeles—was home alone miserable and depressed with no one to hang out with, too. I had tried calling him several times that day; there was no answer. I dialed his cell.

"Yo, the man here," Mark boomed. I could hear techno music in the background.

"Mark, where are you?" I shouted over the din.

"Party." It sounded like Mark was kissing someone. "Who is it?" I heard a female voice ask.

"But it's noon on Sunday."

"Tail end . . . Hey, Joe. Can I call you later?"

"Joe? My name's Kyle."

Mark didn't hear me; he had already hung up.

A few minutes later I drifted off to sleep to the sound of my prison friends being loudspeakered back to their cells.

———

I woke to the jangling of the telephone.

"That was a wingding of a day, cowgirl. How 'bout a date?"

The voice was scratchy and rough. I panicked, picturing a candlelight dinner on Hector's cell bed. Poor Kelly.

"Hello? Girl, are you there? It's Dexter."

Fleeting moment of relief that I hadn't ruined everything with premature sexual relations, followed by another surge of panic. Respond quickly, I advised myself. Say: *Thank you. But that's against newspaper policy.*

I stared down at my unnaturally clean toes, scrubbed six times this week.

"So, when?"

———

Dressing for a date with Dexter was a challenge. Naturally, there were questions galore. Go as me? The me I imagined Dexter wanted me to be? The me I thought he thought I was? How about the me I thought I wanted to be? Don't laugh. You try moving to North Carolina with a suitcase filled with Betsey Johnson dresses. I ended up wearing tight pants and an over-size man's shirt. Think city-country combo à la Shania Twain. I was eagerly awaiting a night of dank country-western bars, bar-becue, peanuts, and beer.

Dexter surprised me by taking me to a private dining club on the University of North Carolina campus—forty minutes away in Chapel Hill. He told me he was a member, obviously trying to impress me. I didn't ask why, afraid to embarrass him if it turned out he was a janitor or plumber or something at the col-lege. When we got to the restaurant, an elegant dining room with brown leather chairs and white tablecloths, Dexter held open the door for me, took my jacket, helped me to my seat. All good signs.

We ordered, then sipped ice water and waited for our salads. I didn't want Dexter to think I was prodding. But I was eager to get him storytelling. I figured he was full of meaty country boy tales about eating squirrel and growing up dirt poor, stories that would further my knowledge of life in the South.

Finally, I rested my elbow on the table. "So, tell me about where you're from."

Dexter coughed. I could feel his cowboy boot brushing up against my leg. "You mean New Jersey?"

I squinted in amazement. "What? I thought you were Southern."

"No. I just came down here to finish my Ph.D., then I never left."

"That's . . . great," I lied, trying to conceal my disappointment. "So, what's your topic?"

"Asian studies. I've been researching Mao's impact on China's university system for a couple of years now. I followed my professor from Stanford."

"Interesting," I mumbled under my breath, as a woman in heels and a tight black skirt approached the table. Dexter winked at her, and they chatted for a few minutes.

After dinner Dexter and I drove to a bar in Chapel Hill for a nightcap. It was small and quaint with a shellacked bar and painted red tables. It turned out that he knew that place well, too. The bartender called him by his first name, and several thirty-something women and slightly younger men sauntered over to our table to greet him.

About fifteen minutes in, the owner waltzed over to our table—blowing kisses at Dexter and then plopping one right smack on his lips. I don't want to sound parochial, but the gesture seemed a little weird.

For the rest of the evening we talked about European and Asian politics, Eastern philosophy, and twentieth-century art. Dexter knew a lot about the cultural backlash in China and the changing role of women in Japan. He had taken up clay shooting because it was becoming an increasingly popular sport in Asia and he was curious about why.

I think Dexter was enormously pleased by how the date was going. I was not. Raleigh cop, forest ranger, tobacco farmer—that was one thing. But the last thing in the world I wanted to be doing was hanging out with an overaged grad student from the tristate area with an overactive social life that probably included a great deal of sex—with women, and possibly men. Still, Dexter wasn't so bad looking.

That night I did what I shouldn't have. I drank. And then I drank a whole lot more.

————

The next morning, I woke up with the unpleasant feeling that I was sloshing around on a very unstable sailboat. I pressed my hands against the sheet I was lying on and watched my fingers spread. I was trapped on a water bed with Dexter snoring beside me. I scanned the room and noticed that a naked woman with legs spread wide was staring me in the face. The oil painting was signed Nora. I recalled that Dexter had told me his ex-girlfriend was a British painter getting her master's in Asian art. On the floor by the bed were half a dozen candles, massage oils, smelling salts, and a half-burnt stick of incense. Certainly, you expect the people you date to have histories. But this man's history was being shoved up my nose—quite literally.

————

Dexter drove me home, goosed his truck up to my driveway, and switched off the engine. I leaned my back up against his glove compartment, and smiled fakely.

Dexter cracked a smile too. "I'll call you."

I was silent.

"Promise."

I slid out of the truck feeling slightly sad, slightly hopeful—at the same time. So he wasn't what I had expected. So he wasn't really what I wanted. So I really wished we hadn't done what we did. Notwithstanding, this was Raleigh. And I was alone and lonely. And this was the first guy I'd been with in weeks. And he had all his limbs. His parts all worked. He talked.

I spent the next few days imagining my life as the wife of a bisexual playboy professor. Trips to Asia. Friends at every bar in Chapel Hill. A life that was half *Jules and Jim*, half *Flashdance*. By the end of the week we had beautiful, artistic children, a home in Hong Kong. We were coauthoring books about Chinese youth and helping the hungry in Vietnam.

By the beginning of the next week, I lay on my bed, stared at my muted TV, and wondered what it was exactly that had made Dexter seem appealing in the first place. Perhaps, sadly enough, the criterion that he had met was the only one I seemed to need these days. He was there. The thought irked me. And, quite frankly, it felt sort of dangerous. I clicked off the TV and lit a cigarette.

A friend of mine once told me, "Sex with someone you don't know is a trauma to your system." And I concur. But what is no sex at all—no hugs, no kisses, no nothing? By the middle of the following week, when Dexter still hadn't called, I knew what it was. It was worse.

———

Mark was not sympathetic. First, I had woken him up. Second, he didn't like the New Jersey bisexual business. "Tell me you don't really need help deciphering this one."

Mark and I always do postdate commentary. Play-by-plays with wise girl-boy insights interjected at appropriate moments. Some examples:

"We're sitting there, and she just starts going on and on about how she's dying for a dog."

I interrupt: "Wants kids."

Ever-optimistic me: "Architect. Took me out for pizza. Then we—"

Mark interrupts. "Pizza? He's not interested."

"What? He bought me two slices. Well, I paid. . . . But he paid for the diet Cokes. . . . Oh God, Mark, you're right."

Ever since Mark had moved to Hollywood, he had been far exceeding me in the entertainment department. For some reason, his status on the mating market had skyrocketed. "I think it's my brain," he had told me.

"What do you mean?"

"I'm a commodity. I live in California. And I have one."

In any event, Mark was now having "encounters" with aerobics instructors and a TV executive who had called him at two in the morning, muttering, "Want a quickie fuckie?"

"Listen," I had told him when he recounted the story to me. "If that turns you on, I can't help you."

For several weeks Mark had also dated an assistant producer who one night invited him over to watch a movie and listen to the radio simultaneously. When he had complained that he couldn't hear the dialogue, she'd grown so angry she threatened to call the police.

"Listen, brainiac," I told him, "you might want to avoid the psychopaths."

This time I was the one making excuses.

"You fall off a golf cart and do the nasty with a bisexual Ph.D. candidate. You know, you don't have to go to North Carolina to do that," Mark yelled. "They're all over Manhattan."

"Mark, the gene pool is very limited here. I can't afford to be picky. And besides, I don't know that he's bisexual."

"Listen, Kyle. Just be careful."

I didn't like where this was going. I decided to joke it away. "That's easy for you to say. You're living in L.A. You're hobnobbing with movie stars. I'm contemplating dates with guys who go to Hooters. No wonder I'm grasping at straws."

"I'd love to learn more about your demise. But, I've got take this call."

Mark was about to put me on hold, a.k.a. the Hollywood hang-up. It boosts Mark's ego to do that. And I'm okay with helping my best friend feel important about himself. But before I did, I needed some reassurance. I needed to know that if it all failed for me, he was not slipping away.

This is all to say I had Chantal on my mind. "Hey, Mark, what happened to her?"

"You're not going to believe it. She's quitting her job and she wants to move out here."

Silence. This was just what I was worried about. I imagined myself crawling back to New York and spending my evenings talking to myself in the rest room at Odeon—while Mark and his older-woman wife read scripts on her antique sofa. Mark would take my silly charcoal drawings down from his walls. He'd stop listing my positive qualities to cheer me up on a bad day. And if he just happened to do it, and I said: "I like that last one. Can you repeat it—ten times, please," he wouldn't be the old Mark. He'd say: "No. I have to get dressed. Chantal and I are going to the opera."

"Kyle?"

"Yes?"

"I can't live with someone who says phooey."

I smiled. "You're still my insurance policy?"

"As long as you resist a shotgun wedding." I could hear him banging his hand against his desktop. He really amuses himself sometimes.

Mark once told me he liked me because I laughed at all his jokes. I'm okay with that. But sometimes I have to be firm. "Promise you won't ever try to write a comedy?"

Mark cracked up. "Come on, Kyle. You love my jokes."

He was wrong. I didn't just love them; I was living off of them.

5

Feeling a little bit maudlin
Since the carnival rode to town.
But I got my smile painted on
Under the neon
'cause the carnival's in town.

TRAILER BRIDE

Sammy Rooster was Windexing her nineteen-inch TV when I stormed into her trailer, knocking over her leather La-Z-Boy with my knee and her kitchen table with my boot. Sammy's china tea set went flying.

"You know, I'm trying to clean here," she said, rolling her eyes. "Can you please try to be a little more careful?"

"Sorry."

I found a spot on Sammy's fridge and crawled up on it. I tucked my head in my lap, pinched my elbows against my stomach. A vase crashed to the floor.

"Jesus," Sammy hollered, waving her dust rag in the trailer air.

This is what happens when you are invited into the home of the Smallest Woman in the World. Things can feel cramped. And forget about using the bathroom.

I had been hanging out with Sammy Rooster ever since she rolled up to the state fairgrounds a week before in her eye-catching trailer. It had a cardboard chimney, painted red and black to resemble brick, a faux front door that didn't really open, and plastic shutters that were supposed to look like painted wood. It made me think of a class trip I took to the Metropolitan Museum of Art when I was in elementary school. We looked at the Pompeii paintings of outdoor scenes and mountainscapes on plaster. They looked so real. The guide told us: "This is called trompe l'oeil. It means deceiving the eye."

Sammy was in Raleigh preparing for the ten-day run of the North Carolina State Fair. According to the sign above her trailer, she was twenty-nine inches. Her job: offer Tar Heels a glimpse of life in the short lane. Her trailer was specially equipped for the task. It was open at the back so fairgoers could watch her knit, flip through *People* magazine, check up on her favorite soaps. All for the low price of a dollar.

As for me, I had been ordered to loll around the fairgrounds and drum up stories before the gates swung open to the public.

Sammy had sparked my curiosity. I was intrigued by her baby doll dresses, her slippers, as small as pears, the way she made candied apples look like tree trunks when she chomped away at them.

Despite her size, Sammy wasn't childlike. In fact, if you looked at her face and not her body, she looked thirty-five, maybe forty. She had crinkles at the tips of her lips that blossomed when she smiled and cue-ball eyes that bulged when she was annoyed. A few days with her and I had come to realize she wasn't really a midget, she was a lady with short appendages. If she could get them stretched out, she'd be normal size. But then, of course, she'd be out of a job.

That Monday I was at her side recuperating from the most recent torture Kip had imposed on me: ten minutes on the Top Spin. The state fair press kit referred to it as a "spinning, plummeting screamer." And Kip, using some warped metro editor logic, had decided it was my job to test it. He said it had to do with safety, and hence police stuff.

I told Sammy about the new ride.

"Good thing I'm a few inches below the legal height for that thing," she said, spraying stain remover on her Oriental rug. "The fair organizers wanted to take some pictures of me on it, just for publicity. I told them if they asked me again, I'd report them to the Feds." Sammy scrubbed her rug with a rag.

Being sixty-two inches myself, I had no such leverage. Twenty other journalists and I had been strapped into seats, raised six stories into the sky, then dropped like atomic bombs. If the seats had come unhinged, they would have crashed to the ground and folded like tinfoil. During the descent, I lost an earring and my voice, and I almost unloaded my elephant ear lunch before unstrapping myself and stumbling out of my seat with Kip's name and a few curse words on my tongue.

After the ride the press department led all the dizzy journalists over to a muddy podium where the state ride inspector recited several safety statistics—provided by the state's insurance company—into a microphone. Among other things, he told us that 95 percent of amusement ride accidents in North Carolina were caused by rider carelessness, rather than equipment failure.

Sammy chuckled when she heard this, her pudgy corn dog arms flailing in the air. "Is that supposed to reassure you? If you're dead you're dead. Who cares if it's your own damn fault. These people are unbelievable. And to think they manage to run a fair."

Since I'd started visiting with Sammy, I'd learned she was not the most chipper person in the world. She liked to vent.

The cost of fair hot dogs, the placement of her trailer, the way the fair manager referred to her by her first name when he greeted her, had all aggravated her.

"I'm not a clown," she had said to me several times since I'd met her—as way of explanation for her unpleasant demeanor. "I don't do happy. I don't do comedy. I do small. That's an important distinction."

That day it wasn't just the Top Spin that had Sammy peeved. Her nemesis, whom she referred to as "a certain headless woman," was acting up. The headless woman, Sammy said, lived and worked "too close for comfort"—a mere two trailers down.

"She called me an egomaniac because I didn't want to move next to the Fun Haus," Sammy screeched. "She wants to switch with me, so she can be next to the Ferris wheel. Can you believe that? The one thing I have at this fair. And she wants me to give it up." Sammy finished with her rug scrubbing, plopped down on her couch, and began poking ferociously at a ball of yarn with two knitting needles.

The headless woman, she told me, was a young, underqualified drifter from San Francisco who had used some coffeehouse connections to get herself on the fair circuit. "Nothing up there," Sammy said, tapping her head with one of her needles.

"Well, are you going to switch with her?"

Sammy sneered at me. "No way. First, I'm not doing her any favors. Second, I don't park near haunted houses. It's bad for my image. I may be small, but I'm not a freak show. I have to set limits. You know, establish boundaries."

I nodded knowingly, pretending to relate. But I didn't. I was in no position to refuse my colleagues requests. In fact, as a cub reporter, I figured that was part of my job, to say yes to everything—except sexual favors—a superior asked. In that respect, Sammy was definitely higher up on the food chain than I was.

Sammy pointed one of her knitting needles at me. "There is only so much I'm willing to put up with in this business," she hollered. "And let me tell you, if you don't speak up, people will walk all over you, especially someone like me. They think they can shove me around because I'm twenty-nine inches. But I know who's got the upper hand." She tapped the needle against the couch. "It's easy to find headless women. For God's sakes. All they are are young actresses with mirrors and imaginations. But me, Kyle, I'm the real deal."

———

Despite Sammy's foul mood, the 130-year-old North Carolina State Fair was nothing to sneeze at. With dozens of rides, 165 food stands, and thousands of judging competitions, it was one of the largest state fairs in the country. With the exception of a six-year break during the Civil War and Reconstruction period and a one-year break during the 1918 influenza epidemic, the fair had run continuously, garnering more public attention every year. Parents shamelessly took their kids out of school. Employees unapologetically skipped out of work. Bosses gave days off. The fall I covered it, 800,000 people came. If New York had Fashion Week and Hollywood had Oscar Week, Raleigh had the fair. I was off cops for ten days.

———

I drove back to the office and filed my Top Spin story. Then I headed for Kip's desk. "I want to write about the twenty-nine-inch lady tomorrow," I announced, plopping myself down in his swivel chair and digging into his popcorn bag. "She wears wool booties with pom-poms on the tips and little dresses with rainbows swishing across them. And she's got this rivalry going with the headless woman. You wouldn't believe it."

I had been on the job for six months now, and Kip was growing accustomed to my tirades, and even more used to my chair stealing. He leaned against the pole by his desk—and fastened his eyes on me. I was about to rest my feet on his mouse pad.

"You don't have your own desk?" he quipped.

I got up. "Sorry."

I sometimes wished Kip had a mood barometer attached to his lapel. How much of his oxford had dropped out of his pants was a good indicator of where he was in the day, but I always noticed that too late. Like after I sensed he wanted to clobber me with my notepad.

Kip's moods were not incidental. They determined the play of your stories and the amount of time he would spend editing them. Whether he would care at all. When he was in good spirits, I could actually elicit gruff chuckles out of him. Sometimes, a whole sentence would come streaming out of his mouth. I would bang my hand against his desk. He'd draw squares on a pad and fill them up with sections for a proposed story. "Here, you lure the reader," he'd say, circling one of the squares. "Here, you teach them. Then you zap them with the 'oh' factor."

We'd be off, in our own world, immersed in some story. When I was sent to write a piece about a shopping mall manager with a secret heroin addiction who died during a shoot-out between police and his dealer, Kip's moon-shaped eyes glistened. "This is not a police story," he mumbled. "It's a story about a seemingly normal guy leading a double life, having an out-of-control love affair with a deadly drug."

But when Kip was in bad spirits, he clammed up. You could carry on a whole conversation with yourself, and he'd pretend you weren't there. You wanted to poke him in the ribs, yell: "Say something." But you knew it wouldn't work. Kip was like the office computer system. When it was down, it was down. And there was nothing you could do but wait.

That afternoon Kip was on state fair patrol. A page designer had just threatened to put a house ad in the center of the main fair page if Kip didn't hurry up and finish editing a piece about the fair manager.

"House ad?" Kip mumbled, pulling out the remaining tucked-in edges of his oxford from his khakis and rolling up his left sleeve.

"What else do we have left for tomorrow?" a copy editor hollered from across the room.

"The emu burger stand almost burned down," Kip replied wearily.

"Good, the prefair piece on the Top Spin that's going tomorrow is illegible," another copy editor shouted.

I smiled meekly at Kip. "Hey, I was sick," I said. "That ride was brutal."

Kip didn't take well to meek smiling. I was still lording over his desk. And I could tell he wanted to get rid of me.

"The twenty-nine-inch lady is already taken," he said.

"How 'bout the headless woman? I already have a jump start on that."

"Taken."

"Largest pig?"

"Taken."

"Kip, I can't believe you. You didn't save anything good for me."

Kip ignored me. "You're covering food. Ten days of meals on the paper."

I could tell he was on the counterattack. If I stayed at his desk any longer, he'd make me write about the cyberspace exhibit.

I fired back one last time. "I expect the paper will also pay for my supply of Rolaids, Pepto-Bismol, and Alka-Seltzer."

Kip's phone rang. "No," he said to me, before picking up the receiver. "But you can help yourself to my bottom drawer." He brushed me away, then mumbled into the phone: "No, we are not putting a house ad on the fair page."

———

I fed Sammy for ten days. I'd go research a food story—tacos, ham biscuits, fried onions—take a few bites of my subject material, jot some notes down on the taste and texture, then wrap up the perishables and deliver them to her trailer.

The afternoon I brought Sammy some barbecue samples, she tore off the cellophane and bit into a rib. "Thanks," she said. "I just love these things."

A gaggle of teenagers in oversize jeans and long rope key chains falling out of their pants pockets were stepping around the corner. I found a spot on the ledge of the trailer and waited. I wanted to see Sammy in action.

Sammy wiped her mouth on her dress. "Oh God, here come the teenagers. They're the worst."

Sammy took another bite of her barbecue stick.

"Look, she eats," one shouted.

"That's gross," another one bellowed.

"God, that thing is bigger than her."

I wished I'd brought Sammy something smaller—like a chocolate chip cookie or a piece of candy.

"I wonder if she gets laid."

"You perv!"

Sammy polished off her barbecue stick and turned on her TV set, loud.

"Hey, little lady. Short lady, yoo-hoo."

Sammy stared at the set and acted as if there was a glass wall that protected her from the visitors.

"Shorty, don't you talk? Shorty . . ."

I looked at Sammy in her barbecue-stained dress and pretended not to hear the young hecklers either.

When they left she clicked off her TV and rested her foot up on her coffee table.

"People are shitty," she said. "You know, the younger ones want to talk to me about the sex. The women want to hear my sob stories. The men want to sleep with me." Sammy plucked a compact from the coffee table and applied some lipstick. "No one wants to sleep with a headless woman, the bearded woman they won't go near. But small, they all want to try that."

"God, I can't believe guys actually want to sleep with you. What sickos!"

The words shot out too fast for me to realize how insensitive they were.

Sammy wasn't fazed. She looked puzzled herself. "I guess they're curious," she said.

I was curious, too. I couldn't help wondering if Sammy could handle a big guy, say a really big guy. But I didn't ask.

———

I spent much of the next week writing about biscuit makers and cherry pie competitions. The next time I visited Sammy, I brought her a bacon biscuit. She was entertaining a middle-aged mother—wearing a Winnie-the-Pooh sweatshirt—and her ten-year-old daughter—in stretchy pants and a sexy halter top.

"Not a fan of pig," Sammy said, poking her nose into the paper bag and grimacing. She handed the bag back to me. "Nice of you to think of me. But I'm more of a steak and barbecue person."

"Isn't she cute?" the mother said to her daughter, before addressing Sammy. "Can my little daughter touch you?"

Sammy put a doughy hand out and smiled.

"You're ugly," the girl said, adjusting her halter top.

Sammy forced another smile. "It's all relative," she said.

Her response sounded kind of pathetic.

When the woman and her daughter left, Sammy flopped down on her couch. "It's like modeling. Some days you love it; you feel like you're on top of the world. Other times, you just feel objectified. Your size is all that counts. You think Kate Moss is the only one who has these worries? And to make matters worse, I've got to deal with the jealousy stuff."

Sammy had had another fight with the headless woman.

"She came over bragging that she got a hundred visitors yesterday. I only got seventy-eight. She thinks she runs this place."

Sammy told me the headless woman had been "trying to destroy" her for months. She was intent on making waves, "because of her insecurity."

"She sounds like a real pain," I said.

"Sure is. You know, her parents are dead, and her brother has some weird disease. But I can't really pity her. This morning she told me I had a Napoleonic complex. I told her she had head envy." Sammy chuckled bitterly. "Office politics. . . . The thing is, the woman doesn't know when to give up."

The situation with the headless woman had been trying Sammy's patience for a while. During a fair in Tallahassee, the headless woman had spread a rumor that Sammy was really thirty inches, and hence not the Smallest Woman in the World. And in Chattanooga, she had told everyone Sammy slept with the guy who watches over the three-hundred-pound pig.

"It was humiliating. . . . Now she just won't stop making little jokes about my size," Sammy said, glancing sadly around her trailer. "And you know what? You never get used to them."

Sammy stretched out a pudgy hand and pressed her fingers against the charm bracelet around my wrist. I'd found it in Shelby's closet when I was eleven. Shelby's father had given it to her when she graduated from high school. It had a silver

Christmas tree on it and a drama honors award that Shelby had won in high school, a little bell, and a cat.

"I like your bracelet," Sammy said.

I felt ashamed at being normal size, at having a head, at working a regular job. I pulled off the bracelet and handed it to Sammy.

———

All the fights with the headless lady had me intrigued. I didn't want to betray Sammy. But I wanted the lowdown. Both sides of the story.

The day the fair ended, I strolled over to the headless woman's trailer. Her ad said she had been decapitated in 1985 when her car ran under a truck. But I'd read in an article written about her the year before that she wasn't really headless. According to Tom, the reporter who had written the story, she actually had a mane of pretty auburn hair that a viewing window and a glare of lights kept hidden from viewers. I paid my one dollar and slipped inside her trailer. The lights shone down on her wiggling body. It twisted and turned like she was possessed. "Hah," a female voice moaned. "Where's my head?"

When my time was up I crawled around to the back of the trailer and tapped on the door.

"It's open. Come in."

Inside, a girl in jeans and a black leather jacket was resting on a folding chair, brushing her hair. She had lips painted deep red and slabs of dark eye shadow on her crescent-shaped lids. She was freshly made up. Strange, I thought, for someone who never shows her face.

"I'm a reporter."

"Can't reveal anything till the fair is over," she said. "Manager's policy. So, I guess you better leave."

"Can we talk off the record?"

"What do you mean?"

"No quotes."

"Well, okay. It depends on what you want."

I asked her about Sammy.

"Who?"

"Pretty small lady." I brushed my arm against my calf to illustrate. " 'Bout this high."

Gasping laughs came out of the headless woman's mouth. "Oh, Sammy." I noticed her lipstick was slightly smeared. I couldn't really tell where her lips ended. "I love her."

"You do?"

"Yeah. We're buds."

"No?"

"Yeah. Wait." She let out a loud hoot. "Did she tell you about me?"

She laughed some more.

"Yes. She did. . . . Why?"

"It's"—she was wheezing with glee—"part of . . . Oh, my God. I can't stop. She is so funny about it. . . . Part of her skit. It's part of her skit."

I looked at the headless woman like she'd just told me she didn't have feet either.

"Our boss, he manages the sideshows here—bearded woman, headless woman, smallest woman. He tells us to create stories. You know, things to get people's imaginations going. Get them here. Did she tell you— Oh God." She was laughing even more. "Did she tell you she feels like Kate Moss? Objectified?"

I nodded.

"Well, he tells us to do that too. I would, but I'm headless. So I tell people nobody loves me for what's in my head. Sometimes I say: 'Sorry, I've lost my head. I can't get ahead in life. I'm not very headstrong. . . .' "

She was wheezing, heaving, out of control.

I turned around and marched out of the trailer.

———————

Sammy was knitting a new pair of booties when I bolted into her trailer for the last time.

"Sammy, I can't believe you. You've been lying to me all this time."

Sammy looked up from her work nonchalantly.

"I talked to the headless woman. She says everything you told me was part of your skit."

"So?"

"But I'm a reporter. I thought you'd tell me the truth."

"Why?"

"I don't know. I trusted you."

"Do you feel like you've been lied to when you go to the movies?"

"No. But I guess I thought this was different. I mean, it's a little confusing."

"Well, it's not my problem if you can't separate fact from fiction." She put her head back down and kept knitting, looping in and out of the wool with her needles.

"What have you told me that's true?"

Sammy set her needles down on her coffee table. "That I'm twenty-nine inches. Not twenty-four. Not thirty. Twenty-nine. Isn't that enough? Why else are you here? You're intrigued. You want to know about the twenty-nine-inch lady. If I were normal you wouldn't give me the time of day. Don't kid yourself. This is your fantasy I'm playing into."

Sammy's words pressed against my cheeks like two hot coals.

———————

It was almost ten and the sky was dimming fast. The string of fluorescent bulbs linking the food and game stands together glowed above the fairway—this time looking more gaudy than exciting. The shrill cries of the kids on the Top Spin suddenly sounded more psychotic than exhilarating. The loud chant of the man at the barbecue stand—"So good you'll slap your momma upside her head"—no longer seemed funny.

There were buzzers and beepers, bells and cacophonous shouts. "Hey, little lady, let me guess your weight. Hey, man, let me paint your girlfriend's face. Hey, kids, don't you want your daddy to git you some popcorn?"

The guy manning the Ferris wheel was caked in grease. I spotted a kissing couple by the Marlboro stand, groping and pawing at each other.

I saw a pretty girl with auburn hair. It was the headless woman on her coffee break. The headless woman wiping her hands across her forehead, the headless woman brushing a lock of hair from her head.

Had anything I'd seen at the fair been real? I stepped up to the emu burger stand and bought my last burger. Worn out, I plopped down on a bench by the world's largest pig. They told me it was an emu burger. *But God knows what's in this thing*, I thought. I took a grainy bite—then tossed the burger in a plastic pail by the bench.

———

When I was seven, I stepped out of a car backseat in Bayport, Long Island and my friend Susie leaned toward me and whispered into my ear: "I have a secret. My mom told me it, about Shelby."

"What?"

"Shelby had a baby die inside her stomach."

My neck got itchy because of my sweater. And my toes dug into the ribs of my saddle shoes.

Susie said the hospital tag on Shelby's wrist wasn't from tonsillitis like she'd told me. It was from getting her dead baby pulled out of her vagina.

"You're a liar."

Susie rested her hands on the pockets of her Sasson jeans. "Ask her."

When I did Shelby lifted up her T-shirt and let me touch her sore belly. "Why do you always need to know the truth, darling?"

What's a broken heart?
It ain't no big deal.
It's not what I have.
It's only what I feel.

PATTY LOVELESS

My father announced family vacation plans the way he discussed all family matters: with the pugnaciousness usually reserved for warlords.

"Kyle," he boomed into my telephone one Monday afternoon in November. "How 'bout we go down to Harlingen this weekend and find out why your brother finds life in the army barracks so much more peaceful than home?"

It was my day off. And I was spending it, kitchen knife in hand, scraping state fair mud of my boots. I rested the phone on my shoulder.

My father chuckled. "Think it has something to do with

Drama Queen?" Drama Queen was one of the kinder nick-
names my father had for Shelby.

"Be nice," I scolded, banging one of my boots against the
garbage can and pondering the thought of skipping town. "You
sound like an asshole."

Ever since my parents had launched permanent war, they
always sounded unpleasant and unlikable when they spoke
about each other.

Harlingen, Texas, a border town of 50,000, boasted an
annual birding festival, a four-lane international highway cross-
ing into Mexico, and Phillip's twenty-year-old military academy,
where, according to Phillip, a year ago a young man had been
expelled for dangling his roommate from a dorm window.
Phillip liked to impress upon us how much suffering he was
willing to endure for the privilege of life away from the family
unit.

My teenage brother's interest in distancing himself from the
people who bore him had surfaced over a year before, when
he climbed up into his second-floor bedroom, taped the window overlooking our loft shut, and announced through a small
crack that from now on out he was only to be disturbed if the
phone rang and the person on the other end wished to con-
verse with him. As for meals, my father's popcorn dinners
would no longer suffice, he announced. "I'll be ordering my
own food. Just leave me money on the kitchen counter on your
way out."

They obliged him. The guilt of warring parents is a powerful thing.

From then on Phillip spent his free time collecting cigarette
ashes in beer cans and enjoying his collection of hard-core CDs
by bands with names like Sick of It All and Madball. He also
researched: Right-wing politics in America and professional
wrestling were his preferred topics. William F. Buckley, Jr.,
became his new idol. In SoHo this is called rebellion.

Then one afternoon in early June, Phillip dropped his books, pulled off his Walkman, bolted down his ladder, and announced his wish for the summer: military camp in Texas. "Please leave a check on the kitchen counter on your way out," he ordered my parents.

"Are you feeling okay?" Shelby reportedly asked him, her Charles Jourdan green suede six-incher pointing menacingly at my little brother's feet.

"No" he replied. "How could anyone feel okay in this house? You people are fuckin' lunatics."

My younger brother has always been good at getting his point across.

When Shelby called me about Phillip's decision, she seemed pleased. "I think your brother realizes he needs some discipline."

"I thought that was your job."

"Oh please, your father has such mixed feelings about discipline."

"Do you have mixed feelings about discipline?" I asked my father a few days later.

"That's just Shelby's psychobabble. The truth is she drives your brother insane."

"And you don't?"

"I hardly think I'm the problem here."

———————

Phillip spent eight weeks performing marching drills in 115-degree weather, feasting on mystery meat and mashed potatoes, and being verbally harassed by a drill sergeant who considered words like *faggot* appropriate terms of endearment for teenage boys. At the end of the summer, he called me. "I'm staying for school," he screamed over the din of the mess hall.

"What do you mean?" I asked—worried my little brother was suffering from heatstroke.

"I mean I'm gaining some perspective."

I was only slightly surprised, really, that my little brother considered military school safer than home.

Now, three months later, the academy was hosting its annual "Birthday Weekend." And my father had already coaxed Shelby's mother, who lived in the neighboring state of Louisiana, to come—as well as Karen, Phillip's blue-haired friend-girlfriend whom he had met a few summers before during an Outward Bound trip in Maine. Karen lived in Queens with her older sister, a law student at Hunter.

George had opted out of going. He had just finished the renovations on his second apartment in the Brooklyn building he had purchased six months before. He needed to stay in town to let his new tenants, three Pratt art students and four cats into the building. As for me, I needed no coaxing and I had no excuses. I threw my knife into the sink and tossed my boots into the air. "I'm there," I told my father.

———

I met my parents at the Harlingen gate in the Houston airport. Shelby was perched on a stool at the gate bar, polishing off a Chardonnay and chatting giddily with the bartender. My father was positioned, across the carpeted aisle, in an empty waiting area, his head buried inside a Winston Churchill biography. Karen was sitting next to Shelby—in her cowboy boots, tent skirt, and nose ring—downing a Miller Lite, her first alcoholic beverage of the weekend. Shelby was not opposed to underage drinking. In fact, she often allowed us a glass of wine or beer on special occasions. "It demystifies the experience," she liked to say. I had always appreciated her outlook. Drinking with parents is a cost-effective way to get plastered. Karen was catching on.

Ever since Karen had started showing up at our house around dinnertime, my family had taken her on as a kind of pet project. Her exact connection to Phillip was unclear. There had been a brief dating stint or a crush or something like that between them. Phillip liked to smack me on the side of my head, right above my right ear, when I asked for details. So I stuck to my hunches. Shelby liked Karen. I assumed it was not because she was interesting or insightful, or particularly fun to be around—Karen really wasn't any of those. I assumed Shelby liked her because she needed our help. "These kids are so poorly supervised," Shelby liked to say.

I couldn't help pitying this blue-haired teenage soul who saw my family as a Brady Bunch of sorts. Shelby, I could tell, liked the idea. It gave her hope—a sense that as a family maybe we were okay.

"Clay, life's a process," I heard Shelby tell the bartender. "And I really believe in people's capacity to change. Your girl-friend might come around."

She hadn't been there an hour, and Shelby was already on a first-name basis with the bartender, immersed in his love woes, carefully giving advice. This was trademark Shelby. She made new friends everywhere: on airplanes, buses, in line at the grocery store. Once, she made friends with a penniless British film student. A few days later, Shelby had hired him to paint our living room. Shelby gave virtual strangers the sense that she cared deeply about their lives; and she did. Age, race, class, these were incidental to her. What Shelby uncovered in people—no matter how seemingly different they might be—were the qualities they possessed that made them like us. It was a trait that I admired.

When Shelby saw me, she patted me on the head. "Poor guy," she whispered. "He's struggling." She took the last chug of her wine. "But who isn't? Are you hungry?"

When we were ready to take off, Shelby shouted to my father from her stool. "George? Where'd your father go? George? I forgot to get cash."

My father poked his head up from his book and shuffled

slowly over. He stared at Shelby with two icy eyes. "You're drunk."

————

The weekend ceremonies began—under a beating sun—with a demonstration of the academy's daily drill. Shelby's mother, whom we referred to as Granny, had met us at the hotel but stayed in our suite to rest with Karen while the three of us attended the short afternoon festivities.

Shelby, my father, and I plopped down on the stainless-steel benches set up on the school lawn and watched as the young cadets stomped through the grass, their pea green demilitarized rifles resting against their wool jackets. I scanned the bodies looking for Phillip.

"Order arms," bellowed the commanding sergeant as the marching bodies formed dark *y*s and *x*s on the grass. "Right shoulder. Left shoulder. Order arms."

My father's face was slowly turning the color of cooked tomatoes. Pearly droplets of hot water were dripping off Shelby's dark Charles Jourdan sunglasses—obscuring her view. I was sweating so hard in my black suit I felt like someone had rolled me up in plastic wrap. The pain was augmented by the fact that all around us the rest of the families were dressed for the beach—decked out in pastel-colored outfits and floppy straw hats. They were hiding underneath big umbrellas and gulping from cold water bottles. We, by contrast, were dressed for ski season in Aspen.

"Jesus, they could have mentioned the weather in the invitation," Shelby said.

"I guess they thought you'd figure it out," my father replied.

"Listen to him," Shelby whispered into my ear. "Your father couldn't crawl his way out of a paper bag."

I remembered a time when Shelby described my father differently. "Your father has an eye for business," she would say.

Or "The thing about your father and I is that, despite our issues, we share the same values." In one of the many moments during my childhood when she forgot I was a child, she told me, chuckling heartily, "Your father doesn't like to have sex as much as some of my other boyfriends. But sometimes, Kyle, it's the quality that counts."

My father rolled his eyes and whispered into my other ear. "She thinks she looks good in those sunglasses. But the people here, they don't want to have anything to do with a woman who looks like that."

Perhaps he was right. But there had been a time when my father had admired Shelby's individuality. He had considered it a sophisticated privilege to attend her cutting-edge, under-ground plays, knowing the buxom woman onstage wearing a costume that included a closet hanger unraveled and draped around her body was his lover. He had liked frequenting the East Village art parties she dragged him to with cool down-town artists who were gay, straight, and sometimes bi. At one time, he viewed my stepmother—with her Italian American roots, sparkly halter tops, fingernails painted hot peach, spicy red, green, or blue—as a sexy and exciting way to thumb his nose at the Upper East Side world he had come from. By help-ing my father gain entrée into Manhattan's antiestablishment, Shelby had liberated him. And sometimes I felt like he should have been more grateful and appreciative.

When the drill was over, we unstuck our sweaty bodies from the benches and panted our way to the barracks where the stu-dents slept. Walking around the campus, I noticed that the school looked like an airport or a community college built in the 1950s. There were redbrick buildings, lush lawns, and a few imposing war monuments. It was so neat, well-kept, it made you want to tuck in your shirt, comb your hair, clear your throat. No wonder Phillip likes it here, I thought. Shelby's din-ing room table newspaper collection would be strictly forbidden in a place like this. As for my father's uncontrollable outbursts, they would be outlawed as well.

———————

A few hours later, after a Marine-quality bed-making demonstration and a tour of the Harlingen fast-food strip in Shelby's rented red convertible, we careened into the spacious parking lot of the San Salvador High School football stadium, where the Bullhorns, the Marine Academy for Boys team, were gearing up for the homecoming game against the San Salvador Hounds.

The stadium's strobe lights were so bright and the *boom-boom-clang* of the marching band was pumping so loudly through the air, I imagined for a split second that the four of us were on a movie set. Meanwhile, teenagers raced past us in football gear, cheerleading outfits, and band uniforms. I was reminded of the Macy's Thanksgiving Day parade. The whole scene seemed so exotically wholesome—like an after-school TV special or one of those parking lot scenes in an Archie comic book. I felt like I was part of something truly American— something I had never seen in my own public high school, where stick-thin John Woo, the Korean coach of our ultimate Frisbee team, was the campus jock and Mark and I were the awkward minorities—being white and non-Jewish.

During the game, Shelby and I nibbled on the tacos she'd bought from a Mexican stand on the ride to the stadium. We dripped hot sauce on our outfits and smudged our makeup while our bench mates, well-behaved in their sandals and ironed Calvins, daintily sipped sodas and nibbled on the Fritos pies they had purchased at the concession stand. They picked at the cooked Fritos slathered in American cheese with their plastic sporks and pierced us with cold suburban stares, the kind that normal people like to give the abnormal.

"I'm sorry," my stepmother said to no one in particular

when it became clear to her that we were the only ones enjoying a Mexican picnic. "Hell, we don't even have football in New York."

Excusing herself to strangers was another one of Shelby's habits. It was, I think, born out of a conviction that people were both aware of her kooky behavior and interested in learning more about its origins.

And sometimes they were. But I think there was something deeper about my stepmother's need to tell the world about her individuality. While most adults preach cooperation and team spirit, Shelby preached freedom. As a social worker, she made the troubled teenage girls she dealt with sign contracts promising that they understood getting pregnant at seventeen was perhaps alluring and trendy in the South Bronx, but also death to their future. One summer, she helped a young gay friend come out of the closet. Before she had grown to hate my father's paintings, she had encouraged him to paint. And she always encouraged me to write. If there was a lesson Shelby seemed destined to teach the world, it was one about self-expression. To her, the world was a wacky place where a lot of people got trapped. And the best revenge was simply to refuse to fit into someone else's box.

But at eight-thirty on a Friday night, in Harlingen, Texas, no one was paying much attention. A player on my brother's team had just scored a twenty-yard touchdown pass, leaping across the field in his oversize red-and-gold jersey like an astronaut doing aerobics on the moon. He'd grabbed the ball, kicked his left leg to the left, kicked his right leg to the right, and bounced past his baffled opponents, who couldn't figure out what he was doing. The entire MAB side of the stadium stood up to cheer, hooting and hollering and banging against the benches. The San Salvador side booed in Spanish.

Shelby and I locked eyes. We were both bored and unsure why these people were so gung ho about the events unfolding before us. Just as the noise died down Karen—who had taken off to get an up close look at the outfits worn by the ninth-grade cheerleading team on the other side of the field—returned with a report. "Those skirts are such the scene," she said, blowing ashtray breath our way. "Totally campy, I'm loving it. Can you not see me wearing one of those out clubbing? I tried to get this girl to sell me one—but she said the cheerleading coach would get mad."

Just as Shelby was about to embark on a lengthy discussion about what will and won't work on the New York City club scene, the band began playing a jazzy rendition of "We will, we will rock you." A scratchy-voiced guy in the scoring booth hollered into his microphone: "Ladies and gentlemen, señores and señoras, let's please put our hands together for Juan Garcia and Julietta Sanchez, this year's San Salvador's Homecoming king and queen."

The crowd clapped merrily.

"Sanchez is a mostly B student who is hoping to pursue a college degree at Texas Tech. His lovely companion is heading off to four years of cheerleading at Florida State. Let's wish them luck."

"Wish them luck?" quipped Shelby, who was an A student in high school. "They're going to need it."

The crowd cheered again as the two stepped off the benches and into a green convertible Camaro, which began circling the field.

The homecoming king was cloaked in a sky blue satin shirt with a petite crown resting atop his slicked-back hair. His coffee bean eyes sparkled as he swayed back and forth in the convertible, waving at the crowd like the winner of a Miss America pageant who was hoping to get an offer for a toothpaste commercial. Each time he swayed, he managed to bump his queen down a little on the seat. He had her wrestling to keep her crown on the entire four laps around the stadium.

"He looks more like a queen than she does," my father said.

"Shhh," I said, holding back a smile. "Someone is going to hear you."

"Well, look at that getup," he replied. "I don't know any straight teenager who would wear a shirt like that."

"This is Texas."

"Precisely my point. He looks like he ought to be on Christopher Street. He's a fag."

"George!" Shelby shouted. This was the second time Shelby had spoken to my father that weekend. I was pleased to see them making some progress in the communication department. "Hell, do you have to use that kind of language?"

"Really, Dad," I said.

"Well, he wouldn't stand out at any New York City club," Karen offered.

"What straight teenagers go to those clubs?"

"My friends," Karen said.

My father chuckled. "But we're not sure they're straight."

Karen kicked her army boot against the bench in front of her. "Just because they go to gay clubs doesn't mean they're not straight," she said.

"It doesn't?" I said, feeling confused.

Several of our Calvin-clad neighbors eyed us cruelly.

"Please," the lady next to us yelled. "This is a family outing."

"Gay people have families too," Shelby said.

"You people really ought to quiet down," the lady responded.

"Because we think it's okay to talk about being gay?"

"Maybe they don't want to hear your garbage," my father replied, delighted that he could confuse the matter.

Fortunately, Granny couldn't hear any of this. She was down at the soft drink booth, chatting with the head of the PTA about her other grandkids. She returned just as halftime was ending, waving a little MAB flag that one of the ladies had given her. I could tell that Shelby's feelings had been hurt by my father's remark. She was starting to twitch and get misty-eyed simultaneously. These were bad signs. I decided to abandon Shelby's ship and sit next to Granny, where the potential for embarrassment was minimal. It was a choice I'd probably pay for later. I figured I'd take my chances.

Life with Shelby was all about alliances. Whose side you bet on was the crucial question. I oscillated often, sometimes sticking up for her, knowing there was mucho payback involved in that strategic position. Like you might get some new clothes. You might get to be on the hit list—as opposed to the shit list—for a while. Sometimes I sided with her because I knew I owed it to her. She had listened to me obsess about a boy for three hours over the phone. Or she had let me wake her up at two in the morning so I could cry about career woes. Maybe she'd taken me to Dean & Deluca and bought fifty dollars' worth of my favorite French cheese or sent me a dress from the sample sale at Dosa, her favorite clothing store in SoHo. Other times I gave up on her and suffered the consequences. This was one of those times.

Karen pried the MAB flag from Granny's fingers just as the game resumed and began making wide streaks above her blue head, bopping us with its tip each time she shifted her weight. The first play was a relatively simple one. Ball thrown, caught by an MAB player in one of the astronaut suits. Player throttled by opponent. Two land on the ground and sway back and forth like a pair of spacewalkers making enthusiastic love on the moon. Ball rolls out from beneath them and stops by the sidelines.

Puzzled, I turned my eyes subtly toward Granny, who was tapping her Keds nervously against the metal floor. "Darn!" Granny hissed, as our neighbors began to boo.

"Darn!" Shelby and I repeated.

"Shit!" Karen yelped.

Granny eyed her disapprovingly and shook her head. So did

several of the Calvin-clad neighbors who were twitching in their seats.

When the referee hit the field and began bickering with the MAB coach, the crowd got hushed. All eyes were on the sidelines.

The referee's hands swished through the air. "It's out!"

"Bad call," Granny mumbled, nodding her head again.

"Bad call!" I repeated a little louder, as more bleacher booing ensued.

The commotion seemed to have an uplifting effect on Karen, who returned from one of her space-outs and began hooting with enthusiasm for no apparent reason other than the sheer desire to hoot. "Be who you fuckin' are!" she yelled hoarsely. "Be fuckin' you!"

I wondered where that came from and figured it was her confused, experimental self's idea of a football cheer.

Granny was blinking uncontrollably. I was hoping to disappear. Our Calvin-clad neighbors shot us one last dagger stare and stormed off.

"What a relief to be able to stretch out a bit," Shelby said. "Jesus, this is not the most comfortable place to—"

Suddenly, a man in a blue guard suit was standing above us, looking down at our taco-sauce-stained bench.

"I'm sorry," he said. "Could you all be quiet?"

Shelby eyed the guy menacingly.

"We've received several complaints about your group. You've been disruptive the whole game."

I thought I saw my father's mischievous eyes sparkling, but maybe they were just glazing over. I pictured him regaling us years later with a skewed tale of how Shelby got kicked off the bleachers at a high school football game in Texas. He was like that, a man who derived a sad delight in collecting stories against his wife, as if it had been a mere accident that he and Shelby had married.

"If you would all stop acting like buffoons, they might let us stay," he said, glaring at Shelby.

I knew this was not good. I knew the tears would now definitely start coming. Black eye shadow would drip down my stepmother's face, like the time in the passport office when the government worker told her she couldn't get three new passports for a flight to Geneva via Iceland at 5:00 P.M. Or the time she'd arrived at Dean & Deluca seven minutes after it closed to buy food for a party she was hosting for seventy-five Swiss tourists on an art tour of Manhattan. She had stood in the doorway, tapped on the glass doors, and begged Dean or Deluca—or whoever happened to be there—to let her in. These were the times when I felt deeply embarrased by my stepmother, mortified really, at her inability to act like everybody else.

"Listen, George," Shelby replied hoarsely, glaring at my father. "I don't need your shit. I'm here to support *my* son."

I looked at my father like a baby wolf knowing mother wolf was about to tear him apart if he didn't back off. It wasn't so much that I cared about protecting him. And it certainly wasn't that I thought he was so terribly wrong. It was just that I wanted the scene to end before it got nasty.

"Maybe you should have thought of that before he moved to Texas," my father mumbled, retreating to the stadium rest rooms.

With one warring party gone, I breathed a deep sigh of relief.

Shelby wiped her eyes with the back of her shirt and muttered an inaudible sentence with the word *asshole* in it.

"Just keep it down, all of you," the guard said apologetically, before taking off, too.

Granny tapped her Keds against the bleacher floor in an official, take-charge gesture. She pulled a napkin out of her purse and wiped off some taco beef we'd dripped on the bench. "Now, let's all just calm down."

———————

There are moments in life when you realize your family is not just different. It's fucked-up different. Your stepmother's got Tourette's syndrome and a tragic case of the sobs. Your dad is a troublemaker, obsessed with who's gay. No one in your family wears Calvins. And your brother found peace at military school. What seemed so ha! ha! funny to you in the past no longer even elicits a chuckle. All the words you liked to use to describe the way things were where you came from—*unique, eccentric, crazy, offbeat*—suddenly seem like poor guises for the truth. Those words were euphemisms, you suddenly realize, for what your house really was: totally fucked up.

When the game ended, we piled out of the stadium and clanked down the bleachers to the muddy ground below. Watching the frenzied crowd head home, I wondered whether normalcy was a behavior you could aspire to, or a psychological profile lost to you if you hadn't learned it at home. Could I catch up with these people in the Calvins?

Phillip had missed the entire bleacher scene because he was sitting with his schoolmates. When he deigned to talk to us that weekend, he stepped back a bit. In his patent leather shoes, with his crew cut and cap, he looked protected. As if unwanted words would bounce off his wool uniform and land in the dust.

When we had stumbled back to our hotel suite, I waited for a fight. In the past, my father would have mocked Shelby. Shelby would have feigned hurt: "Oh, everything is always my fault. How convenient for you."

Instead, Shelby slipped on one of my father's oversize oxfords, settled on the hotel's pullout couch, and clicked on the TV. My father brushed past all of us and settled outside on the cement balcony, alone in a plastic chair. The air in the room was air-conditioner heavy, and the lights were caustic and bright. I stood by the door—holding my purse tightly between my fingers, unsure what camp to spend the rest of the evening in. Then I headed for the bedroom, stole one of Karen's cigarettes, and joined my father outside.

He pulled a cigar out of a plastic Ziploc bag where he kept all his cigars with a wad of wet paper towel. He proudly called it his humidor. He hunched over to light his cigar, and when he sat back up he looked weary. A soldier who might be ready to concede defeat. "She's gotten impossible."

"You used to think she was funny."

He took a puff of his cigar. "You don't think she's funny. No one thinks she's funny. Do they?"

I slipped my fingers inside his shirt pocket and pulled out his matchbook, then leaned back in my chair and lit my cigarette. After twenty years my father was still trying to figure out how he got saddled with Shelby.

"Before, you'd laugh," I said.

"Kyle, that was a long time ago."

"You liked it. You liked the fight."

"It was lust. I made a decision based on lust."

My cigarette made my tongue sting, like those little red hots that I always regretted popping into my mouth.

"What do you mean *lust*? You chose her. You left Mom for her, Dad. *You* got us into this."

"I didn't know what I was getting into myself, Kyle. It's not my fault."

"Then whose fault is it?"

"Kyle, she's changed. She's gotten worse."

"No, Dad. She hasn't changed that much." I crushed my cigarette against the ledge and dropped it on the balcony's cement floor. I glared at my father. "And if you hate her so much, why don't you just get divorced, then? You've driven

Phillip away. I can't be around you two anymore. You can't keep living like this. She can't either."

"I'm not leaving until Phillip goes to college."

"Dad, who are you protecting? Can't you see it would be so much—"

"I'm not having this conversation with you, Kyle. There's nothing else to talk about."

My head felt hot and smoky. My throat hurt. I was sucking words out of it, but they weren't going anywhere. Not to him, anyway. Just into the air and then down, like darts that are missing the mark. By the time I walked inside our air-conditioned hotel room, my words had disappeared. Shelby was in the kitchen—still wearing my father's shirt and fixing herself a drink.

I think I lost it
Let me know if you come across it
Let me know if I let it fall
Along a back road somewhere.

LUCINDA WILLIAMS

At some point after Harlingen, my father began to exhibit strange behavior.

For one thing, he stopped speaking English. Everything became *maravillosa* and *fabulosa*, *bonita* and *simpática*. The words danced across his tongue, leapt from his mouth, merengued across his lips. He was filled with a mirthful positivity that was entirely uncharacteristic.

I first noticed the change several weeks after our trip, when I called to check up on the "state of the union." My father and I hadn't spoken that much since our balcony conversation. And I was still angry at him.

"*Hola, hija,*" he bubbled into the receiver. "*Qué tal? . . . El tiempo en Nueva York está bueno hoy. Un poco frío, pero . . .*"

I pulled the phone away from my ear. "Dad, I don't understand what you're saying."

"*Sí, chiquita, pero un millón de gente en el mundo hablan español. Es el idioma del futuro.*"

"What?"

"*Y sabes, si tú entendieras, esto, podras mirar las novelas. Mucho mejor que las americanas. . . . En un episodio, hay cáncer, incesto.* Talk about melodrama."

"Can I talk to Shelby, please?"

My father put the phone down and went to fetch Shelby.

"Jesus, is he doing it to you too?" Shelby asked.

"*Sí, chiquita.*"

Shelby was worried. She said she'd found a frayed copy of *Spanish, the Easy Way* hiding in the inside pocket of my father's trench coat. One evening my brother George—in Manhattan for the night—had spotted him slinking around the salsa section of Tower Records. When my father realized he had been seen, he feigned surprise and acted lost. "Oh, I can never find the opera section," he told my older brother. Now, Shelby said, things had gotten even stranger. My father was listening to *My Life: Greatest Hits* by Julio Iglesias, buying his shoes at a Mexican store on Fourteenth Street, and keeping Spanish flash cards—to love, to kiss, to touch—by his bed.

"We went to the B's the other night," Shelby told me. The B's were old family friends, originally from Ecuador. "Your father danced till three in the morning. He did the salsa, the cha-cha, and the tango. Danced several times with Ana's mother. You know, she's eighty-three now."

"I thought he didn't dance."

"Until now."

"How do you think he learned?"

"What do I look like, Inspector Clouseau?"

"This is very strange," I said, clicking my teeth. "Well, did you get a dance out of him?"

"Kyle, your father stopped dancing with me long ago," she said. Shelby often shared these unpleasant details about her marriage with me—using a tone that suggested she suspected I was slightly to blame for her misfortune. As for the dancing business, it had always been a sore spot between Shelby and my father. "It's a metaphor," she once explained to me over a café au lait. "Your father is very withholding."

My father's forays into foreign worlds were nothing new. He had always been a compulsive hobbyist. He didn't take a vague interest in a topic. He delved in like one of those female mud wrestlers intent on getting every ounce of her body caked in dirt. He had been a onetime sculptor, ice skater, squider, sketcher, hockey player, opera buff, tennis player, country music fan. He took up rowing when he was eighteen, then switched to iceboating. One summer he became obsessed with urban gardening. He packed the freezer with dozens of wrapped tulip bulbs. "I'm trying to trick them into thinking it's winter," he confided in us. When his tulips came up string beans, he ate them in a ceremonial salad. "My harvest," he said.

This time, though, Shelby said there was something peculiar about my father's passion *"por todo lo que concierne a la cultura española."* Things were appearing in his closet, things she'd never seen before. A silver-topped bottle of Paco Rabanne cologne, a scratchy, thick-threaded sweater from Peru. Suddenly, he was keeping those little Guatemalan worry dolls that fit in a yellow wood box in his underwear drawer.

Shelby said sometimes he even smelled funny. One day, she told me, he came home from work and his breath was all fried bananas. Another time, my brother George spotted a black bean stuck to his collar.

"This?" my father said, looking down at his collar and flicking off the bean. "Must be a jelly bean or something."

———

I hung up with Shelby and called Mark. My best friend had a unique appreciation for my father—and a certain affinity as well. They had both gone to Harvard; they had both lived in the same four-story dorm. They had both been snubbed by the same exclusive campus men's club. My father, because he refused to shave his beard to join. Mark, because he called a guy, who turned out to be the club president, a douche bag at a campus keg party.

"Your father," Mark once said, "isn't marching to his own drum. He's got his own goddamn punk rock band going. And he's like the only one who can hear the noise. There's something endearing about that."

Mark picked up the phone on the first ring.

"Think I should go home for the weekend?" I asked. "My dad's acting up."

"Is he leaving Shelby Post-its on the bathroom sink again?"

"No, they're talking," I said. "He's just acting very spirited."

Mark let out a starchy laugh. "They do that when they age," he said. "My father drinks three bottles of Merlot a night. I said: 'Mom, maybe you ought to tell him to cut down a bit.' She said: 'Leave your father alone. Drinking makes him happy.'"

"That's it, Mark. That's the problem. My father seems happy."

"That's a problem?"

"After twenty years of misery, suddenly he's a Spanish jumping bean, bouncing off the walls and merengueing around the house. Yeah, it's a problem."

"Okay, well go check on him," Mark said.

I hung up and booked a ticket home, abandoning the opportunity to cover the trial of a man who had tossed his wife off a bridge on a foggy fall night.

————

Visiting your childhood home—when you haven't been there for a while—is always oddly informative. You gain perspective. In my case, I stepped into the loft and I noticed that everything was broken. The kitchen tiles were chipped. The washing machine didn't turn on. Several of the chairs around the dining room table had ripped seats. The kitchen telephone had no cord. The grand piano had a crack down the middle of the sound board. Several of the light fixtures in the hallway were missing buttons. My family even had a broken corner, a place where all the broken items—computers and fishing poles, desks and toys—gathered to commiserate. It occurred to me that this was weird. And sad. Why didn't anything in my house ever get fixed? If I asked my father, he would blame Shelby. If I asked Shelby, she would blame my father.

My father greeted me on his throne, a lumpy spot on our fifteen-year-old couch, purchased in 1983, when things were still looking up. A pudgy cigar was dangling from his lips.

"*Chiquita, dame un beso.*"

I gave him a head-to-toe once-over. "Sorry. *No comprendo.*"

A cardboard dish of soupy flan rested by his feet. I eyed it suspiciously.

My father noticed my gaze. "Did you know the best flan is made with canned milk, not the fresh stuff?"

"Really!" I replied, relieved we were actually communicating in English.

"*Sí, chiquita.*"

My father looked only vaguely familiar—like some man you

saw on the subway once and wondered: Where do I know you from?

Gone was his usual uniform: paint-spattered Levi's and a worn and holey T. It had been replaced with a piñata orange dress shirt and stiff black slacks. My father had a silk scarf cranked around his neck. I noticed his new haircut: short on the sides, slicked back in the front. The reassuring speckles of gray were gone. The man I called Dad had transformed into an aging Ricky Martin.

I plopped myself on the couch and slipped off my shoes—noticing a hole in the left foot of my tights. I pulled the quilted comforter Shelby had bought in Virginia over my knees and leaned toward my father. I rubbed my nose against his scalp. "Dyeing your hair, Dad?"

My father squinted, as if to convey a deep sense of confusion about his new look. *"No, hija, por qué tú preguntas?"*

I pressed my fingers against his stubbly chin and tilted it toward me. "Dad, look me straight in the eye and tell me you're not dyeing your hair."

"No estoy pintándome el pelo," he said, laughing boyishly.

My father could watercolor and oil-paint. He could build a chessboard out of colored pieces of plastic from the plastic store on Canal Street. He could read a six-hundred-page tome about Winston Churchill and not get bored. But he had never mastered the art of lying. I didn't need Encyclopedia Brown to interpret this one for me; my old man was getting laid.

I crinkled my nose. "Looks gross," I said.

———

I stepped off the couch and slid across the hardwood floors. The wood felt cold against my feet—even with my cotton tights on. I could feel the sliding grooves and the dipping cracks between the planks of shellacked wood. I wondered if the floors didn't need some work. My eyes rested on three large oil paintings leaning against the wall by the radiator. They were George's. He was storing them at my father's place while he finished up his renovations. Each one depicted a black-and-gray-smudged boxer in the midst of a fight, eyes dripping with paint, crooked nose, an expression that was weary and sad. Once, when I had asked him: "Why boxers?" he had replied: "They're fighting."

On the other side of the loft's main room was the twenty-five-foot dining room table that had arrived—via commercial crane—through one of our living room windows. It was long and dark, medieval-looking. And I always half-expected to see a group of knights around it—downing whole chickens from lead plates and drinking barley wine from wooden goblets. There was barely anywhere to sit at the table, though. A few feet away, stacked one on top of the other, were the once perfect cherry wood chairs that used to surround the table. Now they were marked by their ripped leather cushions that made your butt fall through if you sat on them. They were in the corner, by the freight elevator, along with other things that needed to be fixed.

"I can't eat," Phil would say at dinner, trying to avoid Shelby's gourmet meat loaf, when the broken chairs were still at the table. "I've lost my butt."

"Me, too," I'd yelp.

"What, your meat loaf or your butt?" Dad would ask.

"George, you're not helping matters," Shelby would say.

When my brother George was around for dinner, as he sometimes would be, he too would pipe in: "How can Dad help? He's looking for his butt."

We would chuckle so hard our bellies would ache. Everyone except Shelby. "This is age-appropriate," she would say to my father. "For them."

I tapped on Shelby's door. "Shelby, I'm home."

Shelby wasn't big on official hellos anymore. "Oh," she said, kind of half-grunting.

I climbed onto her bed, a sea of the overlapping cotton sheets we had bought on sale at Bed Bath & Beyond and topped with the handmade comforters Shelby had specially ordered for us kids—before she and my father were married. They were identical shades of faded blue with little sailboats on top—now stained, and ripped at the corners from overuse. They were designed for single beds—so Shelby had two of them draped over her. She was watching a *Falcon Crest* rerun. The VCR was flashing the wrong time.

"I'm miserable down there," I told her.

She and I spoke like this. Our conversations rarely had beginnings—they were usually just extensions of old conversations, or continuations.

Shelby looked up from her *New York Times* crossword puzzle. "This is the hardest move. It's going to get better from here."

"What if I'm alone for the rest of my life—and I never meet anyone?"

Shelby smiled faintly. "Then you'll be an enormously successful reporter, with a great career, a good apartment, and lots of respect from your peers. Kyle, a lot of people would die for a life like that." She wove her fingers through my hair. "Who's doing your hair?"

"Someone in Raleigh."

"Look at these split ends."

"Maybe I want a husband."

"Just make your own money. And worry about a husband later. Marriage is overrated. Take it from me."

I ignored these last remarks. My eyes fell on a dark wood box with painted flowers by my parents' bed.

Inside there was a square photo of my father. His face was pale and pasty, like a piece of soft chalk. He had circles the color of eggplant skin under his eyes.

There was a round photo of Shelby. Her hair was dark and wavy, curled stiffly up in the back.

There was me in candy apple red, dangling a straw basket from my wrist. It had tulips in it, and a pink bow, the color of ballet slippers, wrapped around the birch handle. There was George looking perplexed in a bottle green vest, his straight red hair hanging down to his ears. These were the wedding pictures, still in a box.

Shelby had worn her favorite tea rose perfume. When she hugged me that night, it flew into my nostrils; the scent was spicy and sweet, lavender and lilac. I had smelled it once on a woman marching down the street in a raincoat. I thought she was Shelby. I raced up to her and slid my fingers inside the woman's clenched hand. She jumped.

At the reception, we ate bloody filet mignon and crisp marinated green beans. I remember the long waxy candles, hot and lit. They shone orange blotches on the guests' faces. I remember the stacks of splintery plywood leaning against the dining hall wall. My father said the church had had a fire. The steeple had burned down. The church was like our house, always under construction.

Shelby later told me my father had botched the preceremony interview.

"Are you sure you want to do this?" the priest had asked.

My father had smirked. "No. I'm not sure."

Shelby could have married an abstract painter who was also in love with her. But she chose my dad. "I fell in love with him," she said. "And you."

————

I slid my hand across Shelby's forehead and tilted her face toward mine, the way I used to do as a child. Shelby had always had perfectly smooth, ivory-colored skin. Unlike mine, it never got too dry in winter or too oily in summer. She never got blackheads, like the ones she squeezed off my nose—"Don't move. Stop moving." Tonight she looked haggard, with thin stress lines below her eyes, on her cheeks, by her lips.

"Remember when you bought me two dresses for the wedding?" I asked.

Shelby's mouth split open to form a smile. "The velvet dress was so much more elegant," she said.

We'd seen it together sparkling in a store window on Madison Avenue, a week after we'd bought the embroidered one. Thick and red, overlapping the way dark chocolate batter folds into ripples when you dip it into a silver mixing bowl, it was a princess dress.

"We'd already spent two hundred dollars on the cotton one."

"But the velvet had that beautiful silk bow."

"It was expensive, wasn't it?"

"You were worth it."

————

When my father headed for bed that night, Shelby and I settled into the kitchen on clear stools, in front of the counter with the chipped tiles. I listened to him click the master bedroom door shut. It was the door with the hole the size of a basketball—or a fist. No one remembered how it got there.

Shelby pulled out her pack of emergency cigarettes from a Swiss cookie tin below the counter. She poured herself a glass of icy bourbon. I watched her light her cigarette. The match crackled like a little firecracker. She took a long drag. "Your father's having an affair," she said, exhaling.

I looked down at the grainy floor of our loft—the floor Shelby had polished once with a clunky hard-to-push metal polisher she'd rented on the Lower East Side. I looked beyond the floor, out the window and into a corner of the sky. The night was reaching charcoal blue. It was later than I thought.

"I know," I said, feeling deep bubbles rising into my throat.

"I was hoping it would get better."

"But what have you been doing?"

"I've been trying."

My eyes fell on a pot of popcorn kernels, drenched in oil, remnants of my father's dinner. "Do you think you really are . . . trying? I mean . . . it just seems—"

Shelby interrupted me. "You be married to him for a while."

"He's my father," I reminded her.

"Kyle," she said, taking a long drag of her cigarette. "You have no idea what goes on between your father and me. No idea."

Sometimes it's hard to tell if Shelby is angry with you, or just upset in general.

There is a scene in the John Cassavetes film *A Woman Under the Influence* where Gena Rowlands is on the verge of a nervous breakdown. "Dad," she says, at the dinner table, "stand up for me." The father, befuddled, stands up.

I fantasized for a split second that Shelby would say something like this. And my father would act not like the father in the movie but like the close-to-perfect father I wished, right then, that I had.

But Shelby wasn't one to ask for help. And my father wasn't one to offer. And I was just the daughter. That, for me, has always been the hardest part. When the bomb is about to hit, who doesn't want to yell: "Get out of the way or we're all going down?"

———

I headed back to North Carolina on Sunday, pecking my father on the cheek before stepping into a cab for the airport. From the half-cranked window, I watched him pad up the steel-edged steps of our building. He had one hand buried in his pocket; the other clutched his cigar. His back was bent, his face drawn. He looked like a mountain climber tackling the steepest slope, save for the cigar dangling from his left hand.

"Dad," I said, from the window. "You should really stop smoking those things. . . . You know, they're going to kill you." It seemed like an odd warning—considering the circumstances—but it was the only one I could get out of my ashy throat.

———

On Monday, Kip handed me an assignment about a clerk who disappeared from his corner gas station store. He was forty-seven, the father of four. Money from the electronic cash register and the guy's aging Ford pickup had also disappeared. Footprints on the doormat indicated a tussle. Officials suspected abduction.

The police faxed over a photo of the guy's truck for the photo desk to scan for Tuesday's paper. The bumper sticker above the license plate read: GONE FISHIN'.

Back at my desk, I called the guy's house. "I'm sorry about your father," I said to the young man who picked up the phone. "It must be difficult not to know if he was kidnapped—or if he just took off and left you all."

"Screw you," the kid replied, before hanging up.

I guess I wouldn't want a stranger pounding me with questions about the odd behavior of my family members, either.

The next day Kip approached me. I was fielding phone calls for a follow-up on the convenience store clerk.

"The police called," Kip said. "He's alive. It was a scheme."

"Oh, so he just skipped out of town. Pretended he had been kidnapped because he couldn't stand his wife anymore."

Kip nodded.

"Great story, Kip. How wacky."

"We're killing it."

"Why?"

"This is a domestic affair," he said. "It's between this man and his wife. We don't get involved in that kind of personal stuff. Newspaper policy."

I noticed that the tip of Kip's shirt was hanging out of his jeans. "Kyle," he said, before turning around and shuffling off. "You've got to get better at determining when these stories are none of your business."

Baby, sooner or later . . .
You're gonna have to ride down to the real nitty gritty.

SOUTHERN CULTURE ON THE SKIDS

I darted out of bed the next morning, ready to do what I always do when real life gets unbearable. I slipped into career mode.

I thanked Susan B. Anthony for getting the women's lib ball rolling. And I pictured myself leaping onto some carpeted auditorium stage, preparing to accept the third consecutive Pulitzer of my young career.

I lifted my arm in my bedroom air as if I were holding up my trophy—an Oscar-like gold statue in the shape of a computer. "It never would have happened if I hadn't made the brave move to Raleigh," I shouted at my alarm clock. (I find that fantasies are particularly poignant when they make dubious decisions seem suddenly very wise.)

With those inspiring thoughts drifting through my head, I tossed off my nightgown and scampered to work—suddenly recharged.

———

For eight months I had been slugging it out in the Raleigh police department—drumming up stories about crackhead robberies, bank holdups, and the brave acts of animal control officers who were saving potbelly pigs from going under the knife. The Raleigh police beat was no *NYPD Blue*—although, considering the extent to which the cops surreptitiously withheld harmless information, like the date of birth of a car thief or the eye color of a shoplifter, it was obvious that they thought it was. Without sounding too coy, I sometimes felt like I was hanging out in Mayberry with the likes of Barney Fife—and without the benefit of Aunt Bee's cooking. It is true that, on occasion, my stories landed on the front page—like when I wrote a "hero-for-a-day" piece about a guy who interrupted an afternoon robbery at Pizza Hut by shooting the thief in the thigh, or the time I wrote about a baby who was discovered in the woods behind Research Triangle Park by a Korean lab technician during a Sunday walk with his kids. Otherwise, I was more or less a 3B girl.

My backseat status wasn't going to kill me. But, frankly, it was a little embarrassing vis-à-vis the folks back home. I was having trouble maintaining my image as an adventurous Lois plowing through the New South when most weeks all I had to show for myself was a few shoplifting reports. So I decided to take some action.

"Kip," I said, planting myself at my editor's desk and shoving a piece of morning muffin into my mouth. "This really isn't working for me."

Kip glanced up from the pile of mail he was flipping through. "What?"

"This job." I put my hand on top of the mail pile. "You need to take pity on me and pull me off the cop beat."

By now Kip was used to my melodramatic pronouncements. He let out a guttural laugh. "Did you get another ticket?"

"I'm being serious here."

"Okay." He gave me his standard let's-get-on-with-it look. "What do you propose?"

I hadn't really expected Kip to hear me out. And I certainly hadn't expected him to ask me what I wanted to cover. I scanned the third floor and spotted my favorite piece of newsroom artwork: a black-and-white cartoon on the wall by the library. A giant-size buxom lady in a Scarlett O'Hara dress was standing by a giant-size bulldozer. Her name: Dee V. Loper. She was trouncing on a little homeowner, a mayor, a reporter, and a man named N. Viro Meant. It cracked me up every time I saw it.

"Well . . . hey. Why don't you let me write about the boys?"

The boys were a crew of swashbuckling real estate moguls who were building the city's shopping malls, subdivisions, and roadways. If New York had the Donald, Raleigh had the boys. They were glitzy and gauche—and generally despised. Old-timers insisted they were obliterating the area's charm. Tree huggers insisted they were destroying the environment.

"You know they won't talk to us."

I crossed my arms and looked at my editor intently. "I think I can get them to open up."

Kip was not convinced. He pulled a story up on his computer. It was my cue to exit the scene. "Why waste your time? It's impossible."

Suddenly, I could feel my toenails rubbing against my shoes. In the newsroom setting the word *impossible* had that effect on me. Like the words *no*, *can't*, and *not allowed*, it more or less ensured that I would become obsessed with whatever task had just been deemed out of my reach. In the real world, people take medication for those kinds of obsessions. In Newspaperland, the right obsession and you might win a Pulitzer.

"If I do get them to talk, can I get off cops, get a normal schedule, get a life?"

Kip began tapping on his keyboard absentmindedly. It was unclear to me whether he was truly bored by our conversation, just playing me for his morning entertainment, or really trying to ensure I would take on some new stories. As the frequent casualty of newsroom manipulation, I had come to suspect that editors spent a lot of their day drumming up psychological warfare techniques to coax individual reporters into working. Threats. Flattery. Flirtation. The tactics were endless. And no two reporters, I had come to understand, got the same treatment. Still, I wasn't too concerned about what was going on on Kip's end. All I knew was that I was employing my own warfare techniques. I was intent on winning this game. And I was willing to do just about anything—short of tearing all my clothes off—to get what I wanted. "Kip, this is a pivotal point for the boys."

Kip raised an eyebrow.

"Yes," I said, stalling for time. "It is. . . . A lot of things. . . . a lot of things are going to change for them soon. Kip, you have got to wake up and smell the asphalt!"

I recalled an article I'd read in Harlingen about residents getting peeved that developers were ignoring their concerns. They'd boycotted town hall.

"Traffic. Traffic. Traffic!" I said, repeating the chant I'd read in the article. "Congestion. Lines at the grocery store. Who's to blame? The boys, that's who. Office complexes, houses, shopping malls. That's all they think about. They're building them one after another, luring newcomers here while the rest of us suffer. Do you know what we're going to see soon?"

Kip held back a smile. "What?"

"Marches to every city hall in the Triangle, hatred, political instability, possible riots. We're talking Watts riots scale. And who will be there? Not us. No, the developers won't talk to us. We'll never be able to get their viewpoint. It'll be a journalistic tragedy."

"Whew." Kip was laughing now.

"Unless," I whispered, "I do some stories on them. Get them to open up. Warm up to us. Trust us. Then, when the shit hits the fan, we'll be there, okay?"

I was glad I'd read the editors-only office memo that was sent out the week before: "Concerns about traffic and congestion in the area are mounting. We may want to cultivate our real estate sources better," it read.

Kip was all smiley and happy now. "Okay. But what am I agreeing to?"

I was beaming too. "You're agreeing to let me cover the developers on a full-time basis, if I can do a couple of stories that show they talk to me." I wiped a clump of sweat off my brow. "Then, you give weekend cops to some other poor slob."

I knew then and there that I had two inexplicable things going for me. First, Kip generally thought I knew what I was talking about. And, second, the guy basically liked me. I was by far the loudest, most theatrical reporter in the newsroom. And, quite frankly, I sometimes had a little trouble shutting up. But I always suspected that, for some reason unbeknownst to me, my quiet, pensive editor liked that about me. I guess even in the newsroom opposites attract.

"You know they don't talk," Kip repeated for the gazillionth time. By this point, I knew, he was throwing in a little last-minute reverse psychology. But I decided to feign ignorance.

"Where's the faith, Kippo? Give me a couple of days." Then I raced off. Thanks to Susan B., I was on a mission.

———

My stepmother was on a mission, too.

"You wouldn't believe what I've been through these last few days," Shelby bellowed into my office phone. "I'm exhausted. I've been ordering up old phone bills, credit card slips, researching car rentals and magazine subscriptions."

Shelby had always enjoyed self-imposed projects. She made her own pesto, fried her own french fries. Once she bought an industrial tile cutter and hand-tiled all the bathrooms in our loft. Another time, she took me out of school for ten days and taught me the entire SAT. You wanted to buy the cheapest computer in New York City, Shelby would spend hours researching and, before you knew it, she'd be on a first-name basis with every salesperson in the tristate area.

When I was a kid she would stay up until three or four in the morning and toil on my homemade birthday cakes—once she made a cake in the shape of a roller skate. Another year, she made Phillip a dinosaur cake. One year, for George's birthday, she designed a chocolate chip cookie cut to look like a hockey puck.

"What are you up to this time?" I inquired.

"Up to? I'm investigating."

"Who?"

"Your father, Kyle. Who do you think? We've got to do this. Figure out what *he's been up to*. I can't let him get away with this. Right?"

I mumbled in agreement but wondered silently what exactly my father was getting away with. While Shelby still managed to reach out to almost any stranger who came her way, it was obvious she had more or less given up on my father a few years before. Who was to blame for this, I don't know. But I did know that the anger and disappointment that festered between my parents had gone unattended for so long it was virtually impossible for either one of them to feel anything but numbing indifference when they were together. But suddenly, out of the blue, my father's life was of interest to my stepmother. She now cared to know what he did when he wasn't at home on the couch—reading his hardcover history books.

———

The next morning I marched into the newsroom professionally revived. I logged onto my computer and began searching for stories about the boys.

TOWN COUNCIL CANDIDATE CALLS DEVELOPERS POND SCUM read the first story I pulled up.

DEVELOPERS DO ANOTHER DIRTY DEED read another.

RESIDENTS SAY: "ENOUGH IS ENOUGH. STOP JERKING OUR CHAIN" went another.

No wonder the boys didn't want to talk to the paper.

I clicked out of the newspaper's archives just as Kip passed my desk. I winked at him salaciously, envisioning the day—very soon—when he would take back my beeper, my cell phone, and my scanner, and hand it all over to some other reporter.

"Kipster," I cooed warmly, then winked at him again.

"Your eye okay?" he asked.

I ignored him, picked up the phone, and dialed my first victim. His name: Tiger Flare.

"Positive story about the boys? What are you on, drugs?" the seventy-one year-old howled into my ear.

I yanked the receiver away from my ear.

"I didn't think you reporters were allowed to write those."

The article I had downloaded labeled Tiger "one of the most prolific shopping mall and subdivision builders in the area." His medium: painted brick. His specialty: luxury.

"I love flash," he had reportedly said in a rare interview with the paper. "If you've got the cash, build with panache—that's my logo."

Among other feats, Tiger had brought the bidet to the Triangle, launching what one developer called "a stroke of genius house building that has yet to be rivaled."

Tiger had gotten into the subdivision business in the late sixties—before the walk-in closet and before the zoning laws. As a result, he was one of the only guys around who knew what all the legal jargon meant. As for obscure loopholes, he could recite them in his sleep.

Tiger agreed to meet me a few days later at one of the Triangle's stone-walled, leather-boothed steak houses. Maria had told me the restaurant was a hot spot for Department of Transportation officials and other state politicians. That meant it was also a hot spot for anyone who had a favor to buy or sell. Say, an all-expense-paid golf vacation in Palm Springs for a major highway near a housing development, or a political contribution for a building permit. It was rumored that 90 percent of the area's backroom deals that weren't done on the golf course were done at steak houses. That info was courtesy of Maria, too. Steak houses were a badge of honor for Maria. After she'd spent five years as an investigative reporter, covering pollution, building scandals, and the gross misuse of government transportation funds, the management of one of the more popular restaurants had decided to ban her. She was bad for business, the owner said. "Just because I got a few of their friends arrested. It's not personal," Maria had boasted.

When I walked into the restaurant, I was delighted to discover several of the boys sitting at a table by the door. I recognized them from clips I'd read over the past few days. There was Bo Bo Brown, a wiry fellow in a light-colored V-necked shirt who specialized in golf course communities; Wade Hunter, a low-income housing developer who had a side business selling inspirational CDs and videos; and Mac Doonbury, a man who gave such moving town council meeting speeches about his developments that it was rumored he had once brought tears to the eyes of an enthusiastic city planner.

I detected Tiger's raspy chuckle. "Hee-haw, here she comes," he screeched from his bar stool. I was the only woman in the place.

Tiger was tall and leggy with a washboard waist and short, ropy gray hair. He had a thin, sleek smile and a weathered face that offered one of the few signs of his advanced age. In his burgundy golf pants and his worn tennis sneakers, he looked like an accomplished athlete, pushing fifty. "Well," he said, standing up. "I don't know why you wanted to meet me, I'm just an old know-nothing; the boys never tell me a darn thing." He winked at the guys sitting next to him. "They think I'm too old to shoot the shit."

Limp gambit strikes again. A few months after my first encounter with it, and I was learning to strike back. I patted Tiger on the back. "Not what I've heard. The boys tell me you're brilliant. They say you're amazing, a real one of a kind." I'd never had a conversation about Tiger with anyone.

I could feel Tiger loosening up. He slipped off his sneakers and let his toes dangle in the restaurant air.

I ordered a bottle of wine. Tiger smiled and lit a cigarette— a thin brown stick that looked like a mini cigar. "My only vice," he chirped.

After a few glasses of wine, a few cigarettes, and a discussion about golfing in New York state, we got down to business. I switched into Lois mode.

Lois mode is the supremely confident, self-assured state that female reporters slip into when they're on the job. The Nancy Sinatra boot tune blasts nonstop in our heads. We become fearless in the face of adversity. We get high on the meaty quotes we're beating out of our weakening sources. And we are delighting in the mouth-savoring knowledge that no one is going home till we get the story. I suspect robbing a bank gives you this same power surge.

Sadly, my emotional intelligence has long trailed behind Lois's. Why I can be a flailing idiot on a first date but a no-holes barred go-getter when I'm grilling a businessman about his unsavory government connections is still a mystery to me.

"Tiger," I said, resting my hand on his shoulder. "Let me be straight with you. I'm an outsider. And I need a relationship with you. Someone who can show me the other side.

"You and your friends, Tiger," I continued, "I hate to say . . . are not the most popular people in the world. God knows why. But that's the truth. And you know what you need to do? You need to help them help themselves." I was starting to feel like the MC for a TV fund-raiser for Kenyan orphans.

"Well, I shouldn't talk to a reporter about these things."

"Reporter? I'm not like those lefties at the paper. I'm different. Tiger, I understand what you guys go through. Those NIMBYs can be a real pain in the ass. You need a press person on your side."

NIMBY is an initialism that stands for not in my backyard. It is a reference to homeowners who don't want a nuclear plant, a trash dump, or a tristate shopping mall going up across from their dream homes. In essence, it is a term used for anyone who cares about their neighborhood more than the financial interests of moneymakers. I figured it was a good term to throw around in a steak house.

Tiger took a swig of wine. "Listen, Miss Kyle. I like you. But, girl, if you cross me, I'll deny knowing you. And guess who everyone will believe?"

I decided not to answer that.

"It's a deal, Tiger," I said. Then I did what's called whoring for a quote. "How 'bout a few sentences for my story, Tig?"

Tiger lit another thin cigarette and blew a ring of smoke in my face. "Well, Kyle, me and my boys are special people. And I know you can see that."

I pulled out my pad. "Tiger, you know I can."

"Real wing walkers, you know." Tiger pounded his hand on the bar. "We get a bad rap from those environmental groups worried about trees and mosquitoes." He pounded again. "But we take a lot of chances, and we house a lot of happy people."

I pounded too, just to let Tig know I was following his train of thought. "I know you do, and yours is definitely an under-appreciated task."

Tiger scooted off his bar stool. I followed.

He pointed his cigarette at my face. "Do you know what it's like to stand at a town council meeting and not know whether your three-million-dollar project is going to make you a gazil-lionaire or a street urchin?" he asked, his voice getting louder, his cigarette hand waving in the air. "Imagine the stress. It takes a special kind of person to handle that."

"You know, Tiger, you're right." My voice got louder, too. I was ferociously taking notes and occasionally pounding on the bar—with my pad or my pen or both—for emphasis.

Tiger was pounding, too. Harder and harder. "Then you gotta be nice if it falls through, and you lose three million because some lady is worried about her crepe myrtle bush or some grandpa is grouching about his butterfly farm."

"Tiger, you are so on the money," I screamed.

"Well, it's unbelievably hard," he shouted.

"Difficult."

"Intense."

Tiger collapsed on his stool, exhausted and out of breath. He wiped a dribble of sweat off his brow with a cocktail napkin.

I collapsed on my stool, too. "I know. I know," I managed to whimper. Then I collected my thoughts. "Tiger, that was beautiful. God, those quotes were great. Thank you!"

I glanced at myself in the bar mirror and noticed my hair was messy, my lipstick smudged.

A guy turned toward us. "What the hell are you doing over there, Tig?"

We both ignored him.

On the way out the door, Tiger took me by the table where the boys were still sitting, smoking cigars by now and sipping sherry.

"Boys, this is your girl. Talk to her, listen to her. Be nice to her. She's the first reporter over at that paper of theirs who's got a brain in her skull. She's gonna do us right."

"Well, if that's not a godsend, I don't know what is," one of them sputtered.

"That paper always gets everything all screwy and wrong. We need one of our own in there," another one added. "Welcome on board, darlin'."

I drove home feeling warm and relaxed. I would finally move off cops, never see another drug dealer again, schedule a regular life with regular sources. I would have to see Tiger a lot, keep up our relationship. I would be fine.

These thoughts swam through my brain as I whizzed passed another steak house in the shape of a barn, a Grocery Boy Junior, and a big sign advertising a golf course community on the outskirts of town. I sped up, then realized I was going the wrong way. I did a quick U-turn, all with an easy, satisfied smile on my face—until I noticed a police car, siren blaring, behind me.

Newly annoyed, I pulled over and waited. An officer in a Mister Rogers cardigan marched over. "Ma'am. Did you know that U-turns are illegal here?"

I glanced over at the scanner lying on the passenger seat,

seething. How I wanted to tell my newest cop friend what I truly felt about his colleagues, the lost police records, the way the chief never returned my calls, the way none of the guys would ever be quoted without the presence of the press secretary, who I was convinced didn't exist, how I felt about this no-news town, the way he and his friends seemed to have nothing better to do than to harass me.

"You guys are really unbeliev——" I began, glancing over at the officer's gun. It was big. He had a club, too. And chunky silver cuffs that looked very uncomfortable. "——ably hard workers. . . . I mean, I listen to this scanner all day long. I know how tough your jobs are."

The officer leaned his hand against my roof. "Ma'am, have you been . . . drinking?"

"Oh, no, Officer. . . . Just working. . . . I'm a police reporter for the paper. I write about . . . people like you. A lot of articles about your conduct and stuff, officers' behavior. Your conduct seems very nice, though . . . uh, Sergeant Burney."

Using your power as a reporter to get off a traffic ticket is grounds for firing. I winced, figuring that if I got a DUI and had to take the bus to work every day, I wouldn't be able to keep my job anyway.

Sergeant Burney scratched his balding head and gave me a sideways this-is-going-to-stay-between-you-and-me glance. "Ma'am, do you think in the future you can remember that U-turns are illegal on a six-lane highway?"

I smiled politely. "I sure do think I can, Officer."

I drove off feeling giddy. The bulky sport-utility vehicles in front of me glistened. The gray highway glowed. The massive Hilton I passed shimmered. The possibilities were endless, the hope enormous. Even the towering Church of the Holy Spirit, a six-story salmon-colored coliseum across from a Jiffy Lube, inspired me. It sparkled beneath the afternoon sun like a beacon of faith.

———————

When I got back to the office, I had ten phone messages. A year reporting in North Carolina, and I was starting to suspect that there was some secret high-tech underground gossip network underneath Interstate 40—or a bug planted in my pocketbook. When I first spoke to the mayor of Apex, a town referred to as the "Peak of Good Living," a few weeks before, for a shoplifting story, he'd inquired about my brother in Brooklyn before I could ask about why the shoplifters targeted Apex.

"We heard you're doing a positive piece about builders," a husky voice bellowed into my receiver. "Well, you need to come out and see what we're doing here. We're building whirlpools in all our houses. They're the new must-have."

I got another message from a guy who was putting up a neo-Gothic office complex. "It's never been done in the Southeast," he said. "Just little slabs. Have 'em imported. Stick them up in six weeks. You've got ancient Rome in Raleigh. Built a Champs-Elysées entrance down the street. You should go see it. It looks just like Paris. In this day and age, you don't need to travel. Our motto is: Bring it here."

"We're opening an international hot dog house in the area," a woman shrieked into the phone. "Call us. We have a truck with a giant-size hot dog on the roof driving around. Great photo op."

I was about to erase the last message before listening to it when I heard the voice. It was different. Not brash. Not infomercial. Just earnest. Soothing, really.

"Ms. Spencer, I understand we've sparked your interest." The voice sounded a little shaky, nervous, in a nice way. "My name is William. William Carson. I've been reading your stories for a few months now. You're a good writer, funny. If I can be of help in the developer underworld, call me." He left his number.

Intrigued, I dialed it right away. "William Carson, please. Kyle Spencer, returning his call."

The receptionist must have been right there next to him. "Will," I heard her say. "The reporter girl."

"Miss Spencer, what can I do for you?" He was on the speakerphone.

"Well, umm." Words were juggling in my throat. And suddenly, Lois had disappeared and I was back to my bumbling, tongue-tied self. "I'm, well, you, you know. I'm writing about the developers."

I heard the speakerphone click off. William suddenly sounded much closer. "Hated bunch, huh?" I thought I heard him laugh.

"I guess you could say that."

"Did Tiger tell you about the old man who wanted to preserve his butterfly farm?"

"Actually, he did. Tig is a real talker."

"Very diplomatic way of putting it. How long did it take you to escape?"

"About an hour."

We both laughed now. But this time, I was the one sounding nervous.

"That's stamina. You may really be cut out for reporting on this business, if you could last that long."

"So, you do . . . ?"

"Structures." He sounded vague. Firmly unspecific. "In between trips, vacations."

"To?"

"Africa, Europe. Actually, was in your part of the woods last weekend with a few buddies. Some bar in TriBeCa."

I smiled.

"You know, we could use some tips when we go up there.

You all sure know how to party. I'd say for a bunch of guys like us, it's a bit intimidating." He laughed. "Maybe you could help us, being a New Yorker. Small consulting fee. Hell, you could stop reporting altogether. Write a tour guide for Southerners lost in New York or something."

"So, you got the lowdown on me, too?"

"Hey, you got to be deaf or dumb in this business not to get the lowdown on everything and everyone. It goes both ways. I stub my toe, and the entire state knows."

"So, I'm, what? What have you heard about me?"

"A breath of fresh air. . . . You'd call that a cliché, wouldn't you?"

"Probably."

"Well, I heard smart, too, and pretty. And I know from reading your stuff you're talented. Do I sound like a stalker?"

"Because you think I'm smart, talented, and pretty? I hope not."

William told me he grew up on a farm outside of Raleigh. His parents were in the business. He skipped college, went to Miami instead. Then he moved back. He loved hunting, boats, flying. "I'm kind of a daredevil. . . . Do I sound like a cheeseball?"

Of course, they never do, in the beginning. "No," I said. "No, you, don't."

William was an only child. "People say I look like George Clooney. But that's hogwash. Although you'll see for yourself."

I liked the "you'll see" part.

I rested the phone on my shoulder and wrote his name in block letters on the pad in front of me.

"So, I've got your name, your age, your— Oh wait, you married?"

William laughed.

"For the story," I said, matter-of-factly. I could feel the blood rising to my face. "Readers like to know these things."

"And reporters, too?"

"William, I'm insulted. You think I'd try to pick you up just because you're funny, single, and people say you look like George Clooney."

I hung up wondering whether what I had just done constituted lying to a source.

Well, I'm helpless when I'm tempted
And I'm headed straight for hell
And I've got no resistance
The Devil knows me well.

BROOKS & DUNN

When the story came out, it got top billing, 1A, above the fold. After a dozen interviews, I'd managed to pull together a piece about how the developers were reacting to the growing ire against them. My favorite developer quote: "I just want to be thought of as a nice, good-looking guy."

Everyone read the story differently. Our readers thought it was hysterical. The developers felt their voice had finally been heard. And my editors were pleased that I had managed to convey their viewpoint without passing judgment or appearing biased—something newspaper reporters sometimes have troubling doing when dealing with the rich controversial and/or morally questionable. I've always enjoyed writing those types of stories—where you get to crawl into the brains of people with values foreign to you. Kind of like why I tend to be attracted to "inappropriate men." Relating to people I have nothing in common with is a challenge. A test of my open-mindedness. Not to mention an opportunity to spin the world around and check it out from another angle.

When Kip read my story, he zapped me a two-word e-mail: Nice Job.

I sauntered over to his desk, dewy-eyed. "Kip, so I'm off cops?"

My editor scowled at me. "What?"

"I get to cover the developers now."

"Oh, yeah. Well . . . soon. Keep up the work, and we'll talk about it soon."

"When's soon?"

"A few more months."

That wasn't soon. That was an eternity. That was never. I clunked back to my desk, newly depressed.

I quickly recovered.

———

I figured if I called William to ask him what he thought about the story, he'd be sure to think that, all along, I had been trying to pick him up.

So that afternoon I dialed his number—picturing in my head our small spring wedding.

"What did you think?"

"Well done."

Well done sounded affirming, like: I love you or I want you.

William coughed. "You didn't quote me?"

"Nah, you're good for background."

Background meant real life, love life. And, in my ballooning fantasy, it meant William was getting ready to plan our wedding too.

"Oh . . ."

I heard the scratchy sound of a telephone line.

"Do you want to go flying?"

"What?"

"Flying. My plane. Do you want to take a ride in my plane tonight? Atlanta, dinner?"

The idea sounded risky.

Lois accepted.

————

Seasoned editors tell us that silence is a good way to get a jittery source talking. White-collar criminals often spit out juicy confessions if you can convince them you're onto them. Information leakers usually have an ulterior motive. Then there are journalistic superstitions, rules everyone with reporter blood lives by but never mentions out loud. Here is the deal on life-threatening experiences: If there is good 1A potential for your obit, take the risk. A plane crash on my way to Atlanta with wunderkind over here—I figured even a summer intern would have trouble screwing that up. Especially with the help of a good editor.

"Hey, Maria," I shouted as I switched off my computer and headed for the lobby, "I've always wanted to fly in a two-seater. Something I need to do before I die."

With a quote like that, spoken minutes before my death, my obit was sure to get top billing.

Maria was back from "a personal exploration" of her people. In other words, a three-month sabbatical in Central and South America—with a brief stint in Paris. She had blackmailed the higher-ups into giving her the time off. The paid vacation request, I was told, went something like this: "We do believe in diversity, don't we? Because I know *The Wall Street Journal* does." Maria was constantly being courted by big league papers, who had gotten wind of her reputation as a kick-ass editor. She stayed in Raleigh, I could only assume, because the higher-ups valued her so much. They routinely bribed her into turning down offers. "How 'bout you take the two-month paid vacation, buy a home computer on us, and do a few months of a four-day workweek? Sound good to you?"

If I didn't think she had enough to teach me as an editor, I would have asked her to give me a seminar in office negotiating. Forget "Win, Win." Maria did "I win, I win." All the time.

Maria was buried beneath a computerized diagram of a rat heart when I shouted her way. She was making red pencil marks on the diagram for a six-part series on lab rat abuse in the Triangle. She had the fanatic energy of an editor on the Pulitzer hunt. She looked up from her rat drawing and beamed me her X-ray stare.

"If I ever die in flight, Maria," I said, "I want people to know I was fulfilling a lifetime dream. A desire."

"Chica, do I look like an obit writer?" Maria shouted as I headed out the door.

————

When I was in the car, Shelby called my cell.

"Guess what?"

"What?"

"I got the phone bills back."

"What phone bills?"

"Jesus, where have you been? Your father's. He's been calling Juanita's apartment—for months."

"Who?"

"Your father!"

"Oh."

I felt like I was having a flashback. A reentry into a former life. She sounded frantic. I could feel the tension oozing into my ear.

Juanita was a middle-aged Ecuadoran beautician my family

had gone to for ten years. She trimmed and dyed hair in the kitchen of her rent-controlled apartment, on the edge of SoHo. It was an apartment with several rooms she rented out to friends. Juanita was a neighborhood socialite. And while we would get chopped and brushed, combed and styled, Juanita would entertain her posse of Ecuadoran ladies who had emigrated to Manhattan—young, old, fat, thin, rich, poor. That was until Shelby began to question the quality of Juanita's coloring skills. And Sido, a French stylist who used herbal dyes and served ginseng in her one-bedroom, lured Shelby away. I went to Sido, too. My father had stayed with Juanita.

"I got the phone bills, and he's calling some renter in that house. All the time. Two, three times a day. On my phone."

"Well, it's his phone, too."

"That's beside the point."

"You're right. Shelby, do you think he's having an affair with Juanita?"

Shelby laughed. "No, I know your father. He's bedding some young type. God, I hope she's older than you. A banker. Or one of those razor-thin SoHo sculptor women. Someone who knows Juanita. Maybe a friend . . ."

Suddenly, the details of my father's illicit love life were starting to irk me. The phone line hissed. I felt the hiss go right up my spine. "Shelby . . . I'm busy."

"Too busy for me? I'm never too busy for you."

"Shelby, you're talking about my father's sex life. It feels kind of weird. And anyway, I've got a . . . get-together. A kind of date." I omitted the plane part and my hopes for a quick marriage proposal. "I'm trying here. I'm trying to—"

I heard a snicker. Would it surprise you if I told you Shelby was starting to sound very negative about love?

She hung up, then tried to call back several times on the cell. I pretended I was out of the calling area.

William was perched in front of a computer screen staring at a row of squiggly lines when I walked into the airport briefing room several hours later. He was darker than George Clooney, and stockier, but just as striking. He wore a pair of khakis and a rumpled oxford. The outfit made him appear solid but not pretentious. I gave him the head-to-toe once-over and was pleased to confirm that he was worth a dance with death.

William bolted out of his swivel chair. "Good to meet you." He put his arm around my shoulder. I felt a finger on my collarbone. "I've been accessing the weather," he said. "The winds are a little gusty. But it's gonna be severely clear tonight. The visibility is fabulous. Are you ready, girl?"

I nodded. "Ready."

William marched toward the airstrip: Master of the Universe. I followed, Mistress of the Night.

William's plane was heather gray. It had a nose like a penguin's and wings that were silvery and long—like sticks of chewing gum wrapped in foil.

I slid inside and landed on a white leather seat. It smelled clean, like a man's polished office shoes.

William clicked my door shut and disappeared. I pressed my palms against my seat, making sweat smudges on the soft leather. I wondered if my long skirt had been a mistake. I waited.

I was alone in a space-age cocoon with silver knobs and polished oak paneling, an engine and two wings. I buried my nails, chipped from too much typing, and pretended I was a woman accustomed to dining cross-country.

Dating an amateur pilot, I mused, must be a bit like dating a fireman or a police officer, or one of those Mafia bosses who has late-night secret rendezvous in parking lots. You never know if you're getting your last kiss. I made a mental note to take one of those self-help books on losing a loved one out of the library. Just in case. Death is like that. William and I could survive the night and, heck, next week the guy could be getting gussied up to go three feet under.

The pilot door swished open, and William reappeared. He handed me a headset. I felt an index finger brush against my thumb.

"We can only talk one at a time," he cautioned. "Or else we won't be able to hear each other. Then communication between us gets—"

I interrupted. "Difficult?"

The word *communication* made me think of Shelby and my father. I couldn't help wondering if their problem was that they had lost the ability to communicate with each other. Or was it that they had never learned how in the first place? You always want to know why. What happened? It's like a probing question. But no one gives you a usable quote.

The foam muffs from the headset squished tightly against my ears. They were like the headphones for those early-model Walkmen, only bigger. I scanned the fifteen-hundred-pound heap of metal that was about to lift me off the ground.

"Nice," I said, as if I knew how to evaluate the quality of a single-engine plane.

My eyes rested on a glass-plated panel in front of William's seat: three instruments on the top row, three on the bottom.

"They're the sacred six," William said. "They help you gauge what you're doing."

It suddenly occurred to me that I didn't have the foggiest idea what I was doing. Was this a date? A vacation? A reporter-source get-together? I banished the questions.

William pointed to an instrument. The face looked like a

carpenter's level. His words brushed into my earphones and then somersaulted into my ears. "Turn coordinator. Keeps you from shifting directions too abruptly."

Did he know about my weakness for abrupt shifting?

William tapped a clocklike box with little wings in the middle. "The directional gyro helps you determine which way you are going."

It occurred to me that relying on a man to tell me which way we were going might be dangerous. Even with an instrument, I figured the chances for confusion were high.

He pointed to a round instrument, the top half blue, the bottom half black. "Attitude indicator. Measures our relation to the horizon.

"See, you have this perception of where you are. But you could be totally wrong. The thing about flying is that you have to be willing to accept that what you think is going on may not be. The attitude indicator is the tool you use."

I wondered why we didn't have attitude indicators in our living rooms, at our desks, on dates. Why couldn't I take one of these with me during conversations with family members? For job interviews? Why hadn't Bloomingdale's jumped on this?

It was getting dark. William leaned over to fasten my seat belt. I thanked him and dropped my hands in my lap. I wasn't really wringing them. But it might have looked that way.

———

When we went up I felt the plane pressing up underneath me, my body pushing against the wind. I saw the ground slowly back up. It was that delicious part of dusk when the blueberry sky mixes with the raspberry sun—that round, jammy mess right before darkness descends.

William fiddled with his radio. "This is Twenty-one Kilo-Sierra, taking off from RDU."

"Twenty-one KiloSierra. Contact Atlanta Center 119.3. Good day."

"Atlanta, this is twenty-one KiloSierra with you level forty-five hundred."

"Welcome, twenty-one KiloSierra, glad to have you with us. You're in for a beautiful flight."

We were off.

We went up, 2,500, 3,500, 4,500 feet.

The sky looked open, fleshy, and endless. The clouds looked puffy, like white marzipan balls on a wedding cake. The world got smaller, distances got shorter. William got closer.

"The sky is smooth as glass," he crackled.

I crackled back: "Yes."

———

When we stepped inside the 57th Fighter Group bar and restaurant there were fluffy-collared bomber jackets and thick leather helmets, miniature airplanes and black-and-white photos of World War II pilots with boyish buzz cuts and wing-size grins everywhere.

William put his hand on my shoulder and led me inside. He found a spot near a stone fireplace and took off to fetch us drinks.

I watched him shuffle off. Masculine. Gentle. Courtly and cordial. I thought of the gear I would need for this relationship: a pair of sunglasses, a white silk scarf to wrap around my neck, a leather jacket for long flights. Up there, on clear days, I would always have to remember to thank William for introducing me to the sky, for sheltering me in the clouds. I would have to remember to . . . Then it dawned on me that maybe I wouldn't have to remember anything but a pack of extrasoft tissues. For when he dumped me. Or, worse, explained to me that we were never going to be anything but friends.

"You look pretty in this light," William said, handing me a foamy glass of beer.

I took a swig of beer and blushed.

"You also looked pretty outside, don't get me wrong." William sat down. "And in the plane, too. You just generally look pretty in every light. Oh, you must think I'm a fool."

"No . . . No . . . I think you're adorable."

It was easy and entertaining to drink my beer and evaluate William's rightness.

Charming, George Clooney look-alike, accomplished flier. Soon-to-be-my-husband.

Some of the foam slipped off the lip of my beer mug and landed on my nose.

William wiped the foam off with a napkin.

Quick hands.

He took a sip of club soda. "Love to booze. But not when I'm flying."

Safe, in an adventurous way.

"But you have as much as you want. We don't both have to abstain."

Generous.

We ordered hamburgers with funny names. Mine was named something like a Charles Lindbergh. It had cheese. His was something like an Orville Wright. It had bacon. We split an order of fries.

We covered a girlfriend who hated to fly.

"It's miserable when the people you love don't support you." I emphasized the word *miserable*. I would be copilot.

We covered a mom who had never gotten over the fact that he hadn't graduated from college.

"It's important to be accepting. And that's what my friends

say about me: 'Kyle, you're so accepting.' " I would be so healing.

He told me his father had died in a plane crash. I winced. "My dad is a great guy, a little spacey but smart." You can have him.

William slid his hand across the fries plate—it was one of those three-inch-thick porcelain plates that looked like it would simply never break. He raised his hand and licked some salt speckles off his fingers. "My father used to fly with me. He used to take me up and talk to me about life. Told me the universe was a hard place to grasp. But he always said you could harness it when you're flying. You could wrap yourself around it. You could own it. When he died, I felt like the world had harnessed him. Like he had lost trying to master his life."

I contemplated dropping to the gravelly floor and begging William to marry me. I resisted the urge.

"It's hard to find quality girls here," he said.

I inhaled the word *quality*—which no longer meant filet mignon, or one of those old Volvos that never fails. It was the way you wanted to be identified.

I fidgeted with a sugar packet. William nibbled on a sliver of ice.

I spilled some sugar on the table. He slipped another sliver into his mouth.

"I'm surprised you don't have a girlfriend."

"Yeah, I'm not a loner by nature. Just haven't found the right person."

My mouth felt sloppy and warm. But words weren't coming out. I wanted to say: "Yes, yes, yes." But he hadn't asked a question. I looked at the airstrip. He did too. A warm mouth collided with a cold one. I got an ice cube on my tongue.

He paid the bill. We took off.

————

On the flight back, we saw lighted dollhouses, toothpick telephone poles, and traffic signals the size of twinkling Christmas
tree lights. He said Atlanta was behind us; Raleigh was in front
of us. We were flying above Greensboro.

"Great town to raise a family. Wouldn't mind living there."
He said it like a proposal.

"Me too," I said. But I said it like I meant it. And I did.
No one in Greensboro was cheating with the hairdresser—or
had seatless chairs. Married couples went on dates. Cheshire-
grinned, happy, lifelong dates.

"See, over there? That's a water tower."

William knew his landmarks, even when they were tiny
spots on a map. Even when a marbled sky was draped over
them.

I was reminded of a trip to Six Flags in ninth grade. I was on
the ride where you go up and the bottom drops out. I was suc-
tioned against the sidewalls. Suspended in air. I remember
wondering: What are the chances that the man below will stop
the ride and I will fall?

I held on. My life flashed before me. I am a woman in white
swept away on an airstrip. I am a mother with toy jets in my
canvas bag. I am a gardening grandmother with a flying part-
ner. I am a woman who says: "I love you, now and forever."
Then forever never stops. I skipped past the future and fast-
forwarded to the end. The last gulps of air stretched before me.
If I died like this, I thought, I'd want it known that when I
dropped from the sky things felt fine.

My fingers swept across my seat. I heard the sounds of William crackling. "Girl, I'm taking you down."

We went swoosh and bump. The wind sucked into my
shoes. Rocks tossed around in my stomach. My fingers danced
nervously across my thighs. I felt a surging gust of pressure on
my chest, a spiraling thread went from my head down to my
big toe.

Can I count on you, William? Don't fuck this one up? I held my breath.

I was Amelia Earhart. Cokie Roberts. I was a girl with a momentary streak of luck, a woman who was making friends with fate. I was ready to float around the world, zip through the sky, and ride the clouds on a glassy skateboard with wings. My world opened. My engine roared. I never wanted to land.

That's the breaks
The way the old cookie crumbles
What's been going 'round
Ain't been going my way.

GEORGE STRAIT

A two-seater was doing round trips from the edge of my belly button to the tip of my spine. "Halt all sky-bound activity," I yelled into my microphone. "We have a winner."

I woke up to the phone ringing.

I figured it was Shelby with an update, something about credit cards or my father's secret table for two at the Copacabana.

It was William. "Want to go waterskiing?"

For a second I thought I was still dreaming. Then I saw the matchbook by my bed: The 57th Fighter Group—Atlanta, Georgia. I remembered coming home, plucking the thin cardboard book out of my pocket, letting it drop to the floor, and falling asleep to the breezy sensation that the world was about to tilt my way. "Well, umm, sure."

"The third boat landing, off of Wake Forest Road. Meet me at two. I'll be in a sky blue cigarette boat. You can't miss it."

I dove under my covers, taking the phone with me. I dialed L.A.

"Waterskiing date?" I whispered into the receiver. "What does this mean?"

Mark was not his usual animated self. ". . . That you just woke me up. Do you know what time it is?"

I climbed out of bed and found my watch. It was 6:00 A.M. his time. "Sorry!" I paused to let my apology sink in. "Okay . . . I need some analysis."

I looked at my hair in the mirror as I waited to be delivered to a blissful state of male understanding.

Mark yawned. "He wants to go waterskiing."

"No, sleepy doofus, what does it really mean?"

Mark yawned again. "Kyle, I think you are reading too much into this. Men aren't that complicated."

"Mark, he flies airplanes, water-skis. Don't you think this guy could have issues with danger, pushing limits? Aren't those signs of a potential abuser?"

"Hey, Dr. Freud. Could you put your pad away and just have a good time?"

I entertained the possibility for a split second. "No."

Mark let out a wail. I heard a whack. I pictured my best friend smacking his hand against his forehead. "I hate when you do this," he croaked.

"I know," I answered blithely. "But I'm feeling vulnerable. I need you."

Mark sighed. If he and I had a syndicated radio show— which of course is an idea we both support wholeheartedly— this would be the hour that revealed my wimpy, codependent streak, his commitment phobic–closure issues.

Let me explain. Ever since Mark had been ruthlessly dumped by Caitlin, his girlfriend of two years, on a bench outside the Louvre at the tail end of their postcollege backpacking trip through Europe, he had become an aggressive advocate for the heartbroken, the soon-to-be heartbroken, and anyone who needed advice on keeping dangerous suitors away.

Mark said that being dropped by Caitlin—a green-eyed, wheat-haired girl who shared his lust for Truffaut films—was like being robbed at gunpoint by your kid brother. The way he told it, Caitlin had nonchalantly plucked his plane ticket home out of her college backpack, handed it to him, and then rammed him with the news: "I just feel like we're more brother and sister than girlfriend and boyfriend," he recalled her saying.

"Does this mean we're not going to sleep together any-more?" he remembered asking her.

Ever since then Mark had been suffering from an acute case of posttraumatic breakup syndrome. The main symptom: He did all the wrong things. Mark's recent fling with Chantal was a textbook example. The minute things got serious, he moved across the country.

His other recent encounters were equally ill-fated. He had reportedly told a date she reminded him of Sylvia Plath. On another setup, he had decided it would be a good idea to get honest with a recovering anorexic. "Your stomach isn't flabby," he told her. "But your butt could use some firming up."

Once, I'd watched him cream a girl who had pooh-poohed his attempts at buying her a drink at a party. "They're free," she had said. His response lasted twenty minutes. "Do you think it's easy for a guy like me to come up to you and bare my soul? . . . Here I am, naked. I'm standing in front of you with no clothes on—metaphorically speaking—and you . . ."

At the end of the tirade, the host asked him to leave.

In short, Caitlin had turned my best friend into the kind of guy who makes most self-respecting girls head for the hills.

Except, of course, me. When I looked at Mark's unshaven face, his ragged jeans, the torn Paris T-shirt he still wore five years after the unpleasant trip that had ended love as he knew it, I didn't see an asshole. I saw a sick man. And, if truth be told, I think that's part of what bonded us.

This time, though, at 9:00 A.M. Eastern Standard Time, on a Saturday morning, Mark's usual paranoia was noticeably absent. He was actually suggesting that I be so carefree as to accept a man's word at face value.

"Are you recovering?" I inquired, growing alarmed. He had told me a few weeks before that he had gotten a personal trainer and was thinking of taking up yoga, something about getting his soul in line with his movie career. "Because that's not allowed. I need you with me in the back row of Emotional 101."

Mark let out a quick laugh. "Kyle, you don't have to freak out just because the guy asked you to go waterskiing."

Waterskiing? When would he get it? Waterskiing was not just waterskiing. What a ridiculous assumption. Waterskiing was clearly a well-planned test to see how I looked in a bathing suit.

"Listen, Romeo," I growled. "Go back to sleep. I'm going elsewhere for help."

Mark got defensive. "Hey, hey, who's my competition?"

"Lord & Taylor," I said.

"Didn't they go out of business about ten years ago?"

"Fashion plate, that was Gimbel's."

"Oh."

Sometimes, I wish my best friend were a girl.

———

After three hours of unadulterated torture—my head between my legs in the changing room of the Lord & Taylor bathing suit section—I settled on a sporty black one-piece. If I spread my legs the right way and bumped my behind out a bit, being careful not to lean too much to one side, I looked acceptable. The suit had wide straps at the top, to do what Shelby called "distract the eye from problem areas." It was a constructive solution. And I like to consider myself resourceful.

The boat strip was forty-five minutes from Raleigh. I drove there imagining a day of watery touches, shared towels, fingers caked with thin layers of suntan lotion. Then I had a vision of my stepmother—depressed and alone in her bedroom, watching Saturday afternoon reruns while my father got his hair trimmed. Feeling guilty about my abrupt hang-up the day before, I called her. I owed Shelby this. After all, she had spent countless hours on the phone with me—often late at night—or in the middle of the afternoon while she was at her social work job and some poor kid whose mother was dying of AIDS waited in the hallway to talk to her. It was Shelby I called when I was twenty, in Paris, and in the midst of a messy breakup with a boyfriend whose apartment I was leaving. She talked to me for three hours, providing moral support while I packed. "Just get everything in your bags," she coaxed. It was two o'clock in the morning her time. "Sweetheart, you can worry about folding it all later."

"Sorry about yesterday," I said, waiting for Shelby to ask about my date. She almost always asked. Asked and asked. Analyzed and questioned. This time, I think she had forgotten, completely. It was unexpected. Shelby was not a forgetter.

"Well," she huffed. "Guess what I heard?" Shelby did this sometimes, flipped a switch and suddenly became unexpectedly accusatory rather than supportive. Like I'd cut high school math or failed college chemistry and she'd just gotten the call. That was her other side, the side I wasn't so fond of, the side that scared me.

"Your father has been dabbling for a while, Kyle." Now she was rhyming. Like a singsong school yard chanter. We had a girl in second grade who used to do that: *Spencer is a spender. Kyle, you look like a crocodile.*

"He's been picking up phone numbers all over town."

"Really?"

"Really." The tone was there again. Like a jab, or the way some people say "So there." "Erin called last night." Erin was one of Shelby's friends. She was a divorcée, in love with a married jazz musician. She was helping out it seemed. "She says she bumped into your father a couple of years ago at that Chinese dump he used to go to. He was handing some woman his business card."

"Work?"

"I don't think so, Kyle." Shelby sounded angry.

"Well, what do you want me to say?"

"Well, I don't want you to say anything."

I could tell the conversation was starting to descend. Soon it was going to be all curse words and subtle threats. My attempt at civility had failed. I pretended my phone was going dead. "I think I'm driving out of the cell zone. Shelby? . . . Shelby? . . ."

I hung up.

When I arrived, the strip was packed. There were bikini girls in fluorescent tank tops and water cowboys riding their Jet Skis through the artificial lake. The water was glassy green in the deep part, dark blue on the shallow lips. Cone-shaped shadows from the pines on the bank covered the lake edges like a canopy of floral sunscreen.

William was nowhere in sight. I tried to look casual, even though I was standing on the steamy asphalt and my black bathing suit was starting to scratch against my skin like a flannel nightgown.

I should leave, I thought. I don't know this guy. And he's not here.

When twenty-five minutes had passed, my desperation suddenly dissipated. A sky blue boat slid toward the dock. William was grinning at me, waving his beer can in the air, obviously wanting to sweep me up and twirl me around like one of those wooden toy planes. I was relieved.

"Hey!" he shouted, his arm slicing through the sun-bleached air.

"Hey," I yelled back.

When the motorboat bumped against the rubber dock cones, William seemed to look beyond me, as if he was feeling a little dreamy himself. I noticed his skin was the color of light cocoa and his legs were particularly muscular. I saw us together, sailing around the Greek Isles, or off the coast of Maine. We'd be a boating couple. Lovers with chapped lips and salty hair.

Suddenly, my pleasant reverie was interrupted. I heard a shriek. "Where have you been, Billy? Making us wait like this."

"Hey! We're frying here," a second voice wailed.

I turned around and noticed that two women—one taller than I was, the other shorter, both wearing bikini tops and printed cotton wraps—were standing on the sticky pavement next to me. The three of us walked toward the dock, our beach bags bumping against our legs.

William finger-pointed each one of us. "Binky, Lou-Anne, Kyle. . . . Good you're all here."

An unsettling thought dropped into my head: William had never mentioned the word *date*.

———

When we got on the dock, the girl I came to know as Binky waltzed over to me with her Texas long legs. I noticed her breasts, peeking out of her peach bikini top. They were fleshy and sexy, large. The kind of breasts that inevitably made my smaller ones seem nonexistent. She stuck her hand in my face. "Binky," she said. "Billy's accountant."

"Billy?" I inquired politely.

"Will. William."

I nodded—feeling slightly clueless. "Oh."

"Binky's tough," William said. "So be careful."

Binky made a gun with her thumb and her forefinger and pointed it at Billy's head.

"Hey, wise guy. Don't piss off the accountant. I'm the one who makes sure you don't get audited."

William chuckled. "Calm down, we're going to have a blast."

I don't know why, but right then I was reminded of a story I'd done two weeks before. A private plane dove into a Chapel Hill pond, nose first. The police said the pilot was found knocked up against the glass. He died trying to escape, his fingers scratching against the plane door. Suddenly the incident seemed less tragic. Maybe the guy had been a jerk.

Lou-Anne, William's other friend, winked at me. Her face was small and square. Her eyes were little buttons.

"Lou-Anne's my volleyball pal," William said. "She's quite an athlete."

"Oh."

Lou-Anne flashed me a smile. "Billy said you write. I hate writing. I'm much better at numbers. I could spend all day on a math problem. But when I have to do grant proposals at work, I freeze up."

"I freeze up too," I said. "Sometimes. . . . Like in awkward situations."

"Don't have any of those," William said. "We're all old friends here."

Everyone laughed. I felt like I'd walked onto the set of a

popular sitcom. And I was the only one who didn't think it was funny.

A guy named Billy grabbed the wheel. We lurched forward.

I wondered where my pilot had gone. Where was William?

———

"Billy likes you," Binky whispered.

I furrowed my brow.

"He says you're interesting."

We were on the bow of the boat, lying on our towels. Mine was small and navy blue, not really meant for sunbathing. Binky's was large and jungle green. Tarzan was swinging from a tree.

"He said that?"

"Oh yeah, can't you tell that's what he likes about you?"

William was at the back of the boat, talking with Lou-Anne.

"No."

Binky began making loops with her pinkie nail around the terry-cloth Tarzan. "The guy's got party girls like us for buds. But the chicks he really digs are ones like you—ones he can really talk to. Quality girls."

"Oh."

Suddenly, quality became filet mignon again. Meat. Did Binky consider herself ground chuck? I hoped not.

Binky lifted her head from her towel and wrapped a squiggly around a cluster of her sun-bleached hair. She moved with authority, and spoke with a confident tone—Julie on *The Love Boat*, fixing her do.

"Yeah, he's complex. He always says: 'Binky, I'm a multi-faceted person. I need a woman who can satisfy my more intellectual side.' "

"Really?" I said.

"Yup. He's always doing self-improvement stuff. You know,

ballroom dancing, European cooking classes. He's a cowboy at heart, though."

I nodded in agreement—as if I knew this to be true.

"An anal retentive cowboy, though. You know he keeps little notebooks for everything. He's really big on that." She started laughing. "Even the women he dates."

"He does?"

"Oh yeah, gives them points. Pluses for this. Minuses for that. That's what's so cool about you. He told me, 'Binky, she hasn't gotten any minuses yet.' "

I gulped—hard—and imagined myself yelling: *He keeps notebooks?*

"He also loves shows. That's what he'll be taking you to on double dates. My boyfriend Trevor and I go with him all the time. We rent a limo, drive around all night. He loves that shit."

The word *show* stopped me up. In my world, shows were the Sunday hard-core matinees Phillip used to drag me to. *Suicidal Tendencies* at noon. "Let's go to a show," Phillip would say. "And, uh . . . can you pay?" I always agreed to go—and to bring a pocket filled with cash. My little brother, I was convinced, needed all the supervision he could get.

Inside, a guy—usually bald and tattooed, with a mike stuck up his nose—would yell epithets at the crowd. "I hate my mother. Die. Die. Die."

"Do you feel angry?" I'd shout at my brother, hoping to use the time together in the mosh pit for a heart-to-heart.

"I already have a therapist," he'd shout back, before kicking some kid in the groin with his army boot.

I wondered what a show meant to Binky.

She quickly clarified. "Billy likes going to Garth Brooks concerts."

I knew about Brooks from my favorite late-night show, *Honky Tonk Videos*, which aired after midnight on cable. Brooks was a beefy, Stetson-wearing cowboy with a syrupy voice that cracked when he sang about heartbreak. So maybe this was what William and I shared: a mild, not-too-involved appreciation for country music.

"Billy worships Brooks. He's got his posters all over his house. He even got himself a big-screen TV last year so he could watch Brooks videos and concerts."

I wondered for a split second where Billy stored his big-screen, then decided to push that thought out of my mind. "I do think Brooks is kind of sexy in those videos," I said, smiling at Binky. "I watch them sometimes at night when I have insomnia. But, you know, it cracks me up every time I see Brooks lounging around in his ironed jeans. Like on his porch or something. It's so eighties."

Binky gave me a stern once-over. "So eighties? I don't get what you mean. Billy irons his jeans. . . . Like all the country music greats."

My face burned. Like when you suddenly realize you've been in the sun too long and it hurts to crinkle your nose.

"Oh well . . . whatever. I didn't really mean eighties. More like late nineties. Retro. In a good way."

Lou-Anne was behind the wheel and William was sunning himself on the cushions in the back when he tilted his head toward us and squinted his eyes. "Okay, how 'bout some skiing?" He pushed himself up off his towel. "I'll go first."

He pulled his wet suit out of a canvas bag and winked at me. "Are you having fun?"

I smiled.

He squished lubricant into his ski boots and dove in.

"Pull me out of the hole, Lou-Anne."

Before I knew it, we were speeding through the water with William water-dancing behind us. He had one arm up, one arm on the handle. He scooted to the left, then to the right. He shot orders at Lou-Anne. "Lighten up. Go a little faster. The water's great. You guys are gonna love it."

When it was Lou-Anne's turn, she glided through the lake delicately, like a mermaid tiptoeing on the waves. Foamy water glistened against tanned skin. She looked like she was the star of an ad for the new, improved York peppermint pattie.

"Go, girl," William cheered. He was stabbing his leather cushion with his fist while he steered. "What a woman!"

Binky dove in. She slipped on her skis, then held the handle in front of her.

"Keep it light, keep it down," she said, poking her thumb up. William rammed the engine, and we zoomed forward. I waited for her to fall.

"Watch her, Kyle," William said. "She never falls."

Binky lifted her right leg up in the air and put her left hand on her waist. She was ice-skating in water.

When it was my turn, I shook my head defiantly. "Really, you guys are having so much fun. Why don't you just forget about me? Just pretend I'm not here. I've got this book in my bag, I really want to read and . . ."

William wagged a finger at me. "No you don't. We're not getting off this boat until we see you do your stuff."

I looked at him, positively beggarlike.

William wagged some more.

I slipped on the life preserver, crawled to the ledge. Splash; the water was icy.

William plopped the skis in the water. "Go to it, girl."

I could feel the bottom of my bathing suit slipping up into my butt.

"William, I've never done this before. Bill?"

No one responded.

It is impossible to put on a water ski for the first time and maintain a sense of dignity. I swam toward the skis and dragged one down, under the water and toward my foot. I lost it. It flipped up in the air and landed behind me. I swam to it. I let my leg dangle in the air. The life preserver helped me float. I tilted my head back so I was staring at the boat. I pulled one on, then the other. The first one flipped off. When I'd finally gotten both skis on, I noticed that the rope was stuck in my left ski. When I tried to unstick it, the ski flew up and out of the water, plopping itself behind me. I could see Lou-Anne giggling as she wrapped her hair in a beach towel. When I'd finally untangled the cord, I got up. I was backwards.

I smiled, trying to appear coy. But William's smile was slipping off his face. He was looking more and more bummed.

"Just kneel," he said.

I kneeled.

"Keep your butt out."

I did.

"Relax."

I couldn't.

The engine smoked. The boat jerked forward. The cord slipped through the air. My body went flying. I didn't dive; I didn't land. I didn't slip into the water. I crashed.

Ca-plunk.

"Face plant!" someone yelled.

The engine croaked. The boat swished forward. I went backwards.

"She took a digger," someone else shouted.

Cord lost, foam in my face. Cord lost, ski in the air. Cord lost, I am a waterlogged rag doll with no owner. I am a young girl's silver jack spinning out of control. I am a soon-to-be discarded play airplane with broken wings.

I heard Binky's confident musing. "She's not getting this."

My eyes were smarting from the fuelly water. "Stop."

No one heard me.

The tips of my fingers felt numb. "Stop."

No one looked down.

They were playing, laughing, swapping stories. They were "having fun."

William turned around to grab something from his cooler. I noticed his shorts were sticking against his thighs. They were too short, too tight. They were gross.

"People, I want to stop now," I yelled from the water.

William didn't hear me. "Do you have your skis on yet?" he said, turning around.

I ducked underwater and doggie-paddled to the boat. My breath was watery, cold. It was caught in my throat.

"I'm done, okay," I said, hanging from the boat railing.

———

We were pulling into the dock. I was arranging my stuff, folding up Binky's towel, tucking mine in my bag, getting ready to leap out.

"So, we're gonna go for some food. Have some drinks. What do you think, girls?"

I was the first to respond. "I really need to get back."

William looked irritated, like I was gashing his plans. "Oh, come on."

Binky looked surprised, like I had insulted her after our instructive talk.

Lou-Anne looked worried. "Aren't you hungry?"

"No, actually, I'm not hungry at all." My voice was starting to sound shrill.

William wrapped an arm around my shoulder. "Hey, don't worry if you lost some points there in the water. I still think you're cute."

I put my bag down and undraped his arm, thinking of

Binky's comments about the notebooks. "Points? I didn't real-ize you were keeping score."

William smirked. "Well, I guess you don't know that much about water sports, either."

"Obviously not," I mumbled. "We don't water-ski in NYC."

William put his hands on his hips. "I'm sorry," he said, half-joking, "if our activities aren't good enough for you New York types."

"What do you mean—'good enough'? You are the one who didn't bother to talk to me the whole day."

"Hey, you weren't exactly approachable. You hardly said anything the entire time we were on the boat."

"I didn't know the other guests."

"So?"

"So. Maybe I was nervous. Anyway, I thought this was going to be a date."

The easygoing William was gone. Someone much stricter, more judgmental, and mostly unlikable had replaced him. "That's no excuse."

"It's not?" I asked, looking up at his face. It was taut and beet red burnt. His eyes were little blue stones—sharp and piercing. I hoisted my bag up onto my shoulder and turned toward the parking lot. "I think I need to get out of here."

———

The sun was still beating down onto the asphalt parking lot when I climbed into my car. The seat felt as hot as a diner grill, and the steering wheel was burning the tips of my fingers. I cranked up the air conditioner and wound around the lake to the park exit. I soared past the Holy Church of God and the KFC, the Kmart and the Starbucks. The yellow traffic lines were bleaching the road. The neon signs were blurring the sky. Everything was fuzzy and out of focus, like drunk eyes and all the days you want to smudge away with your finger—as if life were a series of charcoal drawings you could erase from your brain.

I felt stupid and naïve. I didn't want another confirmation that men were assholes, that people couldn't get along, that I couldn't get it together with a member of the opposite sex. Had I been at fault? Had William? I was angry, and I knew enough to know that meant I was also hurt. Words flashed across my dashboard. As if they were scripted there, and I just needed to press the right button and they would somersault out, one after another.

"Fuck you." That was me.

"Screw you." That was my dad.

"You monster." That was Shelby.

The hitting was what everyone deserved.

My hands clutched the steering wheel so hard that my palms were dotted with red splotches. Little heart-shaped splotches that reminded me of my worst Valentine's Day. I woke to snow that morning. Five feet of it. As if a dove white blanket had unfolded outside our loft window. I pulled on the white, knee-length sweatshirt dress that Shelby had ironed the night before and placed by my bed. It was dotted with red hearts—all over the top and bottom, even on the sleeves. I slipped on the backs of my loopy heart earrings and strapped my heart-shaped bag, with the red sparkly beads that Shelby had found at her favorite store on Ninth Street, over my shoulder.

"School's open," the newscaster said.

"You're not going," my father said.

"Let her go," Shelby said.

"You are manipulating her."

"You are using her to get at me."

I could hear the shouting from my spot on our one kitchen stool, where I nibbled on a piece of dried toast. Worried about my parents, I slid off the stool and cracked open the door to their bedroom. I watched my father grab a clump of my step-mother's dark hair and bang her head against the Sheetrock wall—as if he were bouncing a basketball. I watched Shelby reach for my father's chin and bite into the skin on his face—as if she were an animal gnawing on a piece of meat.

"Stop, you're hurting each other," I screamed. Then my mind went blank. I slipped off my heart outfit and climbed back into bed, pulling my pink-and-white Laura Ashley hundred-percent cotton sheets over my head and wishing I could slip into another girl's life.

———

At home, I called Shelby. Suddenly I was feeling that the basic requirements for serenity were floating out of my reach.

"I'm not happy here," I sputtered into the receiver. "I want to come home."

I don't remember her first reply or the other things she said. But I do remember this: "Kyle, your father—he's left us."

I remember how my stomach tilted, my bed got crooked, my room turned into the Haunted House at the state fair. The ceiling was tipsy. The walls were slippery. I put the phone down and watched the plastic receiver float up and out of reach. The phone turned into Shelby's TV set, then her VCR, flashing the wrong time. It became the rippled red dress I wore to her wedding, then one of Shelby's green suede Charles Jourdan heels. I saw our seatless chairs and my dad's cigar Ziplocs, one of Phillip's wool school hats, my Christmas stocking with the fuzzy Santa. Then I saw my parents' loft. The broken light fixtures, the broken stereo, the broken washing machine, the rusty faucets, the chipped tiles, the cracked walls, the peeling ceilings, the door with the fist-size hole. Everything under construction. In renovation. Never livable. Floating away.

11

You keep telling me you're sorry
But I'm never going to listen
To another word you're saying
. . . Please don't speak to me of love.

WHISKEY TOWN

Over the summer, my father said "sorry" a hundred times. He sent presents: a Swatch watch with a little plastic face designed to look like a newspaper, a yellow ceramic cup in the shape of a taxicab, a fifteen-year-old pottery mask he had made during a class we took together in the East Village. He called often, sent letters, left messages.

"It's not you I'm leaving."

"You have a right to be angry."

"Kyle, I wish I had made better choices."

His words were purposeful and well-meaning. They reflected his skill at dissolving families. He had done this before.

Shelby and my brother George were pretty sure that my father was shacking up in one of the rented rooms in Juanita's apartment. At least that's what their sources were telling them. They'd also gotten word that my father might be dating a twenty-four-year-old Ecuadoran law student. And at one point they heard some gossip about a nineteen-year-old aspiring actress from Brazil. But none of the rumors had been confirmed. And, to their collective dismay, they were unable to nail down who exactly had become the object of my father's affections.

On a showery Sunday afternoon, I interrupted his effusive apologizing about his spotty marriage record and popped the question. "Dad, who is she?"

"She?" he inquired.

"Okay," I blurted out. "This is getting embarrassing. How long do you intend to keep this a secret?"

"Keep what a secret?"

"Listen," I interrupted—figuring that with this level of resistance my father was likely to be dating a ten-year-old. "You are really starting to sound like a shady character."

My father took a deep breath. "Kyle, for God's sakes, haven't you figured it out by now?" He paused. "It's Juanita."

"Juanita?"

"Yes, Juanita."

The Ecuadoran beautician who used to badger me about the knots in my hair?

"Dad!" I gasped in horror. "She's your age."

"I can't believe with your reporter skills you didn't figure this out." He sounded genuinely disappointed. "I've been living in her apartment for three months."

Three months with Juanita?

"Dad, we thought you were . . ." I saw scissors. I smelled hair conditioner. I felt the rub of the towel against my wet hair. I remembered Juanita's fingers, the way they raked through my tangled shoulder-length strands. I heard her voice: "You don't brush enough, do you?"

I remembered how Juanita used to chase her daughter around the kitchen with a curling iron. "If you don't go to school, you're going to be a nothing."

"Kyle, she makes me very happy."

"Happy?" I was starting to panic. "This is a joke. . . . Right? . . . Right? . . . Dad? . . . Do I know you?"

I hung up the phone, shaking.

My father's departure had left me feeling like I was floating aimlessly on another planet. Now, suddenly, that planet had blown up. And I was upside down—dangling from a crater.

———

Some affairs are more socially acceptable than others. If my fifty-nine-year-old father had shacked up with a ballet dancer from Louisville, Kentucky, or a big-boobed stripper from Hoboken, New Jersey, people would have shrugged their shoulders and declared: "Good for him."

But throw in a woman more or less his age, give her some hair dye and a pair of rollers, and people want to know: "Does your father have emotional problems?"

The answer to that question—as far as my brothers were concerned—was yes. More specifically: "The lady dyed Mom's hair. Now Dad's bedding her. Don't you think that's gross?" Phillip asked me over the phone one evening. "The fuckin' cleaning lady would have been better."

"Or the chick behind the counter at the dry cleaner's," I interjected.

We both cackled, oblivious to how unabashedly snobby our

beef with my father's new love interest was. Phil may have had a reason. After a year at military school, "sensitivity" was not something he was thinking a lot about. But I didn't have any excuse to make bitter, mean-spirited jokes about someone I hardly knew—particularly since they were the kind of remarks that would have elicited disapproving sneers from me if they came out of anyone else's mouth.

Luckily, my father's meandering didn't make temporary bigots out of all of us. My brother George transformed into Brooklyn's answer to Oprah. His reply to questions about my father's behavior: "The man needs therapy."

————

As the months progressed my father made frequent attempts to stay connected to me. But I felt as if a glass wall now separated us—and the only way I could get close to him again would be to crash through it with my fists and risk hurting him. I had a lot of images like that swarming around in my head. When I pushed my cart along aisles at the grocery store, I would often fantasize about bopping the cart in front of mine and watching the man pushing it go flying into the toilet paper rolls. "I know you're angry at me," my father would tell me over the phone, on the rare occasions when I chose not to hang up on him. "And you have every right to be."

Usually I would tell him: "Listen, this is your life." And then I would lie: "I have my own."

————

Shelby waited several weeks after her initial announcement to phone me again. I was surprised by the delay—but I assumed it was the shock that had kept her away. As for me, I didn't call. Instead, at night, I pictured her alone in bed, wearing my father's shirt—like she'd done in Harlingen—unable to sleep, rereading old mystery novels and doing crossword puzzles from back issues of *The New York Times*. It was one of those images you try to erase the minute it pops in your head.

When Shelby did call, I had a strange, unsettling feeling. She called my father "evil," "horrible," "an immoral man." My responses were brief and supportive. "I know, Shelby. I know, he's an asshole."

"Kyle, I didn't ask for this. I didn't want this. You can't imagine how hard it is."

"I know, Shelby. It's hard for all of us."

Her voice was desperate and coarse—as if she somehow blamed me. "Hard for all of us? What do you mean, Kyle? It's clearly harder for me. Kyle, it's worse for me."

During our next conversation I made the mistake of suggesting that perhaps the blame didn't lie squarely in my father's camp.

I could feel frost on the phone line. "Kyle, I think it's abundantly clear who is at fault here."

In late August Phillip entered college. It was the culmination of a long drawn-out admissions process. Both my father and Shelby had wanted to send Phillip to one of the very competitive, small liberal arts colleges in New England. But he had made that difficult for them by pulling in mostly mediocre grades his last year of high school—even though MAB was not a hard place to succeed at. It was predictable behavior for him. Phil was furious at our parents for making him miserable. And, in turn, he had worked diligently to add to their misery by refusing to do anything that would make them proud of him.

In any event, he eventually got accepted at a well-respected, small, all-boys college in Virginia. But six weeks after classes began Phil, in a drunken stupor, punched his roommate in the jaw, strapped a Walkman to his head, and rode a Greyhound to

New York. He moved back into the loft with Shelby. The detached calm that had enveloped him in Harlingen had turned to rage. It seethed out of him—as if almost uncontrollable. It scared me, and I think it scared him. One night he had gotten so pissed he called my father at three in the morning to call him a fuckhead.

"Wish I had been there," I told him when he sheepishly recounted the tale. "Sometimes, just for fun, I'm going to picture that in my head. . . . But really, Phil, are you okay?"

"No. I'm not, Kyle. I beat the shit out of that kid in school. I could have killed him. Do you ever feel like that—killing someone?"

"Yeah," I replied. "Myself."

––––––––

A few days later my father called. Assuming it was an editor, I picked up.

"*No estoy aquí,*" I said, when I realized who it was.

My father ignored my assertion—in Spanish—that I was not home. "Phil says you're not doing well, Kyle."

"You can't help me."

"Maybe it would just be good to talk about it. Why don't you come to New York and see me?"

"No, thanks."

"I'm sending you a ticket—just in case you change your mind."

––––––––

I planned my trip to New York in October, for the same week Mark had scheduled to fly home for a vacation, and during a weekend I knew Shelby would be out of town. I stayed in Brooklyn on George's couch—not at my father's new place—wanting to avoid any questions from Shelby about my allegiance.

Mark and I met at Sophie's, a loud but cheap dungeon of a watering hole in the East Village that played the Pogues non-stop and served three-dollar shots.

We sat at a corner table by the bathrooms and sipped tequila. It was chilly, in that wet fall way when the dampness just starts to feel like it is wrapping around your bones. The alcohol was warming. "I always knew your dad was depressed," Mark shouted into my ear. "But I didn't know he was misera-ble, too."

I gulped down my next shot and wiped my lips with the back of my hand. The alcohol stung my throat—but felt good in a numbing way. "Well, apparently he wasn't that miserable," I shouted back. "He had to be having this affair for a couple of years. Like Christmas Eve, we'd all be home. And my dad would just slip off the couch and disappear. Last year George made plans to do something with him a few days before Christ-mas. He starts walking around the house looking for my father, you know, saying: 'Dad, what time is it that you want to go to the museum?' And then Phil was like: 'George, who are you talking to? Dad went out for the day.' Mark, he had totally forgotten."

Mark peered down at his glass and then put his hand on top of mine. "That's sad."

For a split second I wondered what it would be like to lick his lips and feel his chest breathing against mine.

———

I met my father on the steps of the Harvard Club—underneath the crimson flag. He was wearing his favorite Shetland sweater and his worn Brooks Brothers jacket with the brass buttons on the sleeves. As always, he carried his *Wall Street Journal* tucked under his right arm. I took it as a comforting reminder that he still read English. He wasn't wearing any of the funky Juanita stuff he had sported the last time I was in New York. I assumed he had done it on purpose—so as not to upset me further. However, his hair was now a new shade: bluish black.

"Interesting," I said, standing on my tiptoes and brushing my fingers through it.

We left our jackets at the coat check and settled into red leather chairs at a round oak table with a backgammon set on top of it. Two men in their late thirties were playing chess a few tables down from us. One had on a pink polo shirt. The other one had on a white oxford button-down.

My father picked up a marble-topped backgammon chip and pressed it between his fingers. "I don't know how this is affecting you."

"Neither do I."

"Kyle, you must be angry with me," he said, still pressing the chip.

"I don't think that's what I'm feeling," I replied, pushing the board away from me.

"Then what is it you're feeling?"

"I don't know." I glared at my father.

"Why don't you try to figure it out?"

I was getting annoyed. "You're not my psychiatrist."

He waited a minute. "I'm hardly trying to be. Kyle, it's impossible for you to feel nothing." My father plopped the chip down on the table. "I've made a lot of mistakes that have hurt other people. I know."

I was furious now. I leaned forward and pressed my ribs against the thick table edge. "Dad, I just can't believe . . ." I glared at him. "Just because . . . This is so . . ." My words and feelings and thoughts were getting jumbled in my head, and my eyes were getting fogged up. The edges of my father's sweater and the sides of his face were growing blurry. I knew I was angry—despite my claims otherwise. But what I didn't know was what the sundry other emotions were that were swimming aimlessly around in my head, piercing and poking at my brain. "You know what. This is fuckin' embarrassing." I was whisper-shouting now. My legs were shaking involuntarily. And from where I was sitting my father looked like a smudged-up watercolor with distorted contours and blended shades. "I mean, couldn't you have found someone else? She doesn't even speak English."

He coughed. "This isn't about Juanita. It's about me and Shelby. Kyle, Shelby was driving me into the ground financially. I couldn't afford to stay with her. She was impossible."

Somewhere, amidst all the confusion, I knew that Juanita's language skills were not the point. But I was feeling vengeful, and mocking her seemed like the most effective way to hurt my father.

"But . . . why, why do you keep doing this? I mean, what were you thinking? Didn't you suspect things would be rocky with Shelby before you married her? Did you think about it at all, Dad? When you married Mom, did you think about that?"

"Kyle, I was too young when I married your mother. By the time I was your age, I was saddled with a family and I wasn't even out of business school. Then with Shelby, once Phillip was born, I couldn't leave. I swore I wouldn't put you through another divorce."

"So you spent twenty years having knock-down-drag-out fights with a lunatic you decided to marry. Dad, I'm fucked up. You've fucked me up."

My father's fingers were gnawing at the leather siding of the backgammon set. I could see the blood rushing to his fingertips as he pressed them hard against the set. "Jesus Christ, I'd buy a VCR with more care than you put into your love life."

My father stopped tugging at the backgammon set and placed his hand on the oak table. "I know you're disappointed in me."

I looked up at him in his fuzzy Shetland sweater with his

corduroy shirt collar sticking out, and his favorite cracked leather belt with the brass buckle wrapped around his waist. He was sloppy—but handsome. I noticed the scar on my father's face from when Phillip caught him with a fishhook, and the wisps of hair I had loved to tussle by wrapping my arm around the back of his head like a snake and touching the tip of his ear with my fingers. I felt his hand on my neck at the departure gate at Kennedy Airport before my flight to Paris—his *Wall Street Journal* between his rib and forearm. It was 1993, I had just graduated from college, and I was leaving to go back to Paris—after having spent my junior year there interning and working as a reporter. He was outlining my recent achievements: I had spent the summer before freelancing in Prague, he reminded me. I had written for *The Miami Herald*. I was flying back to Europe "not to monkey around—but to use your talents. Because most people didn't get this far. Most people don't have the guts. Most people don't have what you have, Kyle."

I saw him in 1985, tired and worn-out from a week of work—shouting at me, his fifteen-year-old daughter, as we engaged in our weekly Friday night curfew combat. I heard him shout: "Twelve A.M."

"Just make it twelve-fifteen," I heard myself shout back.

"I said twelve."

"You don't even trust me."

"One more word and I'll make it eleven-forty-five."

"Dad, I can't even talk about—"

"That's it—you want to make it eleven-thirty?"

"I hate you! Screw you! You are the most uptight father on the whole planet."

"Okay, forget it. You're not going out tonight."

I saw us together in 1980, as we stood side-by-side in the wide, high-ceilinged gallery at the Met, staring at the Ingres lady with the long back. "See, her back is not proportionate—but it looks like it is," he whispered into my ear. "See how interesting that is?"

Then I saw my father in 1973. I smelled the scent of cigarette smoke in his hair as he kneeled down and put his hand on my jumper.

"I feel icky," I told him—using the only words my three-year-old brain could muster up to describe the pangs in my stomach.

"We're not getting divorced because you did anything bad," he replied.

———————

I could hear the waiters tapping the soles of their patent leather shoes against the hardwood floors, and the cackling of a fire in the next room. The men at the table nearby were gone. In their place was a woman in a Talbots skirt with a Coach bag by her chair. The tea I had ordered was lukewarm now. My father had barely touched his coffee. I crossed my arms around my stomach tightly, as if somehow that would protect me from the searing pain in my ribs. He appeared small now, just a fuzzy body sinking into a fuzzy cushion. He was a fuzzy fuckup, a smudged wrecking ball crashing into everything he created. Who wants her father to say: "I know you're disappointed in me"? Not me.

———————

When my plane landed in Raleigh, I rode the bus to my car and was let out in a muddy makeshift parking lot a mile from the tarmac. Around me everything was green, and above me everything was blue. I was facing a sea of open space that sucked me in.

I ambled slowly to my car—being careful not to get mud stains on my pants. And while I walked it suddenly occurred to me that my father was no longer relating to me like the large, towering figure he had been to me as a child. But when, exactly, I wondered, had I become an adult? And what did that mean?

As I drove out onto the highway, these questions slipped away. New York dissolved. My father disappeared. Shelby dimmed. And the Carolina road leapt into the sky. The poppies swam around me. The broomstick trees danced above me. Everything looked new and fresh and pure and beautiful. And there I was. Just me. This part of the world would be mine.

We're pluggin' in the power
Crankin' up the sound.

SHANIA TWAIN

The cop beat was dead. And nothing was brewing on the developer front. Maria was spending the afternoon on her masseuse's bed, and most of the other reporters were at the gym, doctoring their résumés, or home taking naps.

I was skulking around the newsroom looking for a section of the paper to invade. The faith section, a weekly pullout that featured articles on anything vaguely related to worshiping a higher being, looked vulnerable. The editors were so strapped for stories they had threatened that morning to launch a "church-of-the-moment" column on the section's front page. The idea had Maria—who edited most of the stories in the section—rather worked up. And, true to character, she saw a bargaining opportunity.

"Hell, if I'm going to work for an advertising agency, I'd like to at least get paid a decent salary," she proclaimed, before grabbing her purse and taking off for her massage.

That evening after work I lounged in my bathtub, reading the latest issue of *Southern Living* magazine and wondering what I could write for the section. I'd tossed my wet magazine on the tile floor and switched off the tap water when the words of an editor I'd once had in Philadelphia came to me. "When all else fails," he'd growled one news-dead August afternoon, "try the yellow pages." I jolted out of the bathtub, grabbed a towel, and pulled the phone book out of my recycling bin.

"Stories, stories, stories," I repeated to myself, as if the mantra would make some really scintillating topic suddenly appear on the pages. A good article idea, by the way, is Prozac for the bored reporter.

I flipped to the *Cs*—and found that there were fifteen full pages dedicated to churches. One was pushing automatic payment donations, another was advertising its ATM machine, conveniently located just outside the worship hall. The Western Heart Church featured free valet parking. The Triangle Worship Club offered a class entitled "Godly Ways to Lose Weight." Christ, I thought, one-stop shopping. The only thing you couldn't get done at one of these churches was your dry cleaning.

Then my eyes rested on an ad for a church group that offered sex advice for singles. But when I read the small print—"How to Resist the Urge"—I quickly flipped the page.

After a few more flips I spotted the sprawling half-page ad for the Morrisville Christian Rocker Congregation. That's when I knew I'd found my story.

"We'll rock your cross off!" the ad promised.

The idea appealed to me. After all, I was smack dab in the middle of the Bible Belt. So it seemed only appropriate that I would write at least one story relating to faith in the South. Furthermore, the section was wildly popular. It even had an Israeli columnist who wrote faith-based features and a Dear Abby–like Q & A column. She was so beloved, she was often asked to sign the mug shot above her name by fans she bumped into outside the office.

That evening before dozing off to sleep, I called Mark to announce that my newsroom dry spell was over.

"Just don't become a Christian Rocker, okay," my best friend warned.

The advice surprised me. "Huh?"

"Listen," Mark retorted. "I know you."

I was getting defensive. "What do you know?"

"That you went away to college wearing black lipstick and came home for spring break in a grass green sweater and duck boots."

"Hey, it was a preppy campus."

"But you weren't preppy . . . until you got there."

"At least I got over it."

"Yeah, when you went to Paris and convinced yourself you were a French bohemian communist. You were speaking English with a French accent and denouncing the capitalist state."

"Listen, I'm getting insulted here. I didn't ask for an evaluation of my personality. You make me out to be a person with a shaky sense of self."

Mark chuckled. "You said it. Not me."

"Oh, I'm sorry," I shot back—using the most condescending tone I could muster. "Not everyone feels compelled to limit their social circle to the four New Yorkers they roomed with in college."

"Hey, now *I'm* insulted."

I was feeling better already. "Good."

"I still want you to promise me you won't become a Christian Rocker."

I let out an angry yelp and hung up.

———

I drove to Morrisville, a small nondescript town about ten minutes from Raleigh, and stepped into Rocker Heaven cautiously.

"Come to rock with God?" a man in a pair of glimmering green slacks thundered at me.

"Well, sure. I guess I have," I returned, flashing a dumb smile.

Around me in the high school were hundreds of excited men and women—bobbing, gyrating, and rotating up and down. They were waving paperback Bibles in the charged morning air and pointing at the sky with their fluorescent highlighters. Their faces were glowing; their bodies were dripping with sweat. Their clothes were clinging to them like swimsuits. And this was only the lobby.

From my spot in the entryway, I detected the sound of a drum set and the whir of an electric guitar floating from the auditorium—where the church band was apparently warming up. An earsplitting version of Melissa Etheridge's "Like the Way I Do" was pounding against the walls. The song's chorus, "Nobody loves you like the way I do" had been changed to "Nobody loves you like the way God does."

I watched as a man in dusty cowboy boots lifted his hands above his head and began banging them against each other as he strutted toward the music. "I'm ready for him," he yelped. "Ready as I'll ever be!"

"God sees my heart not my clothes," screamed a woman in spandex biking shorts.

The crowd formed a link of swerving bodies, some already breathless, that boogied its way toward the cafeteria. The band broke into another tune, a Christian rendition of Tom Petty's "Won't Back Down."

> *Hey, Jesus, He is the Only Way.*
> *Hey, I will stand by my ground.*
> *And I won't back down.*

I quietly mouthed a few of the lyrics, then followed the pulsating bodies toward the cafeteria. I made a little finger-snapping gesture, then I did a leap and a twist and landed—exhausted—in a metal folding chair.

"I love Jesus," I said to no one in particular. "He's smokin'!"

———

Considering all the hoopla in the lobby, you might have expected the rockers to be tearing off their clothes in the auditorium. But things were slightly tamer than that. Still, there were enough salacious elements to forget for a second that this was ultimately a holy endeavor. The Rockers were basking in sun from windows overlooking the teachers' parking lot and dancing underneath floodlights from ceiling fixtures that were speckled with spitball stains. Onstage, fondling his drumsticks, was the man who'd greeted me at the front door in his sparkly pants. Slithering in front of him was a stick-thin woman in a miniskirt who seemed perilously close to French-kissing her microphone. And a man with platform sneakers was tapping on the keyboard, looking as high as a veteran raver after a few hits of Ecstasy. The band, I would soon learn, was called The Holy Crüe.

I rambled over to the coffee and Dunkin' Donut table, gently snapping my fingers to the beat of the music. I bit into a glazed donut and started flipping through the brochures that had been thrust into my hand in the lobby. "Rock into His Heart," read a hot pink pamphlet. "Now That I'm Rocking,

How Do I Know He's Listening?" read a fluorescent blue one—as if in response to the first. The brochures reminded me of Chinese take-out menus, except there was no Chinese writing on them and they were all emblazoned with the church logo: "Normal people experiencing God."

I was preparing to let out another slew of Christianese when I noticed a woman in purple suede clogs parading around the room like some clog dancer about to break into a jig. She swooped over, as if her clogs were propelling her my way, and wrapped her beefy arms around me.

"First-timer, uh?" the woman cooed, pressing her forehead up to mine, then releasing me from her clutches. "Spotted you right away. Deer in the headlights look. Seekers always have it. I'm Bonnie, the pastor's wife. . . . And you are . . . ?"

"Kyle," I said, pointing at my chest with my thumb. "Just dropped in to—"

Bonnie interrupted me with another bear hug. "Kyle, we're glad you've come to rock with us. We always welcome newcomers. . . . You a newbie?"

"A newbie?" I stared at Bonnie intently. She was tall and lanky, thin as a broomstick, with a contagious smile and long dark hair pulled back in a braid.

"You know, a new suburbanite." Bonnie flexed her left clog confidently. "We get a lot of them."

I nodded halfheartedly—both amused and alarmed by my new title.

"A lot of us guy and gal Rockers are transplants—fairly new in town dealing with, you know, loneliness and feelings of isolation."

I smiled.

"That's where we come in. A pinch of faith. A few bear hugs. And a big swig of God. Kyle, that's the cocktail we get drunk on." Bonnie chuckled. "Are you listening to these guys?" she said. "They are so . . . cool!"

After a hearty rendition of Bruce Springsteen's "Born in the U.S.A."—with the chorus changed to "I was born to love Jesus Christ"—the guy in the sequined pants plopped his drumsticks down and catapulted off the stage. Locks of his long, feathery blond hair lifted a little as he landed smoothly on the cafeteria floor in his Nikes.

He grabbed for his microphone, an ultramodern wiry one, and wrapped the cord around his neck; then he started pacing like a stand-up comic preparing for his skit in a Las Vegas casino. The crowd went wild.

Bonnie clapped excitedly, then sashayed over to the nearest folding chair and dropped into it. I settled into an empty chair next to her.

"People," the man in the sparkly pants began. "A few years ago, the Big Guy interrupted me during my shower. He tapped me on the soapy shoulder and told me he wanted me bad." He flashed a smile and pointed good-naturedly at a few silver-haired ladies in the front row. "Now, ladies, don't get the wrong idea."

Bonnie cupped her mouth with her hand, as if holding back a giggle. "That's Borris, my husband," she whispered to me. "Doesn't sound like a pastor, does he?"

Borris pointed to the ceiling with his thumb and began rubbing his armpits as if soaping up.

"I went: 'Listen, God. Don't you think there are people out there who are a little more qualified? I mean, I bet you can find a better candidate than me.' For crying out loud, people. I was an electrician.

"I told him: 'God, I don't own a suit.' " Borris plucked the creases of his sparkly slacks. "You know, I'm really averse to cutting my hair.' " He pointed at his head. " 'You know, dude,' I told him. 'I'm just not the type.' "

Borris lowered his voice. "Then I heard God say: 'Are you going to do this?'" Borris was whispering now. "I felt like God had just punched me in the stomach." He tilted his head toward the ceiling and joined his hands together so firmly that his whole body shook. "Then I knew," he hollered. "I had to go."

The crowd went wild. A man behind me yelled "Hee-haw!" A woman in leather pants climbed up on her chair and let out a loud, whooping whistle.

"We're the walking wounded, people. All of us. Our souls are tarnished. Our hearts are scarred. And God says: 'Come dance with me. Let me shield you. Let me heal you.' You gonna turn him down? People, don't turn him down.

"Wounds. Scabs. Scars. We're jolted. We're lost. Our world is constantly playing tricks on us. What do you do?"

Borris paused for a second, to let the question really sink in, and then whispered into his microphone: "You turn to God. People, you turn to the Man."

Borris started jogging around the cafeteria high-fiving his parishioners. Then when the cheers died down, he returned to his spot on the edge of the stage, sat down crossed-legged, and looked over at Bonnie. "Bonnie," he whispered into his microphone. "Tell us what made you turn to him."

A thin smile swept across Bonnie's face. She bounced out of her chair like a human rubber band, then raced to the stage like the next contestant on *The Price Is Right*.

"Well, people," she began, a little out of breath. "It was, well, a long time ago. I was lost in my disco and dancing days." She did a little twist with her hips and shot her arms out like arrows—à la John Travolta in *Saturday Night Fever*.

"I was . . . well, people, I was not cool. I was hanging around in nightclubs. I was going for guys with expensive cars and no hearts. I was looking desperately for something more meaningful—but not knowing what."

She raised an eyebrow and looked over at her husband. "Then I met Borris."

She cracked a smile. "And, oh boy, was that ever a meeting. Borris was in our basement fixing our air conditioner. I stepped downstairs to put some towels in the dryer. When I first saw him, I almost screamed. I thought he was robbing the joint. Then I saw the wood cross around his neck. And something happened. A click. Borris looked over at me and, people, he goes: 'Do you need to be saved?'

"And you know what, people? I looked up at that man in my basement and I said: 'Save me!' "

A man roared. Another one shouted, "Thata girl." A little lady in white tennis shoes hurled: "You go, Bonnie."

Bonnie's eyes twinkled. "I thought I'd end up with some club promoter. Instead, I found a man selling salvation. People, this guy swept me off my feet." Bonnie made a stroke in the air with her hand to demonstrate. "And I've been boogying with J. Christ ever since."

"Let us pray!" someone yelled.

"Yes, we should," someone added.

"Oh all right," Borris replied, laughing softly and blushing.

———

Once the crowd had settled back down and Bonnie had returned to her seat, Borris scanned the room again. "Newcomers?" he asked. "Do we have any of those this morning?"

Bonnie jumped back up and pointed at me. "This one's a first-timer, Borris. A seeker."

My face turned the color of a fall leaf.

"Stand up, seeker," Borris shouted at me. "Tell us—what's the hurt that brought you here?"

I rose from my folding chair reluctantly. One hundred curious Christians eyed me with looks of wonder and expectation. I didn't want to lie. But I didn't want to tell my new friends right then and there that I was on assignment. They might throw me out of the cafeteria, toss their highlighters at me, then boo me in the parking lot. I needed an answer quick, a plausible reason why I had just happened to be there that morning.

I coughed nervously. Then I whispered: "Divorce." I spoke a little louder. "My parents are getting divorced."

A soothing *oh* rose from the chairs.

I was hoping that that would be enough and I could sit back down and bury myself behind one of the paperback Bibles on the floor by the chairs. But Bonnie was nodding encouragingly. "Keep going," she whispered. "Tell us more."

I had no idea what to do. So I did what Bonnie told me to. "An affair," I said, hesitantly. "My father was having an affair."

A few people shook their heads in dismay. A few others inched forward in their folding chairs and cocked their ears.

"Go on," Borris shouted. "Let it out."

"It's not my father's first divorce," I continued, cautiously. "It's the second one."

A few listeners gasped.

My heart was speed racing now, and the donuts I'd downed at the refreshment table had bounced to the bottom of my stomach like tennis balls.

"So, um . . . well, anyway. You know, I'm devastated. Torn up really."

"Good for you," Bonnie whispered. "Let it out. We want to know."

"And, well, I'm not really happy in Raleigh, either. My job's okay—but they've got me on the weekend shift. And I don't have a boyfriend—which is really too bad when you don't have any friends. And since I have Mondays and Tuesdays off, it's kind of hard to make any friends. I mean, who is going to go out with you on a Monday night? Frankly, people, I'm feeling lonely and isolated."

When I settled back down into my seat, a tall girl in the

chair behind me put her hand on my arm. A guy next to me in heather gray sweatpants patted me on the back.

What possessed me to do that, I don't know. Maybe it was Bonnie's whispering, or the way everyone in the room looked like they genuinely wanted to hear my story. Whatever it was, it obviously had had a powerful hold on me—because I'd ended up spilling my guts to a bunch of strangers.

"You're going through a transitional period," a man in the crowd shouted. "You're vulnerable."

"Reach out," a lady screamed. "We'll pull you in."

Borris nodded warmly. "Indeed, we will. Let us welcome our hurt friend."

"Yes, we should," Bonnie shouted.

"Welcome her, people! Welcome her to the Man."

Borris bowed his head, and the keyboardist tiptoed up onto the stage and began playing a rendition of "We Are Family" with the lyrics changed to "We Are Holy."

I put my head down with the rest of the worshipers and stared at a spot on the linoleum floor—feeling flushed and oddly relieved.

When the sermon was over I grabbed my bag—hoping to duck out the door before I made any more of a mess. But when I looked up, Borris was heading my way. "Way to go with your testimony," he said, patting me on the back. "I was impressed. That's one of the best ones we've ever had." He poked me in the ribs—half surfer dude, half Washington lobbyist. "Oh yeah, it felt real. A lot of times people just kind of fake it. But you, you were honest. Genuine."

I swallowed hard, remembering my mission. "Borris," I said. "I guess I should tell you now who I am."

I wasn't exactly sure how Borris was going to take my confession. But it was starting to occur to me that perhaps he wouldn't take it well. I could just see him bad-mouthing me to the heavens: "You know that girl from New York. She lied, lied,

lied. Dude, you do what you want. But I wouldn't waste a spot up there on her."

Borris smirked devilishly. "Don't worry. I know what you are."

"You do?" I was surprised—but also pleased that maybe I didn't have to explain anything after all.

"Oh, yeah. You're one of those slick city chicks looking for enlightenment. You never thought you'd need God. But here you are."

I smiled faintly. "No, Borris. Actually, you're wrong. I'm not looking for salvation. I appreciate you guys having me out here. But I'm . . . I'm actually a reporter. I'm here to do a story."

His eyebrows shot up in surprise.

My breath was caught in my throat. "I know I should have said something before I got up there. But . . . Borris, I made a bad judgment call."

Borris was staring aimlessly into the cafeteria crowd now. "I just got such a good vibe from you." He paused for a second. "I felt like: darn, we can help her."

I smiled encouragingly. "Borris, listen. I think you're a great pastor. . . . I'm just not—you know, seeking."

Borris bit his lower lip and shook his head up and down, then looked up at me intently. He offered a half smile—as if he was trying to be a good sport. "Oh, well. . . . No hurt feelings. I guess I can't complain. It's always cool to get a good write-up. Anyway, I should have known. This is not the first time this has happened. It must be our ad or something. You reporter people can't get enough of us. Half the time we end up converting you in the end anyway. Heck, the worst was this Washington reporter who showed up last year. What a fiasco. It took her two months to admit she was doing a story. And we had to prod it out of her. We told her we weren't baptizing her till she came clean. She runs one of the churches out in Las Vegas now."

Borris seemed to have completely regained his composure. "We may save you too—God help us. . . . Now make yourself useful." He handed me a folded chair. "We're stacking."

Borris disappeared out the cafeteria doors—then returned a few seconds later with a slightly bent chair stand on wheels.

I folded up a chair. "So, can I ask you some questions, Borris?"

"Shoot."

"Well, why would anyone want to join this church?"

Borris began collapsing chairs in the back row and setting them on the stand. "You know," he said, resting one foot on the stand and spreading his arms out above him as if reading a bill-board. "We are all just mortals in search of meaning." He paused. "Lost Suburbanites Looking for Salvation." He paused again. "Pathetic People Looking for Grace." Borris glanced over at me. "Which one do you like better? I'm trying to come up with a new slogan for the church."

I collapsed a chair. "I like the first one best," I muttered, bummed that I was having trouble taking control of the interview.

"Yeah, me too. I wish we didn't need a slogan. But these days everything has got to have one. I mean, would one of my kids say: 'Dad, I want a pair of no-name jeans?' I don't think so."

I stopped folding chairs and looked over at Borris. "Listen, Borris, can I do a little interviewing here? I mean, I don't mind helping. But I really should get some work done too."

"Sure," Borris replied. "But could you start collecting the dirty styrofoam cups? There are a bunch under the refreshments table."

I climbed under the table and grabbed some cups.

Borris scanned the cafeteria proudly. "No-stress fun. My PR guy came up with that. What do you think?"

I looked up at Borris from my spot by an unlined garbage can on wheels. I was lining it with a giant-size plastic bag that had been hanging from the handle. "It's concise," I said, dropping my head into the can and smoothing the sides. I stood up and threw the cups I'd collected into the garbage.

"Concise—that doesn't exactly sound like an endorsement. You don't like it, do you?"

I ignored the question. I really wasn't supposed to be offering up my personal opinions while on an assignment.

"So, what else do you guys have?" I asked. Borris pulled a crumpled hot pink flyer out of his slacks pocket and looked down at it. "We've got a lot of singles activities," he said. "Like this one." He waved it in the air. "Solo?" he read. "Come Sing with the Singles."

I walked over to my bag and pulled out my notepad. "Interesting."

Borris whipped his date book out of his back pocket and rustled through the pages. "Well, the Gen X band is probably a little cooler," he said. "They meet on Thursdays. A bunch of twenty-somethings looking for a holy hookup. There's a lot of electric guitar in the band. Then, of course, we've got our Saturday night double-dating program. We call it 'Dinner with Jesus.' And a Wednesday night Bible study class: 'Chillin' with the Gang, Chattin' About the Book.'" Borris closed his date book. "What did you think?"

I blinked and looked up from my pad. "Umm . . ."

"Kyle, no more deception. I think we've had enough of that for one day. I want the truth."

It definitely wasn't my place to critique a church I was writing about. But I figured I'd already violated one tenet—and it seemed only courteous to help after what I'd done. "I don't know, Borris, they're a little commercial."

Borris rested his elbow on the top of a folded chair. "You're not digging the schedule, are you?"

"Well, no, it's just . . . Well, those names are a little . . . I don't know, *cheesy*'s not the word—but something close."

Borris brushed his fingers through his hair and gazed out at the playground. "I know," he said sullenly. "I'm with you." He was talking low now—like all this was just between him and me. He unwrapped his microphone from his neck and pulled the battery pack off his belt. He seemed different now, more natural, like he'd let his guard down and was finally exposing his real self. "I didn't come up with the names," he said, dropping his microphone onto a chair. "State headquarters did. And it's not working. Our target group is all off. We're getting families and stuff. The diehards. You know, Kyle, that's just not what we had in mind."

I smiled sympathetically.

"The thing is, Kyle, when Bonnie and I journeyed down here a few years ago from Seattle, we vowed to go after the people we thought were most needy: the young and searching—all you kids from those messed up families. We didn't want to be a place for believers to hang out. We want to be a place for non-believers to turn the corner. We wanted people like you to see us as an option, an answer to the pain of family trauma." Borris bent down to retie the laces on his Nikes. "I guess they don't like the names either."

I patted him on the back. "Hey, listen, Borris, don't be so hard on yourself . . . the names aren't that bad." I was starting to feel sorry for him. I mean, here he was, an obviously ambitious guy, getting all worked up not about money or some job title he wanted but about introducing people to something he was convinced would change their lives. Sure, he didn't have the greatest taste in music. And he needed to lose the long hair and the sparkly pants. But beyond those small details, I saw something admirable in the guy.

"Borris, maybe you should try to figure out what those people you want to attract are into and then start some programs based on that."

"How the heck do I know what you kids are into?"

"Well, it's not that tough, Borris. I mean . . . seventies music is really hot now. Do some Donna Summer remixes. People my age love that shit."

Borris's face brightened. "Huh? That's not a bad idea. See, this is what I need. Someone with some creative vision. . . . So, what do you think?"

"Think about what?"

"Helping us? You know, maybe taking over the singles committee."

I swallowed hard. "The singles committee?"

"What? You think we're doing a good job?"

I didn't really want to respond to this. But Borris had asked me several times to be honest. "No, not really. But . . ."

"But what?"

If I wasn't careful I was going to get myself in a lot of trouble. I could see my life savings being funneled out of my bank account into the church fund. I'd be planning the single women's retreat at the beach and the holy, snowy ski trip. I pictured myself tapping away at the electric keyboard during a Christian rock rendition of "New York, New York" on the church bus trip to Coney Island. All because I'd happened to get up and spill my guts to a bunch of pushy Rockers intent on converting me.

My feet were taking on a life of their own, and they were heading toward the door. "God. I mean, good. I didn't realize how late it was." I scanned the cafeteria for my bag. "Borris, can we do the rest of this interview on the phone?"

Borris chuckled. "Making you nervous, huh?"

"Nervous? What's there to be nervous about?"

Borris wrapped his arm around my neck. "Really digging us."

"Listen, Borris," I said, removing his arm. "That really isn't why I came."

Borris jabbed the air with his pinkie. "Hey, toughie. There's a place for you here—if you want it. That's all I'm saying."

I tucked my notepad into my bag and gave up trying to convince Borris I was unconvertible. "Well, I appreciate that, Borris. Thank you."

Borris and I left the cafeteria together. "Let's go to our meeting rooms," he shouted to the crowd—resuming his pastoral role. "The Junior Jesuses are in the gym. Holy Wanters are meeting in the third-grade classroom. Don't forget today's topic: If you play hard and pray hard, God doesn't care what you listen to."

I waved good-bye to Borris and swooshed passed the lobby's glass doors, out into the parking lot.

"Hee-haw!" I heard someone hiss as I fumbled for my keys.

———

For the next couple of days, I banished Borris and the Rockers from my mind. It seemed like a logical thing to do, considering what complete and total freaks they had turned out to be. I mean, how could Borris have thought I was vulnerable enough to join his cult of Christian wackos?

Back at the office the following Wednesday, things were hectic. The diversity committee had put me on a blacklist of misfits who had missed their sensitivity training course. (I had wanted to go. But when a colleague told me the class included guessing the favorite ice cream flavors of fellow reporters to illustrate how much we prejudge other people, I had quickly decided there were other things I wanted to do a lot more.)

To make matters more unpleasant, Kip had witnessed me in front of the office—getting another speeding ticket on my way to work.

"It's a conspiracy," I told him, when the officer finally turned off his flashing lights and released me. "They hate the paper and they're getting their revenge."

"So why are you the only one getting all these tickets?"

"Kip, don't you see? They know I'm a reporter. And they're

making an example out of me. Which is why I think you ought to allow me to expense these tickets. Kip, I'm suffering for this entire city's right to free speech. Don't you get it? I'm like the poster child for the people's right to know." When I looked up, he had already gone off to a budget meeting.

Meanwhile, the mayor had spent all day on TV bad-mouthing the paper because the city hall reporter had uncovered a secret meeting government officials had held to discuss a $5 million stadium they expected the public to pay for. The mayor was treating the reporter like an uninvited guest who had crashed an exclusive party.

When the office emptied out at lunchtime, I decided to take a peek at my Rocker notes. I pulled them out of my bag and began to transcribe them. I was typing in Bonnie's quotes when Shelby called.

"That father of yours, what a bastard!"

The word *bastard* lingered on the line. It seemed so out of place as I plowed through a notepad filled with sentences about faith and love.

"Shelby, come on, that's my father you're talking about. Let's not—"

"Not what?" Shelby was screaming into my ear now. "Be honest with ourselves about what kind of person he is?"

I paused for a second, in a meager attempt to find something enlightening to say to my enraged soon-to-be ex-stepmother. But nothing was coming out. It had been a week since I'd talked to Shelby—even though she'd left several messages on my answering machine. And, suddenly, I knew why I hadn't returned her phone calls. I was starting to realize I didn't like being yelled at.

"Shelby," I began, softly. "I was thinking that maybe we could consider not talking about my father anymore. You know, move on to other things. Normal stuff. Movies or something."

"Oh, that's very funny. Do you know what he's done to us?" Shelby began to whimper, then broke into tears. "Kyle," she wailed. "He's left us. Whose side are you on anyway?"

"I'm not on anyone's side."

"Well then, you're on his side."

"No, Shelby, really. I'm neutral."

"I think it's abundantly clear that no one is neutral here. You can't have your cake and eat it too."

"I hardly believe not calling my father a bastard is wanting to have my cake and eat it too. . . . In fact, that doesn't even make sense to me. If you need to do this, I think you should call someone else." I paused for a second to contemplate how far I was willing to go to escape Shelby's wrath. "Like maybe Phillip or George," I added.

Shelby huffed. "You're not seeing things the way they are, Kyle. I don't know what's got into you. I mean, maybe we're just different now and we don't have that much to talk about." She began to bawl again.

I could feel a knot forming in the back of my throat.

That evening as I drove home, the sky began to roar. A dark purple stain formed above me. And rain started to pound down onto my windshield. In front of my house the fall leaves were forming wet clumps on the road, and a large crooked branch had fallen from a tree on my street. It was storm season.

When I got inside, I closed my kitchen window and tore off my shoes and stockings. I could still hear Shelby's wailing in my head: "You're not seeing things the way they are, Kyle. I don't know what's gotten into you." I wondered how much longer she and I could go on like this.

For years, I had sided with Shelby, bashed my father to her, played partner-in-crime. In return, she had delved into my deepest thoughts and protected me. At seven, eight, nine, even fifteen and sixteen, it was a welcome deal. After all, it was Shelby who had helped me gain a sense of who I was. And at a time when my mother was often unable to be there for me, it was Shelby who had shown me, on countless occasions, how much I meant to her. I couldn't go into a grocery store, a dress shop, or a library without remembering how much she had taught me. Shelby was responsible for my fondness for fresh pasta, my weakness for smooth, cotton sheets, the pleasure I derived from cracking open a hardcover book. It was Shelby who had introduced me to homemade chocolate and *Little Women*, Truffaut films, and café au lait. But did years of accepting Shelby's generosity mean I could not become my own person?

Shelby seemed intent on keeping a deal I could no longer afford to keep. And I was hurt and angry that she refused to budge. To me, it was obvious that our old system of relating had failed us. And it was time to move on to a new one. But Shelby was unwilling. Now I know she was probably so caught up in her own hurt that she was incapable of seeing how much I needed her to accept my independence. But at the time, I simply felt betrayed.

I looked around my bedroom and noticed Bonnie and Borris's card lying on my bedside table. I picked it up. Suddenly Bonnie's voice came back to me, too: "Tell us more," she had said. "We want to know." The words seemed kind—so different from the ones Shelby so often launched my way.

I found the phone and dialed their number. "Bonnie," I said. "I think I need to come back to the church—ummm, you know . . . for the story."

You say you want to play country,
But you're in a punk rock band.

WHISKEY TOWN

Bonnie took a swig of piping hot coffee from her ceramic mug. "Deer in the headlights," she joked.

"Seekers always have it," I replied.

"Do we have any newbies here this morning?" Borris added, looking around the room like he was still onstage.

The three of us were nestled in comfy wicker chairs in Borris and Bonnie's second-floor rec room, by Borris's drum set and his weight machine, already reminiscing about our first encounter.

It had been over a month since my first trip to Rocker Heaven, and ever since then I'd been hanging around the worship site almost nonstop—so as to get a really good feel for the workings of the church.

Certainly, I could have reeled the Rocker story in earlier—if I had wanted to do a quick hit. But I saw potential for something deeper, a piece that talked about the power of persuasion. If nothing else, I wanted to show my readers how truly malleable some people can be.

Over the weeks Borris and I had had our fair share of runins. He kept insisting I was in a "transitional period" and needed to develop a stronger "support network." And, while I knew he was right, I kept telling him the Rockers just weren't my style. Still, I'd given in a little and helped out with the revamping of the church's singles committee. It seemed like the least I could do—considering how nice he had been. I'd helped him add an independent film night to the roster of activities. And I had finally convinced him to launch an alternative rock night—with strictly secular bands.

This was my last visit. And, if the truth be known, I was feeling a little nostalgic too. The sun was warming my face. Borris looked cool in his sequined pants. And we were all humming along to "Don't ring the bell to hell," a rewrite of the seventies song "Ring My Bell." Borris had, fortunately, taken my seventies tip too.

He stopped humming and held up his coffee mug. "Bonnie," he cooed. "Could you pass me a sugar cube, darlin'?"

She plopped a few brown cubes of organic sugar into his cup from a bowl on the floor by her chair.

He chuckled. "Aren't we pathetic?"

"Pathetical. But in love," she added.

It was true their exchanges were always a bit over the top. But I enjoyed hearing them. I couldn't help comparing them to the ones most common between Shelby and my father.

"Lover," Bonnie cooed, "tell Kyle about your theater touring days. I don't think she's heard that yet."

I pulled out my pad.

Borris smirked devilishly and took a quick sip of his now sweetened coffee. "I was sleeping around. Sometimes it was twenty-nine girls and me."

"Borris, you wish," Bonnie said, chuckling. She looked over at me. "He was touring Seattle with a Christian rock group. You know, sleeping in church basements. A drummen Jesus." She patted her husband on the knee playfully. "You weren't sleeping with women, baby. You were saving souls."

Borris did a little air drumming for me.

Bonnie gave him the thumbs-up. "You go, baby." Then she looked over at me. "You know, they liked him so much. They asked him to start playing a drum mass at a church outside of Seattle."

Borris looked wistfully around the sunroom. "Those were the days."

"Until they made the mistake of telling you you had to wear shoes."

They both started laughing.

Borris threw his hands up in the air. "Listen, I couldn't be constrained."

Bonnie turned toward me and cupped her mouth with her hand. "If he'd had his way, he would have been playing naked."

"Listen," Borris said, his long hair flapping against his back. "It was the seventies."

"Thing is," she interjected, resting her elbows on her knees, "Borris never considered himself the typical pastor personality."

"I sure didn't," he said, rocking in his wicker chair. "And, Bonnie, you weren't exactly a typical pastor's wife. That's why you're so darn cute."

They were at it again. Cooing and air-kissing.

I don't know if I would have chosen Bonnie's outfit for myself, but she did look cute. All decked out in an electric orange jogging suit with matching clips in her hair, blushing innocently at her husband's compliments.

"Borris, stop, you're embarrassing me."

"Okay, enough of that." He jumped up, grabbed a copy of *Holy Week* from the tiled floor, and headed for what I assumed was the bathroom.

Bonnie gestured for me to come over to the warm wicker chair Borris had just vacated. When I did, she leaned in close to me. "Listen. Are you going to be okay?" she asked, lowering her voice a bit.

The question surprised me. "What do you mean?"

She put her hand on my knee. "When you stop seeing us, I mean. Borris and I are kind of worried about you. We know you are going through a really rough patch. And we know you're just here to do the story. But we think that maybe you've been coming around because we have something here you need. I mean, you've been going to all the church support groups, and you haven't missed one potluck dinner."

"Listen, Bonnie, I hope I haven't led you guys on. But I'm not religious."

Bonnie's talk was making me antsy. First of all, I was really fond of her and Borris. And, second, maybe there was a little part of me that couldn't help wondering—for a split second— what my life would be like if I bagged the story and joined the church instead. At least I'd have some friends.

If Borris and Bonnie were game, we could turn the church into a summer hangout for victims of fucked-up New York families, some of the drug addicts I went to high school with, and teenagers like that Japanese kid I knew in junior high who lived by himself in an apartment overlooking the East River. If

I was persuasive enough, Phillip might come down too and get rid of some of his rage. George might get into it, make some new art, get off the ten-year teary-eyed boxer kick. Bonnie might even let him paint a banner of The Holy Crüe to hang up during services.

"The belief is nonnegotiable," Borris had said to me on several occasions. "But what God is going to do in your life, I can help you figure that out."

Bonnie leaned toward me—as if she knew exactly what I was thinking. "You're a dreamer," she once told me. "That's why we like you. There's nothing you wouldn't consider."

"We don't want to pressure you," she said. "And I know we've been through this before. But you might really want to consider giving us a chance."

Just as Bonnie said this, Borris sashayed back into the sun-room. "All we want you to do is think about it," he said.

———————

Kip was hunkered over his desk with a definite do-not-disturb look on his downturned face when I jumped him.

I was ready to pitch the Rocker story.

"What do you think?" I asked, plopping one of the flyers on his desk.

Kip flipped the flyer over and grunted. "How 'bout a piece about the Howard Johnsons?"

This was a bad sign. Kip never turned an idea down. He suggested, instead, that you write about the ugliest building in town.

"I don't do hotels, Kip. You know that. Besides," I said, turning his attention back to the Rocker idea, "this is a real sociology piece. A look at faith in America. We cannot not do this story."

I pounded Kip's desk excitedly and told him that the Rockers did the Hail Mary Full of Grace prayer to the Hare Krishna Beatles tune, thinking he'd at least grunt a chuckle. Instead, he cringed. And that's when I realized I was pitching to the wrong guy. For me, the combo of rock and religion was fascinating. For Kip, it was offensive. The whole thing was too close to home. Kip was lacking perspective.

"I still think it's a story," I said, waving the Rocker flyer in the newsroom air. Kip knew what that meant. I was going "shopping for an editor."

"Shopping for an editor" is the newsroom equivalent of jay-walking. It's illegal but rarely punished. Successful editor shopping requires decent knowledge of your editor selection and confidence that you actually have a decent story idea on your hands.

In my eyes, there was no contest. Maria was my next stop. For over a year I'd watched her ramrod underappreciated stories onto the front page with the bullish energy of a football coach. Her greatest achievement to date was not one but six stories on the Triangle's rat population. "Fuck me to tears," she had shouted every time a higher-up was in earshot. "There are more fuckin' rats than people around here. Did you know that? This is the best series I've seen in years."

It's unclear whether Maria's impressive show on the front page had to do with the quality of her stories or the pure desire among the higher-ups to keep her quiet. It didn't matter. As long as Maria liked a story, everyone else in the newsroom was obligated to like it too.

A few hours after Kip's rejection, I approached her. She had just made mincemeat out of her new environmental reporter, a lanky twenty-something who had finished tacking his Greenpeace bumper stickers to the bulletin board above his desk. It was clear from the way he had moseyed over to Maria's desk that morning for his first edit that he had naïvely convinced himself he could bully her. Maria had quickly set him straight during a discussion of whether the word *digression* could be used in a story to describe a highway detour.

It was a dance of power she performed for every new male reporter.

"When you're editor, your roads can digress, wise guy," she had told him, propping her Clergerie shoe up on his woolly chair seat. I could almost hear his thighs quivering. "But as long as I'm your boss . . . our roads don't digress."

Say what you will about Maria. But there is no doubt she was a powerful leader in the battle against male chauvinism in the newsroom. Maria didn't rally against it. She squished it with her stilettos.

When the edit was over and Maria had electronically sent the story to the copy desk's in box, I closed my notepad and tip-toed over to her desk.

"I have a story," I said cautiously, placing one of the flyers on the edge of her desk like those blind guys selling sign language cards at the airport. "These Rockers, you know, Christian Rockers. The pastor plays the electric guitar. Would you be willing to edit it?"

Maria shrugged her shoulders noncommittally. But as I veered around the corner and headed back to my desk, I saw her flip open the brochure. "If you can get a photo of the band!" she shouted, craning her neck my way. "Jesus Jams. Rockers Rule. This is a great story."

———

I spent the next few days laboring over every sentence of my Rocker story, staying in the office until four in the morning one night—and driving home at sunup, long after the night editor had gone home to his wife, and the copy editors had left to gulp down after-work beers at their favorite dungeon of a bar, and the little man with the radio had strolled upstairs with the first paper of the day—still warm and slightly inky. I wanted to make sure that I described exactly how Bonnie's clogs were, and how Borris's hair shot up when he was doing a particularly emotional speech, and the way the God Rockers sometimes did Jimi Hendrix riffs.

When I finally handed it to Maria, I awaited gushing words of praise, acknowledgment that I was not the fuckup she had pegged me as. A few minutes later she called me over to her desk. "So, what happened—they converted you?"

"What do you mean?"

"This is great writing—but a total blow job piece. It doesn't even include what they believe in."

"Maria, they believe in God."

"No shit. Most Western religions do. But what about abortion, premarital sex? Did you ask them what their policy is on homosexuality?"

I smiled dumbly. "No."

"Well, you've got to go back and do that. The story needs meat. Give them good writing. But the writing is nothing if you're not informing people. That's our mission."

Maria handed me back the article. And I shuffled off to my desk, crimson-faced. It's always embarrassing to get slammed by an editor, but it's even worse when you thought she was going to love the story and the criticism is stuff you already know. This was basic Journalism 101. But for some reason I had gotten so caught up in my detailed exploration of the church that I had forgotten to get the vitals.

I called the church.

"Rocker Heaven, can I rock you?" a receptionist cooed. "Here we say: 'We love Jesus' with a more alternative style."

"Hi, can I talk to the big guy?"

"Well, we do a lot here, but direct line to heaven—now that's asking a little much."

"No, not God. I want to talk to Borris."

I was bristling.

The receptionist giggled. She put me on hold, and an Amy Grant song blasted into my ear.

When Borris got on the line, I decided to get right to the point. "So, uh, Borris, I have a few questions I forgot to ask you, uh . . . these past few weeks."

I could hear Borris cupping the phone with his hand. "Bonnie!" he shouted. "It's Kyle."

Bonnie jumped on the line. "Kyle, how are you? We miss you."

"Um, how, uh, well, I have some questions, Bonnie."

I heard her slap her hand against her knee. "Shoot."

I decided to start with the softball stuff.

"So, Borris, when you and Bonnie go out with your friends, do you, mm, you know, have a beer?"

"Well, I mean, someone might have one."

"We don't have two or three," Bonnie interjected.

"Okay, what about, well, say a couple was living together? I mean, would you just say no, you can't do that if you want to play the bongos in the church band?"

"Kyle," Borris said, softly. "God really wants to take care of those questions in people's lives. Our job is to create the right environment. The right answers are born out of the relationship with Christ."

"They really are," Bonnie added.

I could just hear a disgruntled Maria towering over my head making me call Borris back, if this were the only answer I came up with.

"But, Borris, Bonnie, what does that mean?"

"I think the Big Guy wants to talk to you about that himself."

"Listen. Not everyone is as popular with the Big Guy as you are. And I'm having trouble getting him on the line. Since you've got the direct connection, why don't you just paraphrase what he would say?"

"Kyle," Borris said, softly. "We know what it's like to be searching."

"Yeah, you can feel lonely and isolated," Bonnie joined in.

"Listen, guys." I was really getting pissed. "What is the church's position on live-ins?"

Finally Borris responded. "The Man up there, he tells me it's wrong."

"And what if you met some guy and you were kind of drunk. And you thought he was hot? And you slept with him."

Bonnie responded to this one: "We just think if you asked him, he'd tell you."

"What would he tell me?"

"Those sorts of moments are not in his plan."

"And so nonbelievers, what's happening to them?"

"He's not down with nonbelievers," Borris said. "Kyle, they don't go to heaven. They go to hell."

"So you guys think I'm going to hell?"

"It's hard when God isn't 'round to pick up the pieces," Bonnie offered.

My heart sank. Suddenly, bohemian Borris and Bonnie seemed like a bunch of neo-Nazis. "Well, yeah, I guess so."

When I hung up the phone, I saved my Rocker file and briskly scanned the pages. I'd gotten the facts to add to the story. But now my opinion of Rocker Heaven had sunk. The church had always seemed laid-back and baggage-free. But, in fact, it was a very conservative place. It was not cool and groovy and real. Not all the things Borris had led me to believe it was.

Still, how could I really fault Borris? It was my job to ask the hard questions. And I hadn't done my job. Borris's job was to try to convert people. And he had nearly converted me.

A few weeks later, during a discussion with the religion reporter, I gained some perspective. "Oh, you should have asked me the day you went to see them. This has happened to me several times with various churches. These folks are running businesses. And, let me tell you, they are good."

It turned out the religious community even had a name for the way Borris and Bonnie had lured me in: seeker-sensitive. In essence, that's when doctrinally conservative churches lure newcomers by seeming very cool, laid-back, and decidedly not conservative.

"The competition between these churches is so intense," the religion reporter explained. "This is one of the only ways they have of attracting people who otherwise wouldn't be interested."

I called Borris and Bonnie several times before the story came out to ask them questions and check facts. The last time we spoke, I think Borris still harbored hopes of converting me. "So, we'll be seeing you soon. Right, Kyle?" he said when I'd finished with the last of my follow-up questions.

"Well, I don't know, Borris," I replied.

"Well, don't be a stranger."

"Borris."

"Yeah?"

"I don't know if I'll be able to make it back to the church. But listen, thanks."

Borris's voice got a little creaky. "For what?"

"I've done a lot of soul-searching. And, well, I basically oppose everything your church stands for—except . . . your kindness. You know, you were good friends to me. You and Bonnie."

"God was your friend."

"No, Borris, you were."

"You were good to us, too. We needed a little down-to-earth jolt. And you know what?"

"What?"

"We knew we wouldn't get you."

"You did?"

"Yeah, Bonnie took one look at you and said: 'This one ain't coming on board. She's one of those liberal writer types. But I think she needs help.' But, Kyle, maybe some other congregation will get you. And you know what? We think you'll be a great parishioner."

"Borris, that's the nicest thing anyone has said to me all day."

When I hung up I had a sad but hopeful feeling in my stomach. I would go my way. The Rockers would go their way. Our paths would never collide again. But I also knew that their kindness would linger with me. I would never look at another Bible-thumper the same way again. The Jehovah's Witnesses, the guys who handed out little Mary cards on the subway, the blue-suited Bible-wielding shouters outside college campuses, I would always hold a special place in my heart for them. I would see beyond their creepy hands, their smelly breaths, sweatpants, and food-stained Bibles and pamphlets. I'd look beyond their political leanings, their overzealous urges to convert. And I'd see people like Borris and Bonnie, people who were eager to give lost souls like me a glimpse of heaven.

14

Down home
Things move at a slower pace
Nobody's in the rat race
And these days, that's a special way of life.

ALABAMA

It was a groper—not God—who ended up saving me from my life of solitude.

His name was Dick Peck. And if he had not reached out and tweaked the left nipple of a young cocktail waitress as she sobbed in his downtown law office while discussing her pending divorce, I might never have made friends in the Tar Heel State. But he did. And I did. And things got a lot less lonely and isolating—as Bonnie would say—after that.

I bumped buns with my first Raleigh friend on a breezy November afternoon. We were squished together on a mahogany bench—inside a Wake County courtroom—watching wide-eyed as a county judge determined the best course of action against a man who simply could not keep his hands to himself.

The hearing would not have gained citywide attention—and neither one of us would have been there—if Peck, a mild-mannered Raleigh attorney, had not also been accused of lunging into several female laps, pawing at numerous crotches, and politely asking one unsuspecting client if she wouldn't mind bending down and performing oral sex on him.

"Just something to keep you in the paper," Kip had said, winking at me good-naturedly, "until you finish the Rocker story."

Kip, I had come to learn, was fond of using story assignments to prove points or punish. In Central America, they call that guerrilla warfare.

———

In the courtroom Peck's attorney—an earnest-looking man in a crumpled seersucker suit—stood before the judge, cradling a thick medical dictionary in his arms. "Judge Briar, with all due respect, my client is not a pervert. He's a sick man. Mr. Peck suffers from an organic brain disease of the frontal lobe that prevents him from controlling his urges."

The explanation floated through the courtroom. I heard a cough, a low giggle, and then the muffled voice of my bench mate, the woman I would soon come to know as Lisa Angel. "Hell, half the guys I've dated have brain disorders," she whispered. "You don't catch them pawing away at strangers."

In the front of the courtroom, the assistant district attorney—an olive-faced man in a cotton suit—tapped his ballpoint pen against a yellow legal pad, then pointed it at the judge. "Disease or no disease, Mr. Peck is still a threat to the women of this city."

"Yeah," the voice next to me whispered. "So are most of my exes."

"Your Honor," Peck's attorney continued. "The court should not overlook the fact that Mr. Peck is taking the advice of his psychiatrist. He is keeping his hands in his pockets or wrapped around his chest, and he is counting to fifty each time he finds himself tempted to reach for a female body part."

This time I was the one who couldn't contain herself. "Tempted to reach for a female body part? This guy thinks women are just one big Kentucky Fried Chicken bucket. He reaches for a thigh. He reaches for a breast."

"What he needs is to go on a diet."

"Or find a live-in lover."

"Come on, would you be his lover?"

"Well, he certainly isn't lacking in experience," I retorted. I scanned the room—looking for any sign of Peck. "Do you know if he's here today?"

My bench mate rolled her eyes. "He's always skulking about . . . walking around trying to— Oh God, here he comes." Lisa bolted off the bench—taking her Coach briefcase with her—and edged toward the courtroom wall. "I can't take the emotional stress of being groped today. The guy's a maniac."

Suddenly I heard a groggy voice whispering into my ear: "Ma'am, are you the reporter?"

I spun my head around, and sitting next to me in Lisa's vacated spot was a little man who had both his hands jammed inside the pockets of a tight-fitting charcoal suit. "I'm Dick," Peck said, sliding his right hand out of his slacks pocket and offering me a handshake.

I nodded disapprovingly.

"This is so frustrating," Peck said. "I can't even shake a woman's hand anymore."

I slapped open my pad and jotted down his reply. "I'm quoting you for my story."

"Good." Peck inched closer to me and rested his bony elbow on the back of the mahogany bench. "I just wanted to say that I wish I didn't have to go through this." I dutifully recorded his comment—then noticed that Peck's elbow was beginning to jerk on the bench ledge. His veiny fingers were dangling like sweaty worms on a fishhook. His arm jerked forward, then backward, then brushed my upper back lightly. One brush. Two brushes. Three brushes. Peck's perspiring fingers plopped down and landed smack on my shoulder.

"Ohhh," he said, letting his fingers linger. "It's so nice of you to do this story."

I bolted up and stumbled into the aisle just as Peck's attorney uttered his final words of defense. "I am confident," he said, "that my client is almost cured."

"So you've been groped by a Dick," Lisa Angel whispered from her spot against the wall. "Welcome to the club."

———

I bumped into Lisa in the lobby. I was chatting with one of the attorneys in the case—making sure I had his name spelled correctly. She was talking to an assistant district attorney. When she saw me she suggested we go to a hamburger drive-in called Char-Grill to get some lunch.

Char-Grill is a pleasant 1950s remnant located in the center of town—near a hot dog joint called Snoopy's and a Honda service station. Lisa and I scribbled our orders for fries and burgers on a slip of paper and slid it through a narrow metal tunnel. A hamburger flipper on the other side of the glass partition plucked it out. He grilled our burgers on a greasy grill and wrapped them up. The guy at the cash register called out our number, we paid and sat down on a stainless-steel bench in the parking lot.

Lisa was a born-and-bred Raleighite, an avid reader of the paper, a prolific divorce attorney.

"Peck's nothing," she told me, pulling the wrapper off her burger. "I've seen it all. Eight hundred divorces, six hundred custody cases, three suicide attempts, and one homocide-suicide—that was not a good day for me. . . . Basically, I've got it down to a science. People are so predictable it's not even funny."

I told her about Shelby and my father.

Lisa bit into her hamburger, then wiped her mouth with a paper napkin. "Your dad feeling impoverished—living in a shack?"

"More like a tenement building. But same idea. How'd you know?"

"Textbook male behavior." Lisa plucked a fry out of her fry bag and plopped it in her mouth. "Postdivorce poverty complex. I see it all the time. . . . Let me guess." She took another fry out and pointed it at me. "He was having an affair—someone you knew. A neighbor?"

"Hairdresser."

"Huh. Not unheard of. He must have needed a boost to his self-confidence. Your stepmother a big screamer?"

"Yeah, actually, she is."

"The quiet ones push the exes toward hookers and lap dancers. The loud ones push the guys toward people in helping professions—nurses, doctors, therapists, housecleaners. . . . Don't ask me. It's just the pattern I see."

Lisa's cell phone rang. "Can you hold on a sec?" She pulled it out of her suit pocket and clicked it on. "Karen, I think you need to vacate the premises. No, he is not allowed to climb in the window to see the kids. I know you think that you love him. But what the two of you have is not love. Karen, Karen . . . are you listening to me?"

Lisa clicked off her cell and put it back in her suit pocket. "Anyway, you'll be fine. That's what I tell all the adult family members of divorcing parents. You'll be fine—as long as you don't try to dodge the mourning and the discomfort of the experience. You have to sit with it. Invite it to the table. Right?"

"Right." I figured agreeing with the divorcing expert was a good idea.

When we were done eating, Lisa and I climbed into her car and drove back to the courthouse to my car. Every now and then Lisa's phone would ring and she'd address Karen. At one point, Lisa spoke with Karen's husband, Bruce. ("Bruce, I'm sorry. But we need to set some boundaries here. You are violating Karen's privacy rights, do you realize that?")

When Lisa hung up she looked over at me intently. "I have no earthly idea why these people insist on torturing each other."

With her accent, her liberal politics, and her use of words like *boundaries*, Lisa was an odd mix of Southern belle, left-wing activist, and self-help guru. Her luxury car had a peace sticker on it. In the backseat I noticed a paperback entitled *Toxic Families*. In the front seat on the floor by me were a Coach briefcase and a pair of preppy pumps.

In high school, Lisa was best remembered for two things: going to the prom with the football quarterback and refusing to stand up for the Pledge of Allegiance in protest of Reagan's support of the Contras.

"It was an upsetting thing. Those poor people. . . . Senior year, I was nominated most likely girl to start a revolution. . . . So how are you liking Raleigh?"

"Well, you know, it's not home."

"What are you talking about? Raleigh is where you live. That makes it home."

The way Lisa was talking sounded mildly comforting. Maybe I *was* home in Raleigh.

Lisa's phone rang, and she clicked it on again and put the receiver to her ear. "No, Joe, I don't think you're going to get custody. You're a cocaine addict."

———

That night after work I got a call from Phil. "Shelby's falling apart," he told me. "She cries all the time. I'm worried about her."

Shelby's well-being worried me, too. But short of sounding coldhearted, I'd have to say it didn't worry me as much as Phil's. "What about you? How are you doing?"

My little brother didn't answer.

I knew that on one level Phillip had it good. He didn't pay rent, food, or any of the other expenses that living with your mother alleviates. But even with these perks, I still didn't totally understand how he could have been so eager to skip town at seventeen to go to military school and now be living under Shelby's roof.

"When are you going to move out, get your own place?"

"Who's going to take care of Shelby? I told you, she's a mess."

"Phil, that's not your job." I felt knots developing in my stomach. The truth is, it was Phil's job. It hadn't used to be—because it had been mine. When we were growing up, I had often been the one to soothe Shelby and side with her and protect her from my father's wrath. But now that I was slowly detaching myself from my stepmother, Phil was filling in for me. "Don't you realize, it's not healthy? You shouldn't do that, Phil. You shouldn't feel you need to do that."

But my little brother did. And there was nothing I could do to change that.

———

That fall, Lisa plucked me "out of the social gutter," as she liked to refer to my former life, and introduced me to the Raleigh club scene—not to be confused with the New York club scene. She invited me to join her wine club, her book club, and the drinking club she'd started when the Junior Leaguers took over her Sunday night supper club. ("You know, the ones who refer to their parents as 'Mom and Dad this. Mom and Dad that.'") She also convinced me to join Raleigh's main gym, where her "circle" went to pound the StairMaster and pedal on stationary bicycles, but mostly to mingle ("Hell," she told me. "I go there three times a week. And I haven't been on a machine in a year.").

Soon, I was rubbing shoulders with velvet-headband-and-pearl girls and men who wore boat shoes on land. I was frying my hair up with curlers, wearing sunglasses and straw hats, attending backyard croquet parties, bring-your-own-meat barbecues, steeplechases, and garden fund-raisers for cancer, AIDS, abortions, and art. Lisa's take on adopting me was "Hell, I need someone I can actually talk to at these damn things."

When, during a backyard oyster roast, I dared question whether I was really suited for this new life, an exacerbated Lisa methodically outlined my options. "I know these people seem a little straitlaced, Kyle. But if you'd rather be at the Long Branch doing the do-si-do with a man in Wranglers, that's fine with me." We were standing on a limestone patio, chugging keg beer from wide plastic cups. "We don't have SoHo in Raleigh. We don't even have a Village. Heck, we hardly have a downtown. We just have WASPs and rednecks. You gotta choose a circle and don't look back. Think of it as integration."

"Okay," I said, taking a sip of beer. "But I don't know about these men. This guy over here is wearing a purple-and-green polo shirt."

"I told you I'd get you circulating. I didn't promise fashion plates." Lisa paused for a second and pointed at the bartender. "How 'bout him?"

The guy had long locks of dark chestnut hair flowing down his back and a long-sleeved tie-dyed T-shirt wrapped around his thin waist.

"Thanks—but the last time I checked, the sixties were over."

"Sor-ree, I just thought you might go for the bohemian look."

"I don't," I said, reminding Lisa that in my limited experience male trawling with her, I had come to understand that that was her type—not mine. Lisa liked Beck look-alikes, scruffy guys in bands and/or grad school. Too many showers in a week and a full-time job was enough to make her lose interest altogether. Her taste may have seemed strange for a chick who dressed like an Ann Taylor catalog model and was an officer in the state's Young Lawyers Association. But Lisa defied categorization. And that's probably why I liked her so much.

I scanned the manicured lawn in front of us. It was a sea of powder blues and khakis. On one side of us, there was an empty pool—with wet leaves coating the bottom. On the other side, there was a makeshift table set up with cocktail sauces and crackers and a huge bucket filled with oysters. A fellow in an apron and rubber gloves was cracking them open with a shucker and handing them to hungry guests. Then my eyes fell on a handsome guy with auburn hair and a crooked, boyish grin. "What about him?"

Lisa winced. "Ugh! A Jesse Helms supporter."

"Can't be."

"Believe what you want," she said, polishing off her beer. "But he's not riding in my car."

I leaned toward her, letting the rim of my straw hat touch hers. "I'm sure he has his own," I whispered.

There were dozens of Lisa's pals at the roast—including Georgia, who worked as a fund-raiser for the North Carolina Museum of Art. Georgia had a penchant for vintage clothes and men with criminal records and was a source of great entertainment to everyone but me. I rarely understood anything she was saying because her use of Southernisms was so prolific. She waltzed over.

"Well, I finally told my mother about Carlton." Carlton, I had come to understand through Lisa's translations, was Georgia's boyfriend, an organic farmer from Carrboro.

"Well, my mother was running around the house like a bat out of hell yelling: 'A Lawrence does not date an organic farmer.' I told her: 'Well, at least you know I'm not getting above my raisin'.' "

Lisa leaned toward me. "That means 'uppity.' "

"And that was just the beginning of my botherations."

"Means 'troubles,' " Lisa whispered.

"I couldn't get the farm boy on the phone last night. Which seemed odd since we've been such karmic allies lately. I mean, I was reading the tarot cards I bought in Asheville, and all these vegetables and farm tools just kept popping up. Anyway, I went on one of my catch-a-thons."

"Spying missions," Lisa said.

"And I saw him with that sooky."

"Huh?"

Lisa was about to interpret—when Georgia interjected. "Get this girl a dictionary, will you? Cow, fat-ass, ho, prostitute." Georgia spun back around so she was facing Lisa. "So, anyway, I think I'm going to have to sharpen that guy's hoe."

Georgia had used that one before. It meant she wanted to beat the living shit out of him.

She pursed her lips together. "I mean, maybe what I really ought to do is break up with him. I never liked the way all that organic stuff tasted anyway." Georgia paused for a second. "So, what are y'all up to?"

"What are we ever up to, Georgia? We're circulating," Lisa said.

"Well, aren't you wide open."

"Gregarious," Lisa whispered.

Georgia pulled the beaded bag she had bought during a recent tour of Austin antique shops up on her shoulder and adjusted her tight hip-hugger skirt so the seam was perfectly positioned. She put her arms around both our necks. "Well, let me give you a little advice, darlin's. The strags are all over the place tonight. Avoid 'em."

"What's a strag?"

Georgia swished a strand of her straight, jet black hair off her face. "Kyle, it's a little word I came up with. A combination of *straight* and *drag*. See, in New York, you have gay guys in drag. They dress like women. But down here we have gay guys in disguise. The ones who still haven't confessed their preference to their mommas. So, they're out there on the straight dating circuit, making like they're marriage material. God almighty, they are such a waste of time. My gay friends want to date 'em. My girlfriends don't. And they don't know what they want."

I had a pretty fine-tuned gaydar. But I wasn't so sure how well it worked on this side of the Mason-Dixon line. "How am I going to know?"

Georgia took a chug of beer, then wiped her mouth. "Fabrics. Velour, felt, patent leather. Those are the clues. . . . Now, also stay away from those nouveau North Raleigh developer types."

"Well, actually . . ."

Georgia pressed her index finger against my mouth. "Discretion, darlin', we keep our mistakes to ourselves." Georgia polished off her beer and held her cup up in the air. "Okay. I've had three of these, I think I need to go talk to a man about a dog."

Lisa leaned toward me. "She's gotta pee," she whispered into my ear.

Now I was getting angry. "Hey, would you stop with the translations? I'm not a total moron, okay. I know what that means."

"Sor-ree," Lisa returned. "I'm just trying to help."

Georgia bustled off.

We were silent for a second, then Lisa inquired: "Did you hear what she told you?"

I nodded obediently.

"Good, that's guidebook stuff. Invaluable."

A few minutes later we bumped into Lisa's other best buddy, a tall and wiry party planner from Charlotte. Adelaide was wearing her usual uniform: a powder blue Brooks Brothers pin-striped blouse, and a pair of perfectly ironed khakis. Her long blond hair was pulled back with a velvet head band. Adelaide had more velvet head bands than anyone I had ever met. Lisa said she had them alphabetized by color and organized in little boxes in her closet—along with the labeled and dated boxes she kept her shoes in and her collection of Chanel blush categorized by shade.

"Georgia just gave Kyle the strag speech," Lisa explained. "Care to weigh in?"

Adelaide nodded enthusiastically, then pressed one hand firmly under mine—as if to emphasize the importance of what she was about to say. I could feel her three gold rings digging into my palm. Adelaide and Georgia, it turned out, were constantly coming up with mating theories that they circulated around town.

"Okay, girls. This is my new one: the Tuna Fish for Breakfast Theory." Adelaide let out a hiss, then looked at me intently. "For every single man, there is a small window of opportunity when single life has ceased to be fun and before another woman has snatched him up. During that short time, a man goes through a holy transformation. His fear is your friend. His crackpot ass suddenly realizes he could be alone for the rest of his life, eating tuna fish for breakfast. Your job is to identify when that period is and snatch him up. I don't care what that therapist guy from Mars says. Men are the waves. They foam, peak, and crash. You need to jump on 'em when they peak and ride 'em to shore."

The theory sounded good—but the truth is, it worried me a little. That night I called Mark. "Are you peaking?"

"What?"

"I'm wondering if I could be missing your window of opportunity."

"I have no idea what you are talking about."

I explained Adelaide's theory to Mark. He laughed. "Listen, I can't go on more than two consecutive dates. I'm so far from crashing, I don't even know if I'm rippling yet."

I breathed a sigh of relief. "So, you're still my insurance policy?"

My best friend moaned. "Yesss."

Mark was someone I needed to keep an eye on. But I was beginning to suspect I needed to be a little more attentive about what was going on between us. The thing about insurance policy guys is that they exist because you're not ready to commit to anyone. If you were, you'd be dating them—or someone else. But the problem with them is sometimes they rush past you. And before you know it, your insurance is someone else's husband. It seemed silly to worry about Mark skipping ahead of me. I mean, weren't we bonded in our confusion about suitable suitors? But I did anyway. After all, once I was ready for a real committed relationship, Mark would have to either step up to the plate or step aside. Either way, I knew Mark would not be my best friend forever. He would choose to become my husband or take a backseat to the man who did. *Ready* was not an adjective I would have used to describe myself—but getting ready did seem like a worthy goal. And Mark was no doubt a part of that getting-ready equation.

————

A few weeks later I was dripping sweat onto a day-old copy of *The New York Times* and pedaling ferociously on one of the stationary bicycles at the Y. Georgia was pedaling by my side. "Where does this thrice-married whore think she is?" Georgia bellowed. One of her many nemeses—a slender divorcée—was climbing the StairMaster in biker shorts and a pair of large, dark sunglasses. "Yoo-hoo. This isn't Hollywood, darlin'," Georgia screamed across the room.

By Georgia's side was Adelaide, who had just volunteered to be a celebrity escort during the week-long run of the Special Olympics, which was being held in Raleigh that year. And she was agonizing over whom she might be assigned to take care of and how she was going to handle the assignment.

"The problem with celebrities is you never know what to call them in person," Adelaide mused, as she adjusted one of her hair clips. "I mean let's say you are escorting Hootie & The Blowfish. What do you call the lead singer? Hootie? Mr. Hootie? Hoot? Are the other guys Blowfishes? Do you say, 'Hey Hoot, are you sure the Blowfishes have enough towels?' "

Georgia tossed her magazine on the gym floor. "I think you'll figure it out."

Adelaide ignored her.

A few minutes later Lisa stumbled through the locker-room doors and climbed onto the bicycle next to mine.

She began pedaling. "So, how was your date?" she inquired sternly. I had been dreading this conversation. Desperation had gotten the best of me and, to Lisa's chagrin and my embarrassment, I had gone on a date with the Helms supporter.

"Date?" Georgia cooed. "How come we didn't hear about this?"

"Well, it was more like a social experiment," I mumbled. "Lisa, I just thought maybe he had become more liberal since the last time you talked to him."

"Yeah, people tend to do that. Get more liberal as they age? Admit it, you were in denial."

Georgia waved her hand at Lisa as if to shush her. "Where'd he take you?"

"Sushi."

"That's not bad for a first date."

"Listen, any first date with him is bad. The guy has a trampoline in his backyard. We talked about breakfast cereals for half the night and colds the other half. I told him I took echinacea when I felt one coming on. He acted like I had just confessed to dropping acid on a regular basis. He's opposed to herbal medicines, I guess."

Lisa cringed. "I hope you got the hell out of there."

I cringed, too, recalling the guy's tennis-themed quilt and his matching tennis-racket pillowcases. "No, I got drunk and slept with him."

Lisa gasped. "With a Helms supporter."

"Pollyanna," I whispered, feeling slightly nauseous at the thought of what I'd done. "I haven't had sex in . . . six weeks."

Georgia stopped pedaling and glared at me.

Adelaide pounded her fists against her bike screen. "I don't give a rat's ass about what this man believes in. You did it with a virtual stranger . . . after sushi . . ."

I was getting annoyed. "Listen, ladies." I had taken to calling my new friends ladies. It suited them. "I appreciate your pearls of wisdom. And I know this isn't New York City. But it isn't the nineteen fifties either. After all, the pill has been invented."

"Kyle," Georgia interrupted. "I don't care what year it is. Let me help you out a little. We are not Florence Nightingales here. We do not do charity work."

I was confused. "Listen, I didn't give the guy a blow job if that's what you're asking."

Georgia ignored me. "Sushi is not—let me repeat—not a sex date!"

"A sex date?"

"Angus Barn is a sex date," Adelaide said, referring to Raleigh's gourmet steak house. "Magnolia Grill, with those fifteen-dollar chocolate tortes, is a sex date. *Les Miserables* is a sex date."

Georgia interrupted. "I thought we agreed musicals are not sex dates."

"Whatever, *Les Miz* is more like opera. But, you get the point, don't you?" Adelaide said. "It's called the law of appropriate returns."

"But I love sushi," I whimpered.

"Kyle, darlin', we all love sushi," Georgia said. "But if you behave like this, you ruin it for the rest of us goddesses. We need to train these scoundrels, Kyle. If they get sex after sushi, think about what they'll try next."

"Coffee."

"Bagels."

Adelaide cringed. "A smoothie."

"The next time you want sushi," Georgia said, "go to the grocery store. Harris Teeter sells it in little boxes for nine ninety-nine. I've had it, darlin'. It's not bad. Ugh. These men make me as mad as a hen."

I was distressed that by sleeping with the Helms supporter I had committed a substantial violation of the local dating etiquette. But I was more concerned, really, about whether or not I'd violated my own dating etiquette. Certainly people—including Republicans—are entitled to their own opinions. And for me political ideologies have never been dating or friendship deal breakers. But I had just jumped into bed with a Republican I didn't even like. Didn't I myself have rules about that?

———

The next morning I woke to the rattling of my phone. I let the machine pick it up. It was Shelby. "If my life gets any worse, I'm going on *Jerry Springer*," she bellowed. Shelby wanted to discuss my father's most recent transgression—buying his girl-friend a subscription to *Gourmet* magazine on their still-shared American Express card.

"Like she cooks!" Shelby continued. "So transparent. He's trying to turn her into me."

"I hardly think that is his goal," I said to the machine. "The guy may be a little wacky. But he's not suicidal."

The next call came from my father.

"Hey, chica, the Ecuadoran president is being ousted again. The politics in this country are amazing. I'm e-mailing you some articles about it. I figured you'd find it interesting."

The third call came from Lisa. "Dot," she yelled into my bedroom. Dot is Jesse Helms's wife. "They want you."

This time, I picked up.

"Who?"

"The committee."

"What committee?"

"The Ten Thousand Angels Committee."

"Who?"

"Us. Georgia's president. Adelaide is the secretary. I give legal advice. The Mindy McCready song 'Ten Thousand Angels.' It's our anthem. It's all about a chick who's having troubling kicking a bad habit of a man."

"Why do they want me?" I wiped sleep from my eyes. "I hardly seem to meet their standards."

"No, actually, they like your perspective."

"What does that mean?"

"They think you need help."

———

Mark thought the Ten Thousand Angels business was a big joke. "Is that like the Hell's Angels?" he asked a few days later over the phone.

"Listen, Mark, some things don't translate."

"Yeah," he replied. "Some things shouldn't."

"I'm making friends. Just because I'm not hanging out with Matt Damon . . ."

Mark was silent for a second. "Hey, I'm sure the angels are great people."

"Come on, be serious."

"I mean, they've taken on charity work like you."

"Mark!"

"I'm really glad. You're making friends. I'm not as superficial and shallow as you think."

"You're not?"

"No, but honestly, what could you possibly have in common with these women?"

"I'm feeling disoriented and lost, and my family has just fallen apart. And I almost joined a religious cult. I hardly think hanging out with anyone I have anything in common with is a good idea right now. It's kind of the point. They're not like me."

———

When I hung up with Mark, I dropped onto my bed and lit a cigarette. There were things I wanted to explain to him, but the words weren't really coming out. Like when you know something is changing inside you but you can't pinpoint what. It had something to do with the way I felt when I drove downtown on a Sunday afternoon and heard the dangling streetlights clanking against city road signs. And the way a sense of peace and calm drifted through my body when, on cold, wet days, the city's tree trunks looked like black chalk. And the sky resembled thin sheets of gray-blue tissue paper.

Winter was arriving. Gusts of wind swept through the city. Rain drizzled down onto lawns and forests. The unspoken feeling had something to do with a soothing sensation that if I could just stay put here long enough, things would be more than fine.

I need a thousand angels to save me tonight.

MINDY McCREADY

That winter I got initiated into Raleigh's three-member Ten Thousand Angels Committee during a midnight ceremony at the Tir na nog Irish pub. I downed three bourbons and a pale ale and was given a photocopy of the bylaws, which included Adelaide's man-hunting tips and Georgia's warnings—as well as a series of rules. I also received a basket with a curling iron, a copy of *Ms.* magazine—care of Lisa—and some incense from Georgia. Attached was a note: "Not that we think you need any of this. But just in case."

My first meeting was held at the PR bar, a dank Raleigh watering hole with fluorescent orange booths and mirrored walls and lots of 1960s decor. The PR bar served as the Ten

Thousand Angels headquarters. In New York, the aging decor would have landed it on all the hottest lists of trendy architectural finds. In Raleigh it was an underappreciated dive.

Georgia whipped out the agenda—which hardly seemed necessary since the committee did nothing of real import, according to Lisa, except rap about sex with ex-boyfriends, boyfriends, and potential boyfriends. ("Which is not to say that I don't enjoy our meetings.")

"Okay, I'm first," Georgia exclaimed. "I dumped the organic farmer."

Georgia and Adelaide applauded.

"I'm dating a drummer from Hillsborough now. It's good. We're on the same spiritual plane."

No one clapped. Adelaide rolled her eyes.

"It's over with the Helms supporter," I offered when it was my turn. I told the group it had halted abruptly—because I had finally come to my senses and vowed never to go near a man with those political leanings again. I failed to tell the committee that the Helms supporter had not returned any of my phone calls after my sushi date. I figured the details were unimportant. The committee applauded for me too.

When it was Lisa's turn, she confessed that she had taken up again with her neighbor—a twenty-one-year-old college senior with a fondness for gas station attendant T-shirts. Lisa had been "getting distracted" by this particular fellow on and off for the past year.

I was the only one who applauded.

Adelaide shook her head disapprovingly.

Georgia jumped in. "Lisa, could you let the poor guys get facial hair before you pounce on them?"

As for Adelaide, she was dating an investment banker from her hometown of Charlotte, about whom she seemed noticeably reluctant to talk.

Before we left Lisa's cell rang.

"I agree with everything you're saying, Sue—Scary Harry should never have snuck into the house and taken the VCR. I'll file a complaint in court tomorrow. Just lock the doors. And don't worry the kids."

Scary Harry?

"I know, it's ridiculous. They all have names for the exes. Scary Harry. Peter Never Pays. Mistake Number 3. One guy calls his ex Betty the Bloodsucker. Aren't you glad we're not married?"

The three of us looked up at Lisa. No one responded.

———

My entrée into the Ten Thousand Angels Committee was not my only victory in the City of Oak. Eventually, my Rocker story did come out. And Maria gave it her seal of approval. "This is the best story in the paper today," she exclaimed.

I didn't expect Kip to compliment me on the Rocker story. The final rule about editor shopping is that the editor who passed up the story will never compliment you on the piece once it comes out. He didn't. But he did something better. He switched me off weekend cops to a regular schedule and local government beat—where I could write about developers.

For my first assignment Kip ordered me to cover a night meeting in Apex, a former railroad hub that was becoming popular among the kinds of transplants the Rockers were luring. The town board was reviewing a plan to transform one of the area's last remaining tobacco fields into a massive housing development. And Kip thought we should be there.

Although I was looking forward to using my access to the boys to write a slew of juicy developer pieces, I didn't have any delusions about a monthly municipal meeting like this; I figured it would be a bore.

Shortly before dusk, I rode down Apex's narrow main drag and parked in front of Town Hall, an unassuming brick building that looked more like a canning factory than a democratic hub. I pounded up the cement steps, barreled into the main auditorium, and dropped my butt onto a pew. There, standing in the front of the room tapping on a cardboard architectural plan with the tip of a silver pointer, was Tiger, looking like he had just returned from a golfing excursion. He was decked out in Kelly green Bermuda shorts and a peach polo shirt, Bucks and argyle socks. He couldn't have looked more colorful. Beside him was Bo Bo Brown, the area's famed golf course community builder. They were obviously doing a project together. Thanks to Tiger, I was on a first-name basis with Bo Bo and had even gone out to see the outdoor shopping mall he had constructed near one of his developments. He had stood in the middle of the parking lot and swept his hands through the air. "This is what I have brought to North Carolina!" he had announced—as if we were staring at the Egyptian Pyramids.

Tiger kept tapping on his cardboard plan. "We believe this is really a quality development being proposed here. There will be living, shopping, and office spaces. It is really state-of-the-art."

Tiger began rattling off names of other similarly designed developments, referring to easements, channelization, and indemnity agreements. Occasionally, Bo Bo would whisper something in his ear and he would throw out another benefit of the proposed plan into the meeting room air. While I gave him credit for his winning style, this was hardly titillating stuff. In fact, I was perilously close to falling asleep on my exceedingly uncomfortable wood pew when Tiger finally finished. I tapped his leg when he and Bo Bo passed me. He winked at me and whispered, "Miss Kyle. What do you know!"

The mayor banged his gavel, and public comment time began. A little man in ivory white tennis shoes and heather gray polyester pants belted halfway up his stomach rushed to the podium. "This," he squeaked, pointing to Tiger's cardboard rendition with a pudgy finger, "is a concrete jungle!"

The crowd cheered.

"You greedy moneymakers would destroy our community just to make a buck."

The crowd cheered some more.

"But the buck is gonna stop here. I do not support this plan. It will clog our roads, kill our wildlife, add to suburban sprawl."

I looked over at Tiger and Bo Bo. They were wincing.

A few minutes later a young man in a Greenpeace T-shirt jumped up and headed for the podium.

"Developers are trying to turn the rural parts of Raleigh into the smog-filled Los Angeles I escaped from," the man cried. "But isn't that what I left? Isn't that why I came here? It was peace I was looking for. Peace." The man made a peace sign with his fingers.

A third complainer, an old fellow with a hearing aid the size of a lima bean sticking out of his ear, rumbled up to the podium. "Our town has more bubble gum than it can chew right now," he cracked. "Our jaws are working overtime!"

The bashing went on for over an hour and ended with a small woman in a patterned sweater and baggy shorts wagging her finger at Tiger and Bo Bo and screaming: "We didn't just get off the turnip truck, you know. This time you two are not going to pull the wool over our eyes."

When the insults were over, the mayor told the crowd that he understood their "grassroots frustration," and a commissioner assured the room full of people that he would "find a light at the end of the tunnel."

Tiger's state-of-the-art plan was sent back for revisions. And the next set of builders stood up for their flogging.

I was stupefied. Certainly I knew that concern about excessive development in the area was going to cause strife. That was the card I had used to get the boys to cozy up to me six months before. But even I had not predicted this level of hostility. These people were livid.

During the following weeks I came to understand that the heckling in Apex was a regular occurrence all across the Triangle—and it was getting worse. In the northern suburbs of Raleigh, environmentalists were up in arms over a subdivision that was being built on an archaeological site where ancient relics had been uncovered. Fifteen minutes from Raleigh, in Cary, residents were fighting a massive storage center in their backyard. And in all the towns anger over lost trees, displaced wildlife, and the disappearance of cherished greenery had home owners insisting it was time to send the developers packing.

———————

A few weeks after the Apex fiasco, on a damp Sunday morning, Georgia called an emergency meeting. Lisa had just been dumped by the neighbor.

When I got to Lisa's house, she was angrily pounding the arm of her futon couch. "That jerk. You know, he sat in his car and stroked my hand and told me I was the most interesting person he knew. . . . Then he broke up with me."

Georgia, who was pacing in a recently acquired 1960s micro mini, stopped and patted Lisa's head. "Remember, you're a goddess."

Adelaide adjusted her head band. "I don't really think he was right for our circle anyway," she said.

"He sucked me in," Lisa whined. "He played Martin Luther King speeches in his car for me. Do you all know what that did to me?"

"Listen, darlin', you can go buy your own Martin Luther King tapes. You can get the whole darn set."

"Yeah," I joined in. "You can get Gandhi's tapes and Malcolm X's too."

"Okay, this isn't a damn record store. What you need to get is a drink." Georgia marched toward the door. Adelaide followed Georgia. Lisa followed Adelaide. I followed Lisa.

We drove to the Rockford, the only bar in town that wasn't playing football. Lisa ordered beers for all of us.

Georgia put her beaded purse from Austin on the bar and smiled feebly. "I have a confession. I slept with the drummer on the first date."

All eyes were on Georgia.

"He brought me a bag of weed. And, well, we got stoned and I forgot myself and I was living in the moment. And he started doing his drumming thing . . . and it's been a while. Basically, I couldn't resist. Don't kill me, please. I know—"

"That's the best news I've heard all week," Adelaide exclaimed.

Lisa clapped her hands together. "I have been vindicated. That's it, we're getting that sex date stuff out of the bylaws—once and for all."

Georgia nodded reluctantly. "The problem is those sex date rules were like communism. You know, in theory, they sounded great. But we're all too greedy for them to work in real life."

"Well, ladies, maybe we ought to take a different approach," I suggested. "I knew this woman in New York—she forced herself to sleep with every man on the first date. She figured if the sex was bad, why waste her time dating him?"

"Mandatory sex on the first date," Lisa said. "Not a bad idea. You all, we could try that for a while."

Georgia looked over at me. "Kyle, you're good. You should consider writing a book of our theories. We need to get our knowledge out to the larger public."

"Yeah," Adelaide agreed, taking a sip of her beer. "What does this guy from Mars know anyway?"

We all clinked our drinks together, and I wondered for a split second what had happened to my promise to steer clear of sex with men I didn't like. I guess I'll have to figure out the liking part before the first date, I thought to myself. After all, who ever keeps her no-sex resolutions?

———

That night I spiraled into bed, still in my skirt and bra. The room spun and the floor rotated, and the ceiling was a multi-colored dome in the sky. I was three sheets to the wind and stewed to the gills, and feeling wide open. And when I looked up, I could have sworn I saw an angel flying above me.

You'll always be around
Deep down.

PAM TILLIS

When eight hundred engraved wedding invitations the size of coffee tables arrived in Raleigh mailboxes in April, the Ten Thousand Angels Committee immediately convened for an emergency meeting at the PR bar. The committee concluded that the Charlotte marriage ceremony of a young Junior Leaguer from our gym to the son of a ruby-haired textile magnate was a prime opportunity for a Mark visit. The $200,000 Southern wedding was expected to be a pristine, elegant affair, the kind, the committee concluded, that a young Hollywood type would love.

The visit was important to the committee because, after a careful review of my romantic record, it had slapped me with the following unflattering title: chronic relationship gasher. The committee believed that I had sabotaged long-term love opportunities with half a dozen suitable suitors—including a college boyfriend who had gone on to become a New York City investment banker; a filmmaker in Paris; and an investigative journalist in Philadelphia. As for my future with the handsome, witty Harvard grad in my life (a.k.a. Mark), the committee feared I was perilously close to sabotaging that too.

A Mark visit, the committee concluded, would give me time to resolve the situation.

Mark, it turned out, was more than willing to make an appearance in the Tar Heel State. For three months he had been dating a stunningly beautiful and well-connected screenwriter—who also happened to be an agoraphobic alcoholic with a penchant for S & M games. "Every Monday morning, I have to explain to my boss why I have handcuff scratches on my wrists. If I don't get some distance, this woman is going to kill me."

———

Mark stepped off the airplane at RDU and waltzed toward me in gabardine pants and a powder blue oxford, square-framed glasses and a thick leather belt. It suddenly occurred to me that my best friend fell into the "handsome" category. In fact, he actually fell into the "very handsome" category.

He rested his head on my shoulder. "Ahh," he said, mock crying. "The agoraphobe broke up with me."

"What happened?" I asked as we headed for my car.

"She tells me: 'Gwyneth thinks I can do better than you.' I told her: 'You should listen to your friends.' "

"Then what?"

"She told me to fuck off, then threatened to get me blacklisted all over Hollywood. Finally, I told her: 'Go ahead.' " I figured it would be less humiliating to be shut out of Hollywood than found dead—naked and handcuffed to a bathroom sink in Melrose. I mean, what do you think?"

I started to laugh and climbed into the car. "You crack me up."

Mark beamed.

As I started the engine, I scanned Mark's face up close. He was long and lean and sat with an elegant slouch that radiated a kind of warm confidence. He had a sturdy square jaw, high Slavic cheekbones, eyes the color of peppercorns. Funny, I had known Mark for almost half my life—and I had never really looked at him.

"You look good," I said, pausing for a second and wrapping my arms around him.

Mark pulled me closer. "So do you."

————

I didn't think escaping the S & M agoraphobe was the only reason for Mark's visit. I think he too felt it was time to sort things out. When we got to my house, Mark dropped his worn leather suitcase on my living room floor. I creaked open my screen door, and we huddled together on my porch steps for a smoke. The live oak in my front yard looked like it was glued to the dark blue construction-paper sky. And the large blades of grass poking out of the ground below looked like little puppet dancers waltzing across my lawn.

Mark pulled out a cigarette from a crumpled pack, then lit it. He took a drag and let the smoke swim slowly into the air. I thought maybe then one of us would venture forth, ask a probing question, or make reference to our friendship and where it was headed. But neither of us did. Instead, we talked around the issue—as if we were asking questions that related to our future without actually saying the words.

"So, has the move here been worth it, the adventure?" he asked.

"Yeah," I said, picking at the porch paint with my fingers. "It's been good to get away. To get some distance. A lot wasn't right in New York."

"Yeah, all those people living in shoe boxes with their cats."

"No, I mean all my family shit. I didn't realize how insane it was. I think I'm turning into a suburban housewife, though. You know—rejecting the morals of my childhood. I have all these Raleigh suburban fantasies now. Me driving my kids around in my car, going to the mall. Eating Twinkies. Playing tennis."

Mark was silent. So was I.

"Could you live in the suburbs?" I asked him.

"Dunno," he replied.

Of course, what I was really asking him was: "Could you live in the suburbs with me?" I just felt completely unable to say the "with me" part—even in a funny, joking way, with reference to Mark as my "insurance policy" and allusions to my hopeless future as a thirty-eight-year-old desperado in need of a marriage license.

———

During most of the drive to Charlotte the next afternoon, the road sparkled like a strip of silver. The sky stretched out like a bowl of blue water—and if we squinted our eyes it looked like we were diving right into it.

Mark and I didn't talk about "us." He didn't bring the topic up. And I was too afraid to. Instead, I just took note of how comfortable I felt in his presence, and how comfortable he seemed in mine. I recalled the way he had rummaged through my refrigerator the night before, after our talk on the porch, the way it didn't seem strange to have his shoes lined up by my fireplace, his toothbrush on my bathroom sink. And I noticed that I banged my hand against my steering wheel like some kind of overexcited hyena every time he told a joke. Then I would scream: "I've gotta pee, dude. Stop making me laugh. I'm gonna pee in my pants."

By the time we were halfway there, Mark had his shoes off, his thick cotton-ribbed socks bunched up at his ankles, and his feet on my dashboard. Cheesy country tunes were spilling out of my car radio. Mark was doing imitations of his mother, a fiery Franco German who headed the women's studies department at a college just outside the city. Her thoughts on family planning: "Vark, 'ave at least two children—in case one dies." Poverty in America: "Vark, vee live on the zupper east side and ve're poor. New York is expensive." Faith: "Vark, people who don't believe in higher power 'ave no imagination."

In between his imitations Mark would figure out a song's lyrics and sing along as he tapped his hand against the glove compartment.

Mark cracked open his window and began singing along to the George Strait tune "I'm glad I had the nerve . . ." The song is about a young man getting up the nerve to ask his wife to marry him. I wondered if it was just coincidence that he had chosen this song.

———

When we careened into the church parking lot, we skirted past members of the wedding party who were posing on the lawn for photos. We burst into the packed chapel. I hiked up the long formal dress Adelaide had helped me pick out so I didn't get grass stains on it. Mark had an undone bow tie flapping on his neck.

Inside the cavernous lobby, Lisa was chatting with the bride's brother, a Web designer from Boston who sported a goatee and a several pierced body parts.

Adelaide—wearing a "little black dress" and pulled-back hair—was conversing with Chuck, a Duke Business School student from Houston she had spotted on occasion at the bride's house. "Now, Chuck, did I ever get a chance to tell you about my time as a celebrity escort?"

Outside on the patio, Georgia—who had sworn off men after a messy breakup with the drummer—was ushering the bride's ninety-two-year-old grandfather to the coat check. She was wearing a tweeded Jackie O–like suit she had bought at a yard sale in Chapel Hill.

Mark and I—awkward amidst total strangers—hobbled over to the lobby's brochure-and-Bible table. Mark picked up one of the Bibles and started flipping through it as if it were a magazine at the grocery store checkout line. Lisa and Adelaide swooshed over.

"Welcome to Charlotte, Mark," Adelaide said, waving her arm as if she herself had built the city. "We like to call Charlotte the Wall Street of the South."

Mark smiled good-naturedly. "I wonder why they don't call Wall Street the Charlotte of the North?"

I elbowed him in the ribs.

He jumped. "Ouch. So the city is . . . ?"

"Well, it's mostly bankers and finance types—which is fine," Adelaide said, leaning in toward Mark and lowering her voice. "But I actually prefer Raleigh. Charlotte is too much about keeping up with the Joneses." Adelaide stood upright again. "You know what I mean?"

Mark shook his head. "No."

"Mark," I exclaimed, pretending to laugh. "Stop." I looked over at Adelaide and lied: "He knows exactly what you mean. He hates all that stuff. Keeping up with the Smiths is one thing—but the . . ."

Just as I was fumbling pathetically for the end of my sentence, Georgia bumbled over and blew into Mark's ear. "Now, have I not heard wonderful things about you? So is everyone in L.A. as handsome as you?" Georgia winked at me, then whispered something to him.

A few minutes later we all headed to the bathroom and left Mark with the Bibles.

"See how we did that? You gotta make the viewing seem easy—it relaxes them."

"Mark is always relaxed. . . . Anyway, what did you tell him?"

"I told him your window was wide open."

I cringed. "Oh, that's appealing. Do you realize what that sounds like to someone who doesn't speak your language?"

Georgia ignored me and began adjusting her Jackie O skirt.

Adelaide was ignoring us both—rummaging through a series of flowered makeup bags so as to begin her seven-layer lipstick application. Suddenly, she pointed one of the seven lipsticks at me. "Marry him," she said. "Did you hear me? He's adorable. And for God's sakes, he speaks English—which is a lot more than I can say for a lot of those Frenchmen you dated." Adelaide had been particularly turned off by the foreigner phase of my love history chart.

Back in the lobby Mark, oblivious to the attention he had garnered while we were in the bathroom, had finished his Bible reading and made several abortive bow tie–tying attempts. Finally, he let out a loud and piercing "Oh fuck, Kyle. I need you."

I bowed my head and covered my face with my hands. "We're in a goddamn church," I said.

Lisa, who had finished talking to the Web designer, walked over. "He loves you," she whispered as she headed into the chapel.

"That's not the question," I whispered back.

———

Swiftly and probably not accidentally, organ tones began to filter through the church, and Mark and I settled into one of the pews.

Eight groomsmen—each in a tuxedo jacket—careened

down the aisle in dark leather shoes, followed by eight brides-maids in silver slippers and long, satiny, powder pink dresses. Then the wedding march began, and the bride—in a white chiffon dress, and a swaying white veil and white lace gloves and a white train that swept like a wave behind her—swooshed past us and joined the groom at the front of the church. The mood was elegant and exciting. And I had been to so few weddings that the romantic air felt exotic and dreamy to me.

Once the music quieted, and the church took on an air of meditative calm, the minister began to speak. "Our denial of our dependence is our denial of each other," he said. "Relationships overcome loneliness and isolation, for surely companionship is promised and confirmed in love. . . ."

More words came, and they flowed through the aisles and up into the balcony, where the organist was playing.

The Charlotte Country Club—where the reception was being held—was hidden behind a modest residential neighborhood and accessible only by winding back roads, many with no signs on them. The photocopied map that had arrived with my invitation said it took ten minutes to get there from the chapel. It took Mark and me two hours—partially because of my limited map skills and partially because we had a run-in with a member of the Charlotte Police Department.

We were pulling out of the parking lot of a convenience store, after inquiring about directions, when a sirening car inched up behind us.

"I've got this drill down pat," I told Mark, yanking down my window. "So don't worry."

"That worries me," Mark replied.

I smacked him on the leg and smiled at my newest officer friend, a black man in knee-high leather boots. He looked like a member of the Village People.

"Ma'am," he said, "do you know what you are doing?"

I could hear Mark's mind responding gleefully to that question.

"No, sir," I replied, offering up the kindest smile I could muster. "I don't." I figured, judging from my last encounter, that officers in the Tar Heel State didn't appreciate literal responses to their questions.

"Well, I will tell you, then. Ma'am, you are driving." I guess my rule only worked within the Raleigh city limits. "Yes, you are driving in the state of North Carolina with a Pennsylvania license plate. And I guess you haven't realized that?"

"Well, Officer, things have been really busy."

"Oh, so you haven't had time to obey the law? May I see your license, ma'am?"

I handed over my license, and Mark and I watched as the trooper marched back to his cruiser, the heels of his knee-high boots clicking against the asphalt road.

"YMCA. It's good to be at the YMCA . . ." Mark began making letters with his arms. I guess he too thought the guy looked like a member of the Village People.

"Stop," I muttered. "You're disturbing the peace."

Mark put his hands down and pulled out a cigarette. "So, this happens often, does it? Why doesn't that surprise me?"

"Enough from the peanut gallery," I retorted. "You're lucky to be with me."

Mark furrowed his brow. "I am?"

We lit our cigarettes with the car lighter and inhaled.

"Georgia told me your window was wide open," Mark whispered, blowing smoke rings into my car. "What the hell does that mean?"

"It's Southern-speak," I whispered back. "I'm having car trouble."

When the officer returned he handed me a pink $125 license plate violation ticket.

"Thanky, Officer."

"Thanky?" Mark repeated.

"Shut up," I wailed, putting on my blinker and preparing to forge back onto the road. "They like that."

———

Eventually, we spotted the club's wrought-iron fencing and rumbled in. We passed a little rose garden and could see the sloping golf course in the distance. We looped up and around and finally found the parking lot—hidden behind a bunch of bushes about ten miles away from the two-story dining hall. We climbed out of the car and began our hike.

"Listen, please don't tell anyone about the ticket."

"What ticket?"

He was usually good about secrets.

When we got close Mark and I walked toward what appeared to be the front door—only to discover a sign with an arrow that read: "Please use other door."

We followed the arrow, and kept following the arrow until we realized we'd gone around back, through the golf course, and landed back in front of the clubhouse where the sign was.

Mark clutched his stomach. He was sweating a little. "I think I'm getting dizzy."

"I thought you were good with directions."

"Directions? You didn't tell me I needed a police car detector and a compass. Jesus Christ, I left my toolshed in L.A."

"Very funny."

"Seriously, why do I always get lost with you?"

"Because you never get us unlost when I get us lost."

"That's my job?"

"Sort of."

Mark stopped. "I feel like I'm married to you."

"Listen, I keep track of these things. You're not."

———

When we finally navigated our way inside, we found Lisa on a cushioned bench by the coat check—nursing a Bloody Mary with a celery stick poking out of it. The Web designer from Boston, it turned out, was in love with a Norwegian rock star who had recently shaved all her hair off for a music video.

"I'm competing with a bald woman," Lisa whined. "And she's winning. What does that say about me?"

Mark sat down on the bench uninvited and put his arm around Lisa. "You're a Porsche. He's looking for a jalopy."

I left the two of them to their car conversation and went to get Mark and me drinks. When I came back Mark was still on the cushioned bench, regaling a gaggle of women with the tale of how some famous actress almost ran him over in the studio parking lot. Mark got a few laughs then segued right into his oft-told story of how he was some young starlet's date in a recently released film.

"I didn't see you," Adelaide said.

"Okay, well it was a ten-second scene. But still . . ."

Georgia raised her eyebrows as if impressed. "Still."

"It was so random how it happened. The director says to me: 'We need a young geeky guy.' And I start to look around, thinking, How are we going to find a young geeky guy? And when I look up he's pointing at me. 'You,' he says. 'I'm talking about you.' "

"God, he's adorable," I overheard a young woman in a knee-length polka-dot dress whisper to her friend.

———

When Mark's impromptu comic show was over, I nudged him. "Let's go outside and have a cigarette."

We plopped down on a marble bench on the edge of the

club's brick walkway. A few feet in front of us was the circular driveway and the dining hall where the reception was being held. Behind us were pink azaleas. Mark pulled out two cigarettes from his crinkled pack and lit them with a silver lighter.

"I've missed you," he said, handing me my burning cigarette.

"Yeah, well. Me, too."

The air was pleasant but not too hot, and the sky looked like a piece of royal blue ribbon with white dots painted on it. I took a drag of my cigarette and felt the lavender-scented garden air race through my body and swim into my heart.

"Mark," I said, blowing the smoke out.

"Yeah?"

"Do you know that I love you?"

I could feel Mark breathing against my neck. The music from the wedding band filtered out of the club's main building, and the bulbs from the ballroom's low-hanging chandeliers sparkled against the large windows. Light from the windows made slivers on the grassy patches beside us. And above us—on the second-story porch—a man in a dark suit leaned over and kissed a small girl in a layered ankle-length skirt.

"I love you too," he said.

Suddenly my stomach was churning and my chest felt like it was being split in two. I wanted to kiss Mark, and then I didn't. I wanted to wrap Mark up in my arms—and then the thought seemed wrong, like French-kissing your brother. I knew that I loved him. And then I didn't know what that meant. And then I realized—sitting there, my heart bouncing against the bottom of my stomach—that Mark didn't either. Because surely if he knew he would have done something. He wouldn't have been speechless, just smoking and waiting and holding on to the edge of the worn bench, not moving. And suddenly us not knowing seemed like the clearest sign in the whole world. It didn't matter what Lisa or Adelaide or Georgia thought. My heart told me Mark did not want me as a fling, or a crush, or a suitor, or a heartbreaker, or even a lover.

I let my cigarette drop to the gravel and took a deep breath "Come on," I said regaining my composure. "Let's go inside and find the others . . ."

Mark looked up as if he'd just woken from a very confusing dream or missed his cue onstage. His eyes had grown dusty. He dropped his cigarette and put his hand on my shoulder. "Yeah, right," he said, pressing his fingers against my back. "We should do that."

———

Around midnight, we all headed back to the hotel suite that Lisa, Adelaide, Georgia, Mark, and I were sharing. Chuck, the Duke Business School student, who was good-naturedly currying favor with Adelaide in hopes of getting a sleep-over invite, came too.

Adelaide, perhaps inspired by our presence, wasn't biting. After several whiskey sours and a glass of sherry, she let out an ear-piercing yawn.

Mark was sitting on a wicker chair by the suite's round table in a white T-shirt and tuxedo pants. He looked over at Chuck. "So, bud, how you getting home?"

Chuck put his drink down, picked the phone up from the side table, and put it in his lap. "Well, I'm staying with . . . my . . . I don't know if I'm going to be able to find him." Chuck dialed the operator, mumbled a few words, then hung up. Mark handed him the phone book. Chuck flipped through a few pages, then closed it.

"Hey, buddy, you're going to have to do better than that. Have some respect."

A few minutes later, Chuck miraculously uncovered a slip of

paper with the name and address of the college friend he was staying with. He reluctantly bid his adieus and left us. Mission accomplished, Mark promptly fell asleep.

Adelaide and I were sharing a queen-size bed when she asked: "Did you tell him about the Angels?"

"No, why?"

" 'Cause he was acting like one."

"He's just like that, Adelaide. He's a good guy."

"And he's funny as shit," shouted Georgia, who was supposed to be asleep in the next room.

Adelaide spun around and gave me her scary, bug-eyed look, which I could detect even in the dark. "Marr——"

"Listen, I'm sorry to disappoint you ladies," I interrupted, pulling myself up. "I know you have the best of intentions—but Mark's like a brother to me."

Lisa chuckled. "That never stopped anyone down here."

"Well, I'm sorry. I'm not from down here. Anyway, you told me to resolve it. I took your advice."

A disenchanted Adelaide huffed.

"Well," Lisa interjected, hoping to lighten the mood. "Closure is good. Boundaries are key. It's important that the two of you understand what you have."

"Thank you, Lisa. I appreciate your approval."

Lisa switched off the bedroom light. "Don't get huffy with me," she quipped. "You're lucky I don't charge you."

———

At the airport I stood by the glass wall that looked out onto the tarmac and watched as Mark's plane flew up and off. As I stood there with one hand pressed against the glass and the other one wrapped around the silver armrest on the waiting area seats, it occurred to me Mark and I had both carefully avoided a dramatic scene or a head-on collision or a conversation that left one of us stung. I suspect there was a reason for that. I suspect neither one of us wanted to turn the bond we had into fodder for the kind of hit-and-run-romance tales we both delighted in regaling our friends with.

Maybe I should have felt rejected as I drove home from the airport, or lonely, or abandoned, or unsatisfied by all that was unsaid between us. Instead, I felt loved. And I imagined Mark flying above me—spilling peanuts on his neighbor's lap and asking the stewardess nonchalantly: "Have you ever wondered why they don't call Wall Street the Charlotte of the North?" And I imagined he was feeling loved too.

Maybe a great magnet pulls
All souls towards truth.
Or maybe, it is life itself
That feeds wisdom to its youth.

K. D. LANG

That summer, so impressed by the cost-cutting options in Ecuador, my father bought a shack, a sawed-off shotgun, and a four-cylinder Fiat in Quito and pronounced the town his new second home.

"The country's a fuckin' hellhole," Phillip commented a few days after hearing the news. "And he's racing down there to live?"

I tended to agree with Phillip and enjoyed my opportunities to convey this sentiment to my father.

"So, Jorge, if you are going to apply for citizenship," I sputtered into the phone a few nights later, "you better get crackin'. I hear there's a real backlog down there—Americans just clamoring to get into that country. Oh, wait, I think I got it mixed up. It must be the other way around. I wonder why that is."

Jorge wasn't listening. Jorge never listened anymore. He was in love. She packed him lunches, told him fabulous jokes. Her brothers were a riot. Her friends were amazing. The Spanish language was beautiful. And Juanita, she called him *Mi Amor.*

———

That summer my father returned to the States for a brief stint so he and Shelby could sign their final divorce papers, divvy up the family's broken furniture, and sell the loft.

This time Phillip had this to say: "That's fucked up."

At nineteen, out of school and still grappling with his own independence, he still considered the loft home. And with it gone, I think my little brother felt that he had been pushed out of his comfort zone before he was ready.

My brother George, immersed in his own building issues, was not fazed by the sale.

I, for some reason that seemed to defy all psychological profiling and any predictions that Lisa, the divorce expert, would have made, was ecstatic. With the loft out of the family legend, I was enlivened by a sense of karmic grown-upness. I was a free agent, beholden to no one, attached to nothing. I could get on with my life, and for some reason I could finally forgive my father. I never told my father I forgave him. I never even told myself. I just began to think he was funny again. And I began to want him to be happy. Why and how I got to this point is still a mystery to me. But I think it must have had something to do with my own attempts—as feeble as they may have been—to forge a life in Raleigh and my father's willingness to acknowledge that his departure, his marriages, his life errors were enough to make any kid of his—even an adult kid—angry. Acknowledgment goes a long way.

A few weeks after the papers signing, my father announced he was going down to Quito to get his teeth fixed. "I'm starting my new life cavity-free," he told me, an air of boyish anticipation filtering through the phone line. "You can't imagine how cheap dental care in the Third World is."

I pictured my father strapped into a rusty swivel chair with a piece of barbed wire sticking out of his mouth. "Yeah, Dad. Really. I can. Are you going to be okay down there? I don't want you to come back in a coffin."

"I did some research. It's perfectly safe."

"Dad, they called the last president El Loco. They threw him out. He took off for Panama with a suitcase filled with dollar bills." I was repeating the laborious political tales my father regaled me with each time we spoke. "You've spent the last three weeks listening to another Ecuadoran revolution on the radio. The Indians are rioting in the streets."

"They have a near-perfect voting record. Everyone votes down there."

"Everyone voted in Communist Russia."

"I'm going to be fine."

"Well, just be careful. Okay?"

"*Sí, chiquita.*"

"And listen, Ricky Ricardo, I'm impressed with your budding language skills. And, really, I'm glad you're happy. But please, speak to me in English. You may consider yourself Ecuadoran. But I still live in America."

"Okay," he replied sheepishly. "I hear you."

––––––––

My relationship with Shelby did not fare as well. A few months after the sale of the loft, I invited her to come down and visit me.

"Oh, that would be convenient for you, meeting me on your own territory," she replied.

"Shelby, I was just thinking it might be nice . . ."

"Do you know where your father is now?" she asked. "He's gallivanting around Latin America. . . . That bas——"

"Listen," I said, sternly. "I thought we agreed that—"

"You know, Kyle, talking to you is like talking to someone with an ear infection. You're off balance. And you're stepping on my toes. I don't fault you for it. But that doesn't mean it doesn't hurt."

I wasn't exactly sure what Shelby was talking about. And the thing that seemed the most markedly changed was that there were a few minutes there when I wasn't sure I really cared.

————

A few weeks later Shelby called again—for a "talk."

"So . . . ," she said, puffing into the receiver. "I want you to know that I feel very constrained, Kyle, when I talk to you these days. And, frankly, I don't know what to say to you anymore."

"I don't know what you mean," I replied, my adolescent attempt at playing dumb.

"You know exactly what I mean. If I can't talk to you about what has gone down between your father and me, well, then I don't think we have anything to talk about."

Shelby was threatening me—as she had done countless times before. But this time her threat felt more hostile and out of line than scary.

"Okay," I said, mustering up all my courage. "Well, hey, you know, maybe we don't have anything to talk about right now."

When I hung up the phone, I suddenly felt anxious. But there was another part of me that was curious and excited. As the weeks passed, I began to feel an odd sense of relief. As if, by pushing Shelby back, I had uncovered a corner of myself that I didn't even know existed, a part that Shelby had never wanted me to know about, a part that knew better than she what was best for me.

For the next few months, I mourned Shelby's lemon squares, and the little silver dots on Christmas cookies, the way she was so damn smart, the witty phrases, her caustic humor ("He's not the sharpest tack in the box"), the skirts and scarves she would leave on my bed when I came home for break, the trips to Dean & Deluca, her funky leather handbags and crazy gloves, her large earrings and killer lipsticks, the way she could sit with ten of my friends in a bar and be perfectly comfortable. But I also came to a bittersweet realization that Shelby had spent a year trying to convince me that my father had left me. And when I refused to believe her, she was the one who took off. On bad days I faulted Shelby. On good days I missed her. But mostly I felt as if my brain was a foggy windowpane that was slowly defrosting.

———

A few months after this last conversation with Shelby, I shared with Mark my new theory on parents. "See, what happens is they get stuck at some age and they stay there for life. If you're lucky, your parents stopped somewhere pleasant—like as subdued three-month-olds. But more often than not they get stuck at more problematic places. My dad's not so bad. He's a rebellious sixteen-year-old—still jumping out of his bedroom window at night to hang out with his girlfriend."

"What about Shelby?" Mark inquired.

"She got stuck at the terrible twos. She's in her crib throwing tantrums. And she'll be there for life."

"Ooh. That's bad."

"That's our challenge. To make it past the toddler stage and teenagedom. How do you think we're doing?"

"Maybe we ought to get back to each other on this in a few years."

"Yeah, I feel stuck somewhere at around seventeen."

It was quiet. Then Mark laughed. "When you get past high school, come back and get me. I'm going to need an extra push."

Well, just beyond Virginia's, southern border
Is a land that I am happy to call mine.

ROBBIE FULKS

By late summer, almost two years after my arrival in Raleigh, I became afflicted with the classic reporter dilemma, succinctly described in the title of the Clash hit "Should I Stay or Should I Go?"

One minute I'd be on the phone with Mark musing about my plan to move back to New York and write a book. The next minute I'd be tootling around town—collecting prices on up-for-sale bungalows and inquiring about the quality of the neighborhood elementary schools for my unborn children.

Once, staying in Raleigh would have seemed unfathomable to me. But if the past year and a half had taught me anything, it was that home was an ever-changing and often unpredictable concept. Suddenly, the Southern Part of Heaven was seeming like an all right place to be.

Sensing an opportunity to keep me in town, Lisa and Georgia put their own flailing love lives on hold and decided to concentrate on mine. They figured the one thing that would keep my new, more evolved self around was a serious suitor. I was done chasing cowboys and crackers, they informed me. I was ready for a man of substance.

"Someone older," Georgia told me one afternoon, in the locker room of our gym, as she pulled a 1950s wraparound skirt around her waist and made a knot with the belt.

"Someone settled," Lisa added, pulling off her basketball shorts. "You know—mature."

————

A few weeks later Georgia spotted a flyer at our gym for an annual reunion of Raleigh divorcés. Her aerobics class, the kickboxers, and the stationary bicycle spinners had all been invited.

"Let's forget the commitmentphobes for a while," Georgia told us. "We'll try the ones who did commit and then fucked it all up. Second time around, you know, they might have learned something."

————

That Saturday the three of us stood on a shag rug in a Raleigh living room, by a leopard-skin chair and a wicker basket with a book inside entitled: *Fifty Ways to Avoid Reincarnation—Or Getting It Right the First Time*. Milling around us were dozens of divorcés chatting about how their souls were feeling and "how important it is to center one's life."

"It's the Middle-aged Zenners," Lisa whispered, using the

title we had given this demographic group after overhearing their "holistic" chatter numerous times in the women's locker room.

Georgia chuckled, then spun around. She pointed at a little African sculpture of a black man with an erect penis sitting on a mahogany bookshelf by the door. "I guess Southern belles get this way when they age," she proclaimed, shaking her head in dismay.

I eyed the sculpture. "What, horny for Africans with hard-ons?"

"No," Georgia chided. "Rebellious . . . You know, they get divorced and make up for lost time. They missed the sexual revolution," she whispered.

I rolled my eyes. "So did we."

Lisa adjusted the strap on her Coach bag and interrupted. "Yeah, but we weren't alive yet. These people were getting married and doing diapers while their little brothers and sisters were discovering free love."

I cleared my throat, annoyed that the purpose of our visit—me—was being ignored. "Thanks for the theories on American subcultures, ladies. But can someone please tell me how I am supposed to meet my soul mate at a New Age keg party?"

"God helps those who help themselves," Georgia exclaimed before lunging into the crowd. "How's that?"

"I thought you were a Buddhist," I shouted at her back.

Georgia twisted speedily around and wagged her finger at me. "Hey, enough with the religion seminar. You have work to do."

I rested my elbow on Lisa's shoulder. "Do you see what I put up with? The lone Northerner, and I get treated like a retard."

Lisa wasn't paying attention to either one of us. She took a quick look around the room and frowned. "These people are in delayed adolescence," she remarked—before taking off to find the keg. "I see it with my clients all the time!"

———————

Lisa was resting on a fluffy, chintz-covered couch—holding my now-flat beer—when I approached her with a napkin filled with Goldfish and tortilla chips. Beside her was a needlepoint pillow that read: STAR LIGHT. STAR BRIGHT. WHERE OH WHERE IS MR. RIGHT?

I plopped down next to her and funneled some fish into my mouth. "Do you think we're safe?" I asked, biting into a chip.

In front of us two men in Docksides were stripping off their golf shirts. A man in canvas drawstring pants was gyrating on the dance floor. Another guy in a short-sleeved paisley blouse—circa 1959—was banging his hands against a table a few feet away from us—as if he were getting ready to climb on top of it.

"No, you don't, boy," a woman in a denim mini shouted from across the room. "The last party, J.T. took all his clothes off and danced on that thing for half the night. I'm still trying to get the scratches out."

There seemed to be only one man in the entire room who didn't look potentially dangerous. He stood with his back up against the edge of one of the wood-paneled doors in the living room—tentative and slightly out of place. From my spot on the couch, I could tell he was tall—almost as tall as the door. And handsome. Even in the darkly lit living room, I could see the angles in his face and the way his chin seemed sharp—as if it had been etched in charcoal.

"See anything of interest?" Lisa asked, sounding like a bird-watcher on an early-morning expedition.

"Him," I replied, nodding toward the door. "Any info?"

Lisa bit her upper lip and squinted at our subject. I had grown to know this look well. Lisa was flipping through the Filofax in her brain. "Jules Blackman," she began. "Software whiz. Mid-forties. Wunderkind. Very smart. Your paper writes about him a lot." She paused. "Mission accomplished?"

I nodded.

"Good, we'll get him to call you. Now, let's get out of here—before the cops come."

We pushed ourselves up off the couch and headed for the exit. Georgia was by the door—talking to a tall man with shoulder-length red hair. I recognized him from the local news channel. He was an environmental professor at N.C. State and a well-known antisprawl activist.

"He's very spiritual," she whispered merrily as we swooshed passed her. "He's the guy who saved Umstead Park."

————

Jules and I decided to meet before work at a coffee shop across from a tattoo parlor and a vintage clothing store.

"A morning date?" he had asked on the phone.

"Like eleven?" I had said, feeling mature.

"Like eight," he had said, sounding amused.

He was standing by a stainless-steel cafeteria chair—a rolled-up *Wall Street Journal* under his arm—when I walked into the café. He had on a pair of faded jeans that were frayed at the bottom and a chalk gray T-shirt that matched eyes hidden behind wire-rimmed glasses. He was by far the oldest person in the café. But if it weren't for the salt-and-pepper speckles in his coal black hair, you wouldn't have been able to tell this. He looked restless—in a boyish way. Even a little excited.

"Thanks for meeting me early," he mumbled, shyly.

"Oh," I lied, brushing my hand in the air and plopping down in the chair next to him. "I'm a morning person."

He sat down at the table too—and ordered two coffees. I noticed he had a pair of runner's legs and thick, muscular arms.

"With my kids it's a bit tricky sometimes."

I smiled softly—trying to appear comfortable with a date's use of the term "my kids" to refer to people who already existed. Of course, I wasn't comfortable. Just curious.

A coffee grinder buzzed in the background. Then there was silence. Jules broke it. "You know, I have three. Two teenagers and a nine-year-old."

I looked at him intently. Then cracked a smile. "So, you're experienced with young people?"

When we rose to leave Jules brushed a finger across my wrist—as if accidentally—then raised it quickly. I noticed his hands were the color of burnt almonds and his lips were shaped like half-moons. I wondered—for a second—what it would be like to touch them with my tongue.

On the drive to work I could still see Jules's skin, how it was dark and peppery. I replayed in my head the way he had leaned over and kissed the side of my cheek when we left the café. Three kids, I thought, as I careened into the newspaper parking lot. That's a lot.

———

Jules's house was a renovated bungalow, circa 1920, perched at the bottom of a knobby hill. Big lawn. Floor-to-ceiling windows. A back porch that looked out onto a canopy of live oaks.

The living room was decorated with large abstracts and flooded with light. The kitchen was painted a deep yellow and brimming with organic foods. In every room of the house there were books and CDs piled high on shelves and every piece of sports equipment you could imagine: hockey pucks, soccer balls, softball gloves, and tennis rackets. A high-ceilinged hallway with studio lights separated the bedrooms from the living area. The walls of the hallway were dotted with vacation collages and color photos in clear plastic frames. I noticed one of them was Jules and a teenage boy playing touch football and another was him and a young boy carving pumpkins. There was one of him and a teenage girl posing with a golden retriever. And another with him sweaty and red-faced in jogging shorts and a number tag on his chest, tearing across the finish line of a 10 K marathon.

It was Friday night. Jules had invited me over for a glass of wine. We sat in wicker chairs on the back porch and drank. A whole dark green bottle down our throats.

Jules told me he liked to read novels set in the wilderness and listen to alternative country bands in small Chapel Hill venues. He took swing lessons, collected the paintings of local artists, and had climbed Mt. Everest. He told me his divorce— four years before—had been brutal, the worst thing that had ever happened to him. He called it "an unwanted, soul-searching experience."

Sitting there in his white T-shirt and jean jacket, Jules looked supremely cool—like an old rock star or an aging poet—as if the benefits of age had relaxed him and unfortunate experiences had opened him up.

I noticed his voice was slow and soft—like a spoon sliding through a sliver of melon. And it soothed me. I sipped my wine and listened. His words punctured the air—like sliced-up sentences that were falling from his mouth. *Love, family, future.* The words mixed with other words, then with the wine and the night air and the dew on the tree branches above of us. The mix seemed exotic and exciting—like options, Mark would say, that I wanted to explore.

Jules set his glass down on the porch railing. "I haven't felt this way in a long time," he said, looking over at me. "Not since my wife left. And that was a while ago."

I set my glass down too. "What do you mean?"

He was silent for a second, then he placed his thumb on my knee. "I trust you."

I stared through the porch window at the color photos in the hall. They seemed to be growing bigger and brighter as the sky went from late afternoon blue to evening black. In every photo Jules was huddling or crouching or kneeling—so as to envelop his kids with his arms, or lock them to his side, or pull them tightly to his chest, as if he was swooping them up and shielding them from bad news, inclement weather, or the dark. I wanted to trust him, too.

When evening fell and we could no longer make out each other's faces, Jules picked up our wineglasses and the empty bottle and kicked open the screen door. I followed him into the house.

"If you need to go home, you tell me?" he said.

I sucked in my breath and rested my eyes on the shadowy space between Jules's upper lip and the edge of his nose. "Okay."

In the bedroom I pretended the circle shadows on the ceiling were hearts. Jules touched my hair. I crushed his chest with my elbows and yanked off his glasses. His eyes looked like two slivers of pale sea glass. His face tasted salty, like ocean water. His fingers were slipping and sliding. I was losing limbs, discovering skin. We blinked together and then dove. I saw waves and sky and a white-hot sun.

"Just keep looking at me," he whispered. "And hold my hand."

The next morning the bed felt like a house. And Jules's face and the edges of his body felt familiar, like a road when you've ridden it a few times and know the bumps and curves and where the turns are most pronounced. It was exciting the way his scent had filtered through the strands of my hair—and the way his fingers got tangled around my legs and tied knots around my waist like I was the Sunday newspaper being bundled up.

———————

Jules talked about his kids—Carter, seventeen, Sarah, fourteen, and Tyler, nine—all the time. He used words like *funky* and *smart* to describe them. He showed me Carter's artwork, provided updates on Tyler's soccer games, glowed when he gave detailed accounts of Sarah's school plays. He referred to the three of them as "best friends for life." And he wanted me to meet them right away.

"But what if this is just a fling?" I asked him. "How do you think they'll react to that? One day I'm there. Then I'm gone."

"This isn't just a fling," he told me.

"Well, even if it isn't, maybe I'm not ready for the kid part. I need some time to get used to the idea."

"Darling," he said, planting a kiss on my forehead. "That's okay. It's all okay."

———————

The Ten Thousand Angels had mixed emotions about the Jules situation.

"I think you're taking this a little too fast," Lisa told me at our next meeting. "And if you start carpooling the kids to and from soccer practice, be prepared for me to do an intervention."

Georgia viewed the whole situation a little differently. More of a personal victory in her life than a social victory in mine. "I'm good," she said encouragingly—to herself—when she heard the news. "If you stick it out, two months, I'll take you out for sushi. . . . I knew the chi was right that night."

Adelaide was disapproving of the age difference, but thought, for her purposes, Jules would do. "You need to work on your relationship skills," she told me. "You can practice on this one."

———————

But I wasn't so convinced that this was turning out to be just practice. Jules had captured my attention in a way I couldn't quite explain. Suddenly, I was into everything he was into: long walks, bird-watching, white wine, and calm. I was reading software start-up magazines and the self-help books he threw my way. I was shopping at the Great Outdoor Provision Store and using middle-aged phrases like "centeredness" and "mindful existence."

I liked the idea that we could be a city-country couple—simple but sophisticated, youthful but wise. Jules was sexy and lustful. But he was also a kind of foil. I saw him as an opportunity. What he promised was a healthier life.

Lazing around in his bedroom, Jules and I swapped fantasies about ranches in New Mexico and pieds-à-terre in Paris. Together in bed at night, we talked about our families—and a lot about divorce. We shared that same scratchy, stitched-up wound. And that bonded us tightly. I loved that Jules was a good father, that he cherished his children and treated them like equals. But in a deeply personal way that I was almost embarrassed to admit, what I especially loved about Jules was his sadness.

———

As for Mark, he too was moving on—or back—depending on how you looked at it. He and Caitlin bumped into each other at a studio executive party a few weeks after his visit to North Carolina. "I told her: 'I'm the best you can do.' And she agreed." They were dating again by the following week.

To help him over this new hurdle, Mark said, he too was working on his relationship skills. He had sought the advice of a professional. "I'm making progress," he told me one night over the phone. "I was a shell of man. Now I'm coming out of my shell."

"I think you're mixing metaphors."

"Who cares? Remember how you told me you were seventeen? Well, my therapist says I'm still at ten. But he thinks I can get to seventeen in a few months."

"Congratulations."

———

Things were heating up on my new beat. Distrust of the developers was mounting in the suburbs. By August, Joe Miller, a computer executive who had made millions on the sale of his software firm, announced he was running for town council in Raleigh's largest suburb. Soon he was whizzing around town with his "slow-growth" posters, bad-mouthing Tiger at luncheons and coffee klatches.

"Build?" he screamed during a talk at a country club breakfast. "They can build their brains out—but not at our expense."

I met Miller a few days later at Applebee's for lunch. He showed up in tennis shorts, downed a cheese-and-chili burger, then invited me over to see the work on the domed ceiling in his foyer. It was being hand-painted—like the Sistine Chapel, he told me. "Guys have been lying on their backs working on it for weeks. It's not easy. I've got the largest house in the development—the only one on two plots."

I congratulated Miller on his home size, then opened my pad.

"So, what is this about the developers spying on you?" I asked, referring to a rumor that had hit the suburban town hall.

"Oh, they're doing drive-bys, taking pictures, classic intimidation stuff. But I'm not budging. I'll pump as much money as I need to into this election. We're going to win—because we're saying what people want to hear. I'm taking back this town, Kyle. I represent the little guy."

I hardly considered residents of a town where the median household income was $65,000 little guys. But I guess everything is relative.

"That's admirable," I said.

The editors loved it.

"You're really cracking things open over there," Kip told me one afternoon. "We've never really done this kind of up-close reporting, out there, talked to those developers, gotten into the minds of the residents."

Even Maria was getting a kick out of my inside status with the boys.

"Hey, Tig," she heard me coo on the phone one afternoon. "God bless. And have a great weekend."

"God bless?" Maria yelped, craning her neck around to my desk. "So that's how you get those geezers to talk to you. Not a bad strategy!"

In Maria's world, that was a compliment.

———

The Christmas of 1999, Jules and I bought a pine needle Christmas tree at the Farmers Market and decorated it with colored lights and glass ornaments from boxes we pulled down from the attic. I helped him shop for soccer balls and skateboards for the kids at the sports store in Cameron Village. I even made present suggestions and chose a scarf for Sarah at a clothing store near my house. Bit by bit, I was growing more comfortable with the thought that Jules's children might actually become a part of my life.

At his office Christmas party, I drank Asti Spumante from a fluted glass, smiled confidently at his associates, and made casual remarks about the future—as if to say, "Don't think I'm temporary."

The party was held in a two-story Victorian that one of Jules's associates was renovating. Together we toured the house and remarked on the recently finished moldings, the hardwood floors, and the restored cabinets.

"Neat, huh?" he said, winking at me.

After dinner, I stuck my index finger on a sliver of wax dripping down a candle in a sterling silver holder. He stood behind me and wrapped his fingers around my hand.

"I love you," he whispered into my hair. "Did you know that?"

I felt my heart being pried open with his breath and fingers.

———————

On the drive home, along I-40, I couldn't help seeing our future reflected in the car lights ahead of us. We would be like Annette Bening and Warren Beatty, Liz Phair and the forty-year-old music producer she married. We'd be like a couple that Lisa's mom once knew. The woman married her best friend's father, and they were happily married for thirty-five years. My mind was like a checkout girl, scanning in one element of our new life after another. We'd sell the small brick house and build a large Greek Revival with a two-story porch and a wrought-iron fence—or a Victorian—or something else we could work on together. We'd build a writing room for me and a separate wing—or perhaps an entire house a few acres away—for the children. We'd put in an indoor swimming pool and tennis courts. We would rent a studio in New York City for weekend trips, and rent a house in Brittany for the month of February. Jules would take up painting in his spare time. He'd want to take vacations to Los Angeles. Together we'd learn Italian and buy all our clothes at Prada outlets on trips to Rome.

I pressed my fingers against Jules's flannel suit pants and breathed a sigh of relief. The car was toasty warm, and champagne bubbles were swimming around in my head. I felt safe, home free.

I can read the writing on the wall.

THE MAVERICKS

Even though I knew I was ready, the thought of meeting the children still gave me the jitters. Jules assured me it would be fine. He had the kids half the time, so if I wanted to spend more time with him, he told me, I had to be willing to spend at least some time in the same house with them. The introduction would be nothing formal, Jules promised. Just a quick pizza dinner.

"What will I talk to them about?" I inquired.

"Don't worry," he reassured me. "You'll figure it out."

———

At the Formica table lined with waxy cups and a stainless steel silver napkin holder, I didn't figure anything out—except how much other people's children could frighten me. Jules and his three kids were already seated when I arrived. They were sipping icy Cokes and looking cranky—as if they had been dragged there against their will. I was petrified.

"There are only four chairs," muttered a lanky teenager. He was stretching toward adulthood with Jules's gray eyes and a smaller version of his angular face.

I could feel my own burning with splotches of apple red at the insinuation that there was not enough room for me.

"Carter," Jules reprimanded, affirming my guess that it was Jules's seventeen-year-old son who had launched this insult my way. "I think that's beyond rude. Go get Kyle a chair."

Jules rose to give me a kiss, and Carter pulled himself up and disappeared. I noticed he wore shoulder-length hair and an oversize workman's shirt—unbuttoned at the bottom, presumably to show off his silver belly ring and a tattoo next to his navel.

"Teenagers are from another planet," Jules joked apologetically.

I was feeling too queasy even to feign laughter. This was ten times worse than a job interview. A hundred times worse than a first date. Someone was doing somersaults in my stomach. And I wasn't sure I was going to get through this without losing my lunch.

"Yeah, they can be so . . . stupid," interjected a little boy with orange freckles on his cheeks and a bowl haircut. It was Tyler, Jules's nine-year-old. He was wearing a Durham Bulls baseball cap, backwards, and sitting next to his father. I looked over at him and smiled. A potential in, I thought.

When Carter returned with my chair, I sat down, and we all ordered from our plastic-covered cardboard menus. Carter and Jules's fourteen-year-old daughter, Sarah, struck up a conversation about her boyfriend. She had a long face that was framed by curly locks and a tight-fitting T-shirt with the words BAD GIRL printed on it. "He's been acting like a total doofus," she told her brother, pulling a Magic Marker out of the back pocket of her Abercrombie & Fitch jeans and drawing her name on the paper place mat in front of her. "He like freaked on me in drama yesterday. I think he has some repressed anger issues."

The adult-child discrepancy confused me. But I figured it was a paradox particular to teenagers that I would have to get used to.

During the dinner Jules made frequent attempts at group conversation. He told the kids I was a reporter, worked for the local newspaper, had lived in Paris. I smiled intermittently, trying to appear relaxed—even though I seemed to have forgotten how to speak.

Meanwhile the kids kept their eyes on each other— occasionally glancing over at their father but never exchanging glances with me. Jules had told me a few days before not to worry; they were very shy with strangers. I understood what he had said—but they certainly didn't seem shy with each other.

When Carter finished his pizza, he wiped a piece of tomato sauce off his cheek and threw his balled-up napkin across the table and into his younger brother's lap.

"Carter, gross!" Tyler boomed.

"You guys are such babies," Sarah yelled.

"Okay, Tyler, Sarah. Let's all calm down," Jules interjected.

I nibbled on my pizza crust and wondered if I could really take care of someone else's kids—particularly if the three of them turned out to be totally unlikable. I wondered how Jules could have stood being around them this many years. Didn't he dread getting up in the morning?

"Guys, did you know Kyle's from New York?"

Carter let out a half mumble. "That's cool."

———

Jules paid the bill, and the four of us picked up our belongings and headed for the door. Carter lagged behind to talk to some buddies from school. Sarah rested her arm on her father's shoulder. Jules held Tyler's hand. I walked behind them. Alone.

What was I supposed to do? I imagined myself asking Jules later on that night. They didn't seem very interested in me. And, by the way, you weren't very helpful.

Back at the house we all piled out of the car. I felt deflated—like I'd failed a test or disappointed an editor with a lousy story. I was dreading the inevitable discussion with Jules about my dinner table incompetence, convinced his laid-back demeanor about the matter was a cover-up for deep disappointment.

A few hours later Jules and I were sitting in the kitchen sipping wine when Carter barreled in—in his stocking feet—to pour himself a glass of orange juice. "Dude, you've gotta tell me about New York." I looked up from my wineglass and realized he was talking to me. "That's where I want to go to college. It must have been amazing growing up there."

Carter shut the refrigerator door and slipped back into the living room with his juice glass. "But like later," he shouted my way.

Jules winked at me. "I told you they're from another planet," he whispered, kissing me on the cheek. "But you never listen to me, dude."

A slight smile crawled across my face.

———

For New Year's Jules and I took a trip to New York. We stayed in a prewar suite at the Gramercy Park Hotel, overlooking the residential garden with the black wrought-iron fence. It felt strange to see my hometown from a visitor's perspective. But grown-up, too—as if my world now encompassed so much more than just New York.

We strolled along the snowy, tree-lined streets with the large brownstones draped in browning ivy, ate curried chicken at an Indian restaurant in the East Village, bought CDs at Tower Records. Together we went to the flea market on Spring Street to buy a wool hat from Guatemala for Sarah and to Pearl Paint on Canal Street to buy art supplies for Carter. We didn't tell anyone we were coming. It was our secret trip.

On New Year's Day, we sat on an enclosed patio at a café in Chelsea and drank espresso. Jules looked handsome in his white oxford and creased khakis. I noticed a few added specks of gray in his hair and the way women passing us on the street were staring at him—hard. He was awed by New York—having been there only once before—but not so comfortable. His unease was reassuringly childlike—as if he needed me and he felt okay with that.

We had picked up a *New York Times* on our way to the café. He was flipping through the glossy pages of the Sunday magazine. He stopped at a photo spread of contemporary California kitchens. He turned the magazine around and pointed at one of the photos. "What do you think of this kitchen?" he asked, hesitantly.

I crinkled my nose and made a light dismissive gesture with my hand. "What are you talking about?" Magazine spreads were not things Jules paid attention to.

"I'm talking about our future." Jules rested his elbows on the table and leaned toward me. "Kyle, I want to spend the rest of my life with you."

The words glided across my brain and I gulped hard.

————

Back in Raleigh, I began to feel superhuman and scared—as if unknown possibilities were opening up to me, and old ones were suddenly gone. Jules's avowal had come fast, and a part of me knew to look for the one-eighty, the turnaround, the pull-back, or the pushaway that men are known for when they scare themselves by moving forward too rapidly and getting you to expect big things too soon.

"Just make sure you don't say things you're not sure of," I cautioned Jules a few weeks after our trip. "It would be mean."

Then I brushed aside these scary thoughts, and we began to plan. Like we had done before—but now it all seemed more legitimate. We would swish balls down the squeaky aisles of Raleigh's main bowling alley, down beers from red Coca-Cola cups, and decorate our bedroom. Rugs from Bulgaria. A chest from India. Some pottery from Chapel Hill. We would lie on Jules's living room carpet, listen to Barry White CDs, and plot our new careers. I would freelance. He would build computer systems in the attic. We would eat light lunches together in the late afternoon and take walks after dinner in the woods behind his house—sometimes with the kids, but mostly alone.

One Sunday, while lounging in plastic lawn chairs at the neighborhood indoor pool, we listened to a bunch of kids dipping in and out of the pool. "Marco . . . Polo . . . Marco . . ." Jules looked up at me. His face was dry. "What do you think about the name Marco?" he inquired.

I pulled some lotion out of my straw bag and handed the bottle to him. "For what?"

"Our child."

The words warmed my tongue, and I clapped my hands together and shook my head—as if I were a toddler myself and I had just received a toy.

On days like these Jules would often tell me how different I was from his wife. Less judgmental. More open-minded. Laid-back. Not uptight. I took these as compliments. After four years of postmarriage fumbling, he told me, he had finally found the right fit. Me. The feeling was delightfully unfamiliar.

Sometimes, I would find myself unable to stop giggling, ecstatic. Other times, I was secretly afraid that this was all going to come crashing down.

———

As the weeks passed, I began to spend more time with the kids. When Jules had to work late or go in early, I'd drop them off at school, pick them up from soccer practice, take them out for sushi, or make them lasagna. I recorded their favorite foods and kept track of what colors they liked. In my spare time I began perusing specialty clothing stores—no longer just for me but for Sarah, too. In February, for her birthday, I bought her a pair of cowboy boots like the ones I had seen several of her friends wearing. But hers were better—red with a stitched snake crawling up the leg. They were expensive, $200. But they were worth it. And so was she.

"How did you know I wanted these?" she asked, pulling on the left boot and looking obviously pleased.

I laughed. "Because I'm paying attention."

Six months in and Sarah was always courteous like this—but never tremendously outgoing or forward. Her silence didn't really perturb me, not nearly as much as I thought it might. I gathered she was still trying to determine what I needed from her father and whether those needs were likely to threaten her own. The divorce had been hard on her. And Jules said she had "discipline problems." She was constantly failing a class or getting into a fight with a teacher. But it seemed to me that she was just angry. I liked all the kids, the way they were spontaneous—always bumbling around the house, entrenched in projects that seemed so removed from the world of work and responsibility. But I related to Sarah specifically. And I figured that as time passed Sarah would come to see that.

———

The weekend after Sarah's birthday, Jules and I drove to Cala-
bash to meet his mother, a ruddy-faced widow who spent much
of her time at garden club meetings and in the local library,
where she volunteered. She greeted us for dinner in a pretty
knit dress and a pair of Miranda pumps and regaled us with
tales of how her next-door neighbor was so "brainless he
couldn't pour piss out of a boot with the directions on the
heel." She served us crispy fried chicken, a tomato-and-string-
bean salad from her garden, and a rich banana pudding—
which, she apologetically warned us, was store-bought. I was
nervous—but eager to appear courteous, not too young. I wore
a long, unflattering skirt and my hair pulled back tightly in a
bun so as to look as severe and serious as possible.

After dinner in the kitchen, while Jules scraped off the china
plates and I threw away the wrappings from the pudding, she
leaned over to him and declared: "Isn't it nice you have someone young to provide you some comfort?"

I pulled my hair out of the bun and headed for the
bathroom.

———

"Comfort!" I screamed during the car ride home.

"She has some limitations, Kyle. She is a little closed-
minded."

"I don't care what kind of limitations she has. I'm not your
nurse."

Jules laughed. "Hey, they get paid better than reporters."

I tapped him on the head with a clenched fist. "You are not
making me feel better."

Jules grabbed my fist with his free hand and squeezed it
tightly. "But I love you, does that make you feel better?"

A half-moon smile curled up onto my face.

That night the kids were with their mother. We blasted
Lucinda Williams and drank whiskey sours. I stood on Jules's

bed in my underwear and lip-synched her lyrics—one hand holding my drink, the other pointing at Jules, my hips gyrating, my hair falling into my eyes.

> *Not a day goes by,*
> *I don't think about you.*
> *You left your mark on me.*
> *It's permanent.*
> *A tattoo.*

I was screaming the lyrics, as if performing for a room filled with concertgoers—almost wailing.

> *Pierce the skin and the blood runs through*
> *Oh . . . baby*

I was clutching my chest now, tilting my head dramatically toward the ceiling.

> *The way you move is right in time*
> *The way you move is right in time*
> *It's right in time . . . With me*

Jules was standing in the doorway, watching me and laughing.

> *I stand over the stove in the kitchen*
> *Watch the water boil. And I listen.*
> *Turn off the television.*
> *Ohhhh . . . baby.*

> *The way you move is right in time.*
> *Is right in time.*
> *Is right in time with me.*

When I was done, I flopped on the bed, feigning exhaustion. Jules grabbed me by my ankles and kissed the side of my hip. "My girlfriend's a rock star . . . and a nurse."

I grabbed for a pillow and clobbered him with it. He pulled me toward him. "You make me laugh," he whispered into my ear.

"You make me feel perfect," I whispered back. I could feel my heart pounding against his chest.

Jules took his glasses off and placed them by the bedside table. He was silent. "My wife would never do these sorts of things," he finally said, his eyes glazing over a bit. "Never. She wasn't very spontaneous." I placed my hand on top of his and gripped it tightly—not knowing whether this comparison was a good sign. For a split second I wondered if Jules didn't sometimes think more about her than about me.

That night, I dreamed I was the sole human in a family of fairy-tale bears. Mama Bear came and stole Papa Bear away from me.

———

A few weeks later, Jules and I were driving through Oakwood, admiring the renovated Victorians. We passed the shingled house with the gingerbread siding. The icing pink shoe box with the square porch. The bungalow with dormer windows that had been added in the seventies.

Jules stopped the car in front of a massive Greek Revival mansion. "Listen. I've decided I definitely don't want to get back together with my wife. . . . So, I was thinking that—"

A hand grenade exploded in my stomach. "What?"

"Well, I didn't want to alarm you—but, well, she's been asking me to come back. . . . Of course, I said I didn't want to."

"But you thought about it? After you told me you wanted to spend the rest of your life with me? And you never mentioned it?"

"Does that make you nervous? It shouldn't—but I understand how it could."

"What do you mean you understand? . . . And she's your ex, by the way. Can you stop calling her your wife?"

Suddenly I began to wonder if there had been signals I hadn't caught. Nuances I should have looked for. Should I have worried more about all the times he mentioned his wife? Should I not have trusted him?

"Kyle, it's important for both of us. For the kids. Dee wants to be friends again."

I stared down at the soiled car mat beneath my sneakers. "But what about me?"

"Darling," Jules said, resting his hand on my skirt. "You're my lover."

Lover sounded temporary, inconsequential, like a French harlot or a one-night stand. It sounded like the name for someone who was getting too greedy and expecting too much.

"When I think of having sex, she's not the woman who comes to mind—don't worry."

"Just the woman you think of for everything else?"

Jules pressed his hand against my knee. "Be sweet."

After that it seemed like a third person had slipped into our relationship. And Jules wanted to make sure I knew she was there. Suddenly, he was mentioning Mom all the time, and each time it felt like a piece of meat stuck in my throat.

"When your mom and I were your age, she used to make her own skirts out of jeans," he told the kids one morning.

This must have seemed like an invitation, because suddenly it was open season for them, too.

"Mom says if I want to go to soccer practice she'll pick me up." "Mom says that when you guys were in school, the math you were taught was really different."

Sometimes, at the end of a day like that, I felt like I was going to die choking.

One afternoon in the cereal section of the grocery store, I put a hand to my neck and feigned a slit throat. We had just bumped into Mom's sister.

"You're not mature enough to handle this, are you?" Jules asked as we left the store.

I shoved my hands in the pockets of my sundress. "I am."

Jules started the engine. I could tell he was angry. "If you're not this isn't going to work."

———

The Ten Thousand Angels said it was too early to consider a fast exit.

"He's got some issues," Georgia said, lighting a cigarette. "Good luck finding someone who doesn't. Just take a deep breath. You're getting as jittery as a betsy bug. And you're doing that fleeing thing again."

We were at the PR bar on a dead Tuesday night. The emergency meeting had been convened for my benefit. And I was downing a fruity drink with vodka.

I bit my lip. "What about a time-out?"

Adelaide took a sip of her whiskey sour. "Remember, you need to work on your follow-through."

"But I'm not sure this is the guy I want to follow through with. He's all enmeshed with the ex."

"That's normal for a divorced dad," Lisa said. "And healthy."

I glared at Lisa. "Healthy for whom?"

———

I wanted the Angels to be right. So I made an effort to help Sarah out with the French class she was failing, to talk to Carter about his summer plans to take an art class at Parsons in New York. I tried to be patient with Tyler when he got cranky and overtired. But things were changing. And the changes seemed beyond my control. Jules still talked about us together in the future—but the future kept getting further away. He told me not to take it personally, to calm down and be patient. But his words infuriated me.

In late March, Jules and I had planned to take a trip to Puerto Rico—but two weeks before we were scheduled to leave, he canceled. We were lying in my bed, right before sleep, when he dropped the news. I bolted up as if propelled off my pillow. "What's going on?"

Jules looked sad, even a little disoriented. "I just don't want to be away from the kids for more than a few nights. Anyway, I'm tired."

I was confused. "But isn't that the point of a vacation?"

"Kyle, it's not going to happen. Sarah's been acting up again. Tyler's been having trouble sleeping."

I could feel a lump growing in my throat. I was stunned and hurt. Pissed as hell. "I think you're doing this on purpose to keep me at a distance. We're getting close and now you're jumping ship. Putting up all these obstacles."

My voice was getting stronger, more powerful. Jules's voice was getting softer.

He coughed and got out of bed. "I think you're being paranoid."

"Admit it," I shouted. "You're having trouble moving on. You're using the kids to keep a distance from me. You're doing a one-eighty, a turnaround. And you didn't even warn me this was coming."

Jules began putting on his jeans. One leg, then the other. "Why do you always need to be the center of attention?"

I jumped out of the bed and looked at him pleadingly. "Because I'm your girlfriend. What's so wrong with that?"

"This situation. That's what's wrong. I have three children, Kyle. That's not going to change. I have a family."

My nightgown felt like a tent. I could feel it brushing against my calves, tightening at my neck. "And you have an ex-wife. But you treat her like you're still married to her."

"Kyle," Jules said, turning around and heading for the door. "She's part of that family."

————

The next day at work my computer screen was nothing but a fuzzy blue blur. I tried to pay attention to the story I was writing, but my eyes were salt pools. And every time the phone rang, I grabbed for the receiver—hoping it was Jules. He didn't call.

At three I drove home and plopped myself on my porch steps. The cicadas were chirping into the afternoon air, reminding me how perfectly suited they were for their role in the world. I was envious. My life was not so simple. And I was beginning to wonder if I would ever be suited for anything I chose. It was becoming obvious to me that my "fresh start" at a family was more convoluted than I had originally wanted to admit. Sitting there, it dawned on me that perhaps it was more than just our shared divorce experiences that was attracting me to Jules. Perhaps, with him I was also seeing an opportunity to wedge my way in between two disgruntled parents and save a bunch of divorced kids. That possibility made me feel queasy.

————

If things were getting testy on the personal front, they were no better at work. Joe Miller—the loudmouthed computer engineer who had vowed, a few months before, to win a seat on the town council of Raleigh's largest suburb—was in high gear. He had promised to put an end to unchecked sprawl and the developers' tyrannical reign. And the developers were livid.

Miller spent that spring cavorting around town telling residents the boys were to blame for all their problems. He ran large, alarming ads in area papers. One headline read, TAX-PAYERS: YOU PAY FOR GROWTH. Another ad—entitled CONFLICT OF INTEREST—implied that the developers' relationship with local officials was too close. He held afternoon coffee klatches, campaigned at soccer games. He routinely mocked the size of the developers' yachts—and one time, during a talk in a neighboring town, he referred to the development community as "pond scum."

Tiger called me all the time as did other developers.

"I don't want to be mean but . . . that Miller man's talking out of his ass. You can't run around town and behave that way—and have people like you," an irate builder boomed into my office answering machine one morning.

Bo Bo and the rest of the boys followed suit with their own feverish calls—insisting that I take note of their feelings and get their viewpoints into the paper whenever I could. I did my best to keep them happy. But they were becoming increasingly paranoid and would occasionally accuse me of outlandish feats—like making a secret pact with Miller to help him win.

Old-timers, like the guy who owned the tuxedo rental store in town and the folks who ran the soda shop, were also worried. "He's gonna destroy this town. People are going to think we're closed for business. He's sending out the wrong message," the tuxedo rental guy told me one afternoon.

To bolster their position, the boys put their support and a lot of their money behind the town council incumbent, a cheery dentist who liked to refer to the building community as "our friends, the developers." Also running was a little-known arborist who vowed to spend less than a dollar on his campaign.

I had fallen upon an enormously entertaining story about suburban living gone awry. I was writing about a town outgrowing its roots and questioning the motives of its founding fathers. I identified.

Daily, I pumped out quick hits, and I tackled longer pieces

for the Saturday and Sunday papers. A few months into the campaign season, I wrote my first big in-depth takeout about the three candidates. Miller was in the nut graph, and his kooky behavior and outlandish personality stole the story. The developers were red-hot mad.

After a week of the silent treatment, I telephoned Tiger. "What's going on?" I asked him.

"Miss Kyle, I don't know what you are talking about."

"Tig, 'fess up."

"The boys think you've sided with Miller. You acted so nice, and then when Miller came around you sided with him."

"I didn't side with him. What are you talking about?"

"They think you did. They think he blindsided you. They think all the stories you've done have been big blow jobs."

"No," I said. "I'm neutral. I'm unbiased."

"Well, I'm just telling you what they're telling me. They think you betrayed them."

"That's ridiculous. He's a good story. That's it. He came in here like a bat out of hell. I had to write about it."

It took only a few weeks for Tiger and the rest of the boys to stop returning my calls. Miller won the election with a landslide vote. And they more or less blamed me.

————

"May I ask who's calling?" Tig said into the phone a few afternoons after the election. It was my third attempt to reach him that day.

"Tig, it's me. Kyle."

"Kyle?"

"Tig, it's me. You know me."

The phone went dead.

Tiger never returned my call. And most of the other boys stopped returning my calls too. None of them were ever at their desks anymore. They were in transit, at conferences, out to lunch, on vacation.

At town hall meetings Tig stopped winking at me. During breaks, he and the boys would huddle alone together, swap stories, smoke butts—and ignore me. I had been frozen out.

Another reporter adage: When your best sources stop talking to you, it's time to move on.

———

In May, Adelaide proved that her wave theory worked—at least for her. She jumped a surgery resident from "a good family" in Atlanta and rode him to shore. After a few weeks of speed-dating, they were engaged.

Georgia disappeared into the vertiginous void of the newly in love. She and the red-haired professor she had met at the divorcé party discovered they had more in common than their affinity for Umstead Park. They began spending evenings together immersed in elaborate cook-a-thons that appealed to their highly competitive spirits and shared an obsession with vegan meals.

As for Lisa, she decided to put the man hunting on hold for a while—and try home hunting instead. For much of that spring she dragged me through one new living room after another, ordered me to knock on closet walls, test bathroom sink pipes, crawl through crawl spaces, and listen to her incessant chatter about electrical service installation, ceramic tile subcontractors, window hangings, and doorknobs with Clarence, her real estate agent and husband of her law school buddy who promised to find her a "starter home," "fixer-upper," in an "up-and-comer" of a neighborhood.

One Sunday afternoon Lisa, Clarence, and I found ourselves touring a brick one-story, circa 1940, inhabited by a guy who cleaned gutters. There was a hole in the kitchen wall and another in the bedroom wall. Both were covered by plastic lining and masking tape. The front yard hadn't been mowed since the Civil War, and the backyard served as the neighborhood dog park.

I took one look at the house and declared it an unnatural disaster.

Lisa took one look and pronounced it her new home.

Clarence, apparently, agreed. "Lisa, you need to jump on this," he shouted at her from the yard. "This is the last dog on the street."

"I think I can work with this," she shouted back as she poked her head out the hole in the kitchen wall. "Kyle, you have no earthly idea how much potential there is here."

On the drive back to Lisa's house, I glumly noted that if she worked fast enough she could have a housewarming party by the end of the summer.

Lisa glanced my way. "Whatsa matter, you don't think I can do the renovations?"

I stared out the window at the drab-colored Suburban ahead of us. "No, it's not that. You're just making me queasy with all this house-buying stuff."

"Why?"

"I don't know. Clarence is really intent on selling you a house."

"Kyle, he's very good at what he does."

"That's precisely why I'm worried."

Lisa tilted her head my way. "Are you repressing your true feelings here?"

I stared ahead. "The truth is, I'm not making any progress in the home department. I don't even know where my home would be."

"I thought you were planning to stay here for a while."

I looked down at my hands. I was fidgeting with them in my lap. "Maybe my plan isn't working."

A few days later I had a dream that I gave birth to a little baby boy and handed it to Jules all bundled up like a birthday present in a pale blue flannel blanket.

Lying beneath his comforter the next night, my elbows resting on his ribs, I said to him, "Remember when we talked about what we would name our kids? Well, I want to have a child."

Jules drew a circle on my shoulder with his index finger. "I'm not so sure anymore about more kids."

I rolled over and faced the wall. "You know, I'm not so sure anymore about you."

"Darlin'," Jules whispered into my ear. "Do you have to worry so much about the future? Can't you just live in the present?"

I ignored him.

That night, I lay on my back—naked—and peered at the crepe myrtles blossoming on the other side of Jules's screen door. The live oaks, pear trees, dogwoods, and magnolias were all aflutter. Another spring was nearing. I was thirty. And the intensity of the newness Raleigh had once offered had disappeared. The chirping of the cicadas every night was beginning to annoy me. The thought of another blistering hot summer was making me itchy. And I was getting sick of living in a town where the police had nothing better to do than stop speeders like me. I wanted to know when I could get a decent Indian meal, and why I had to spend so much of my time whizzing around in a metal box on an asphalt strip.

"Jules," I whispered into the darkness. "Do you think we're really that compatible?"

If I had a horse
I'd ride off into the sunset
If I had wings, I'd fly off
In the sky so blue
If I had the time, I'd spend my whole life dreaming
But I'd wake up still in love with you.

BROOKS & DUNN

I tore open the envelope, already suspecting what the letter inside would say: "You're going to jail!" it read. I threw it on my bed, annoyed.

It was the third warning I'd received that week. The others were equally menacing: "Don't wait to get legal help!" read one. "You're in big trouble!" read the other. One included details on North Carolina prison life. All included business cards. Apparently, I was on the mailing list of every young attorney in town. And for good reason.

Three years in Raleigh, and I was one ticket away from a costly stint in driving school, and only a few points away from losing my driver's license completely. In other words, with my fines alone, I was fueling the local economy.

Unfortunately, speeders in the South are a detested group. On the hierarchy of lawbreakers, they are lower than shoplifters and white-collar criminals. And when they are from the North, they are considered even more reprehensible, on par, probably, with crackheads who hold up convenience stores. I am convinced that if I had made a habit of barreling around town all liquored up, few Tar Heels would have cared. Some would even have applauded me for my zest for life. But speeding while sober, I came to realize, was, by its very nature, viewed as a personal affront to the values of the region. At cocktail parties people cracked dumb Northerner-in-the-South driving jokes at my expense. My own traffic attorney, whom I had on retainer, had ordered me to her office one afternoon for a stern lecture on my careless ways. ("If you can't slow down for yourself, for Christ's sake, do it for the people of this city," she had yelled from her oak desk, wagging her finger at me.) Even Lisa, my best friend in Raleigh, refused to ride in a car with me behind the wheel. (When I suggested it once, she glared at me with wolfish eyes. "Give me the keys," she hollered. *"Now!"*) There was no way around it, there was a part of me that no one in North Carolina would ever like.

If I had harbored dreams of staying in the Tar Heel State indefinitely, the reality of my road woes began to sour them— as did the prospect of losing my license completely and riding around the Triangle on an unair-conditioned public bus with my friends from the homeless shelter. As the months wore on and my tickets piled up, I began to suspect that these were signs that it might be time to get out of Dodge—for good.

That fall, more signs presented themselves. Maria surprised us all by arriving at work one day in an oversize sailor suit and announcing that she was going on maternity leave. The news filtered in—then out. I was busy trying to get Tiger to return my calls.

A few mornings later I padded into the office and was greeted by a piercing silence, quickly broken by a soothing whisper from the other side of my desk partition: "Good use of quotes," the little voice said. "This is fine."

Good and *fine* were not Maria words.

I looked down, and poking out of Maria's side of the wall were a pair of Dr. Scholl's.

I switched on my computer and quickly zapped off an e-mail.

"Your replacement wears comfortable shoes," I wrote. "I miss the stilettos . . . and the ball busting."

"You don't need me anymore," came the reply. "You can take it from here. Anyway, you don't need fashion advice."

"Blasphemy!" I replied.

"Fuck me to tears, where's the confidence? There's not a reporter in the newsroom who would have spent three months hanging out with a bunch of Christian Rockers—in Doc Martens no less."

"That was moral depravity."

"Whatever it is, your obsessive persistence works."

"Are you calling me obsessive?"

"Don't you have some developers to abuse?"

"I'm going to miss you."

"*Yo también.*"

—————

A few weeks after Maria's departure, Kip made his own bomb-dropping announcement. He was exhausted from manning the metro desk and was heading downstairs to be a sports columnist.

"Treason," I barked, marching over to his desk when I heard the news. "How could you do this to me?"

Kip mumbled something about being worn out, his kids never saw him, he'd worked these crazy hours for five years.

"I don't care about your kids, Kip. I have abandonment issues. And you're triggering them."

Kip shrugged his shoulders and stared down at his keyboard. I could have sworn I saw a silvery speck in his eye.

Before he took off Kip finally got to see the Howard Johnson's piece he had been trying to convince one of us to write about. He wrote it himself—thirty beautifully choreographed inches about the ugly duckling architectural giant, unwanted and unloved, that scarred the City of Oak's skyline. Only Kip could write a story about a chain hotel and turn it into a masterpiece.

When Kip did finally pack it up and head downstairs, I went to visit him often.

"I'm feeling antsy," I told him one afternoon, leaning against his desk and sipping a cup of watery coffee from the cafeteria. "My sources are all clamming up—and I don't even give a shit. Kip, I've interviewed these guys so many times, I could recite in my sleep what they'd say if they were talking."

"When are you leaving?"

"What do you mean?"

"Maybe it's time to move on."

"Well, no, I've got this guy I'm dating . . ."

"Who? The old guy?"

I nodded.

A fact of life in a small newsroom is that every one of your colleagues knows about your personal life. And many of them have in-depth opinions about it—which they are rarely shy about sharing. I think it must have something to do with our collective respect for the First Amendment.

"This is the one with kids, and an ex, right?"

"Yeah."

"You'll never have this guy. Kyle, you're in over your head."

My face burned with embarrassment. Kip and I never talked about my personal life—particularly not like this. "Anyway, you're too nice to play the evil stepmother."

I smiled. But I was getting angry. Kip didn't know what Jules and I had. He knew nothing about our relationship.

Kip looked up at me intently. "Kyle, you could go to a big paper now. You're ready. I don't want to see you held back for something that will eventually make you miserable."

It was probably the most Kip had ever said to me, and I was seething.

"There are openings at *The Washington Post*. They want young reporters like you. You could go somewhere like that."

I shuffled back upstairs, pissed that even my editor doubted my ability to make this relationship work.

————

A few weeks later, I was resting my head against two feather pillows and threading my fingers through Jules's cotton string blanket when it hit me that Kip was right about the miserable part. I untangled myself from the sheets and slid barefoot to Jules's bathroom. Standing in the doorway looking around, I noticed a pair of children's boxer shorts bunched up on the floor. Above them on the counter sink were several bottles of shampoo and containers of makeup that the kids' mother had brought back from a trip to London. All the objects surrounding me were someone else's. I peed and tried to imagine myself in this bathroom in five years, still surrounded mostly by things that were not mine.

As I walked back to bed, I stopped in front of the family vacation collages hanging against the flowered wallpaper in the hallway. They felt like raised maps of a future I wasn't sure I wanted: Tampa, Florida; Portland, Maine; the Grand Canyon; Disney World. I stopped and scrutinized them up close: the baseball tickets, the Mickey Mouse ride passes, the grains of Grand Canyon sand glued to an egg-stained place mat from a diner in the Rocky Mountains. A thought popped into my head: Jules didn't have a collage of anything I'd ever wished to see. There was no China collage or Australia collage. No post-cards of the Leaning Tower of Pisa. There wasn't anything from New Delhi or Miami or the Museum of Modern Art in New York. As I stood there at two in the morning in a one-story brick bungalow, it occurred to me that the man who lived in this bungalow didn't dream of renting a house in Brittany or restoring a Victorian on a tree-shaded street. He didn't want a pied-à-terre in New York or Williams-Sonoma utensils in his kitchen. He didn't care if he ever left the country. If he had wanted any of those things, they would already be in his life. The stamps would be on his passport. The collages would be on his walls, the utensils in his kitchen. It was the most obvious of thoughts. And it had just occurred to me.

I shuffled to my bag in the living room and pulled out a lighter and a cigarette, then went back to the bathroom and smoked it. Crouched on the tiled floor, I blew smoke rings up into the air, then I threw the rest of my cigarette into the toilet and tiptoed back to bed.

———

The next day, Jules and I took a walk.

We padded along the sidewalk, passing rows and rows of low-roofed brick-and-limestone homes. Jules stopped in front of a small two-story and reached for my chin with his fingers. "You need to get out of here."

I squinted, more in denial than dense. "Get out of where?"

"Raleigh."

I lifted myself onto my tippy toes and tugged at Jules's faded yellow collar. "Are you breaking up with me? I mean, why is everyone trying to kick me out of here?"

"Could you be happy here?"

"No."

"Then, yes. I'm breaking up with you."

I began to cry.

Jules draped an arm around my shoulder. "Sweetheart, you should go home."

"That's mean. I thought I *was* home."

And, indeed, I had hoped that with Jules I could make a home, that perhaps he would want me enough to change his personality, his desires, his whole life. I had thought that maybe we would change together.

"For you, Kyle, this is just a stopover."

The words clicked—the way the truth you know but don't want to admit does.

"How do you know that? How come everyone knows that but me?"

"Because you're trying so hard not to notice. You have the look that Sarah gets when she's in a store trying to convince herself a dress that is too small for her fits."

"That's awkward."

"No, it's endearing."

"Then why don't you want me, Jules?"

"Because I can't give you anything you want."

We walked back to his house in silence. It was one of those fall days in Raleigh that feels like deep summer—when you can practically feel the pollen swimming through the air and the sun beats down onto lawns so brightly it makes the blades of grass look like they are wet. I had a sweater on, and I kept it on as we walked—even though I was sweltering inside.

Back at the house Jules handed me a paper grocery bag, and I filtered through his rooms slowly—filling it up. I plucked my toothbrush and a plastic bottle of Clinique foundation from the bathroom, my orange sleeveless T-shirt from the bedroom. I found a pack of my cigarettes in the kitchen, three books I had left in the hallway, and my Lucinda Williams CD by the stereo. I dropped the objects in the bag, picked it up, and drove home. I felt like my stomach had just tumbled down a hundred flights of stairs without me.

———

A month later, the ringing of my phone lurched me out of my slump.

"We're looking for young reporters," an editor from *The Washington Post* bellowed. "We've heard good things about you."

Kip came to mind. I smiled.

After four grueling years of journalistic dues-paying, I was about to get my payback. A few years in D.C. and I would be a regular guest on *Meet the Press*. I would dine with the president. I would have Bob Woodward's telephone number in my cell phone memory bank, and a few Pulitzer finalist stories in my clip file. George Stephanopoulos would call me to swap scoops. I let these pleasant images swim around my brain.

The editor coughed. "You'd cover the suburbs. Virginia, Maryland, maybe somewhere along the Eastern Shore. It would be a good start."

A good start? Yes, I should have thought of it that way. And I wanted to. But I didn't. After close to ten years of striving, pushing, driving to get to the next paper, suddenly it was seeming less important to prove to myself that I could withstand the torture of another move. The Washington suburbs, I knew, would lead to Annapolis, then maybe Baltimore— perhaps eventually D.C. But by then would I want the prize? I suspected maybe not.

———

A few weeks later I got a call from a book editor in New York.

"This guy named Sourian has been all over both coasts, promoting your book idea."

"What book idea?"

"The one about South Carolina. He said you've been working on a great proposal for months."

I was a bit taken aback. "Well, first of all I'm in North Carolina, and I haven't really thought that—"

"Yeah, he said there're all these great scenes. A really hot guy from L.A. comes down for this Houston wedding. . . ."

I inhaled a swig of air. I wasn't sure whether I wanted to kill Mark or promise him a cut.

"You mean Charlotte wedding."

"Oh, great—so you've got some Virginia in there too."

I made a last-ditch effort in the name of American geography and in protest of the Manhattan provincialism I had so often been accused of. "Listen, I'm in North—"

"We don't need to get bogged down by details. How's the writing coming?"

"Really well," I lied.

———

For weeks, I oscillated between pursuing the dream paper—*The Washington Post*—or the dream life—writing a book in New York. I revised my résumé, corresponded with *Post* editors, thought about whether the Baltimore Newcomers Club welcomed smokers and whether Adelaide's pull in Raleigh could get me in the Junior League in Virginia. Meanwhile, I spent evenings downing cups of steaming coffee and plowing through my book-writing guidebooks. And on Sunday afternoons, I devoured bags of chocolate Kisses and shuffled through my old reporter pads looking for potential book scenes.

Still, I was undecided about my future.

Then, one night in mid-November, I had an unsettling dream. I was curled up on the hardwood floor of an empty Victorian two hours from Baltimore. There were buckets of frozen clam chowder stuffed in my freezer and boxes of saltwater taffy in my refrigerator. Issues of *The Washington Post* were scattered throughout the house with my articles splashed across the front pages. I had a booming career, accolades from editors framed on my wall, and requests for speaking engagements piled on my kitchen countertop. But none of this mattered—I was paralyzed. I couldn't lift myself off the floor.

Those next few weeks, I worked feverishly on my book proposal. A month later, I sent it off. And a few days after that I got a call from New York.

I called a shipping company, prepared my resignation speech at the paper, and booked a flight home. Suddenly, New York—the toxic danger zone—was feeling less like a place to escape from and more like a place to rediscover.

———

Lisa and the Ten Thousand Angels had not wanted me to leave. But they finally stopped threatening to chain me to my porch each time the topic of my departure was broached. I convinced them my mating prospects were probably better in New York City.

"Ladies, I know you have my best intentions at heart," I announced at our last meeting. "But, let's face it, I'm not exactly prized Raleigh material."

"She's right. We need to let her go," Adelaide said. "But, Kyle, we want to see some progress in the man department. No more divorced fathers, please." Adelaide glared at Georgia. "Girl, you need to settle down with someone realistic."

"You deserve that," Georgia piped in. "You're a goddess."

"It's okay to need a man," Lisa added. "We all need love."

I was getting annoyed. "Okay, are we going to start singing 'Kumbaya' now?"

"You're making progress," Adelaide added. "I mean, I think you're really getting ready to meet the tuna fish man."

"And if that doesn't work, you can always come back," Georgia said.

We sat on bar stools and downed our beers. Adelaide sipped her whiskey sour. Lisa draped an arm around my shoulder. Georgia called out for four tequila shots. When they arrived, she raised her glass in the air. "New York better thank us— we're lending them one of our angels."

Adelaide waved her glass in the air. "And she's hot."

Lisa lifted her glass. "And gettin' healthy."

Adelaide took my glass and raised it to her lips. "And she ain't shabby."

Lisa picked up her beer mug. "And she's a looker."

Georgia followed. "But she ain't a—"

"Georgia," Adelaide interjected, practically falling off her stool. "Please!"

I wish, for the story's sake, I could say that we had some deep, scintillating conversation about my future. But we didn't. That's the way the Ten Thousand Angels were. It wasn't really in the words.

The next morning, on my doorstep was a basket. Wrapped inside was a dozen velvet head bands from Adelaide, tarot cards from Georgia, and a book, *Keeping the Love You Find*, from Lisa. And there was a note: "Not that you need any of this. But just in case."

That afternoon, Lisa and I shuffled through the airport parking lot—nursing our hangovers and lugging my two suitcases to the check-in counter.

Once inside and past the metal detector, I noticed the Carolina basketball T-shirts in the gift shop, the jars of barbecue sauces, the Raleigh Junior League paperback cookbook, the color photos on the airport walls of the new homes that the boys were building, and the copies of the paper I no longer worked for. We had some time to kill, so Lisa and I sat down in two of those scratchy seats in the waiting area.

"I'm in denial," she said.

"About what?"

"You leaving."

"Don't flee the discomfort," I said, half mocking, half real. "Invite it to the table and sit with it."

"Listen to you."

"I spent a year and a half with you. You'd think I would have learned something."

Lisa waved her hand in the air. "I knew you needed to go home."

"You did?"

"Of course." Lisa pulled a date book out of her Coach purse. "But, listen, I'm coming the seventeenth, okay? You're making plans, right? I don't sleep on floors, FYI."

A jingling went off in Lisa's pocket. She pulled out her portable. "Larry, listen, I know Horny Harriet wants both the cars. But I'm going to do everything I can to prevent that. Just, Larry . . . Are you listening to me? Do not try to run her over again. Larry, it's illegal!" Lisa clicked off the phone. "These people are ridiculous. They need more help than we do."

————

Lisa waited as I slipped through the gate.

When the plane took off, I pressed my face against the plastic window and watched as the streets became thin white lines of Christmas tree lights. And the cul-de-sacs became mazes on a piece of paper. Raleigh's highways turned into strips of overlapping spaghetti. Homes transformed into plastic

Monopoly pieces and the city's lakes into little puddles. I peered out into the clouds and watched the plane whisk upward into the glass blue sky, just as a neatly dressed flight attendant approached me.

"Care for a cocktail?" she asked, unlocking my tray and plopping a square napkin on top of it.

I took a generous sip—more like a gulp—and wondered what time it would be in Los Angeles when I landed. Mark had promised a few days before that he was going to start dating healthy women. I wanted to ask him about his progress.

ACKNOWLEDGMENTS

I am ever and forever grateful to my cool, crackerjack editor, Jenny Minton, for being one-hundred thousand times more than I could possibly ask for in a writing mentor and a friend.

A word of thanks also goes to her level-headed assistant Megan Hustad for her kindness and patience. And special thanks to Julie Doughty, who was there from the beginning and offered much-needed insight at crucial points during the writing process. Russell Perreault and Renee Louis get kudos for believing in this book and helping me envision ways to reach my readers.

Many thanks also go to my ace of an agent Elyse Cheney for her continued support and guidance along the way.

Heartfelt hugs to Roy E. Mashburn, Caroline Hall, Ken Whelan, and my grandfather Alfred C. Sheffield.

I am indebted to the following home owners and/or renters for generously offering me places to write: Harvey and Gaye Tudanger, James and Miss Ray Coker, my father George H. Spencer Jr., and my mother and stepfather Edie and Ward Mauck. I hope that one day I can repay their kindness by removing the diet Coke stains I left in their home offices.

I love, love, love my family for letting me tell this story—and for eventually threatening to lock me in a room with a laptop if I didn't finish it. But special thanks goes to my brother George H. Spencer III. He gets three dozen hugs from me and a permanent spot on my saint list for buying me egg rolls and doing my dishes while I wrote.

Then there is Seth . . . who cleared off the coffee table, and then his desk, then his apartment, and then his life, for me . . . and Pookie . . . and the book. I am forever his writer.